The Child's Generation
Child Care Policy from Curtis to Houghton

Aspects of Social Policy

General Editor: J. P. Martin

Professor of Sociology and Social Administration,
University of Southampton

Also in this series:

Social Policy
A survey of recent developments
edited by MICHAEL H. COOPER

Provision for the Disabled
EDA TOPLISS

Efficiency in the Social Services
ALAN WILLIAMS AND ROBERT ANDERSON

forthcoming:

Capitalism and Social Welfare
A comparative study
ROGER LAWSON

Penal Policy
A. E. BOTTOMS

JEAN PACKMAN

The Child's Generation

Child Care Policy from Curtis to Houghton

BASIL BLACKWELL · OXFORD
MARTIN ROBERTSON · LONDON

ISBN 0 631 16590 8 (cased)
　　　　0 631 16600 9 (paperback)

First published in 1975 by Basil Blackwell
& Mott Ltd. Oxford, and by Martin Robertson
& Co. Ltd. London

Printed in Great Britain
by Western Printing Services Ltd, Bristol
and bound by The Pitman Press, Bath

Contents

Acknowledgements

First, I would like to thank the Devon and Oxfordshire County Councils and their Social Services Departments, for permitting me to use their old Children's Department records. These helped me to recall and understand afresh many of the events described and discussed in this book and I hope that the extracts chosen, by way of illustration, will also bring them alive to its readers. In their cheerful, practical way, Isobel Dashwood, in Devon, and John Lindsay, in Oxford, dusted down the files and helped me to find my way round them and I am grateful to them both.

Special thanks must also go to Bill Jordan for more advice, guidance and assistance than a colleague could reasonably expect. I am also immensely grateful to Barbara Kahan (who bears full responsibility for involving me in child care, in the first place), to John Martin, Michael Power and Harry Turner, all of whom read and commented constructively on the manuscript. The errors are still mine, but some of the improvements are undoubtedly theirs. My sincere thanks too, to Colleen Hutchings, who produced an impeccable typescript with great speed and good humour.

Finally, my thanks to all my old child care colleagues and to the children in care, whom I knew, enjoyed and remember so well. I have tried to express some of what they taught and shared with me, in the pages which follow, and I hope that they will therefore regard this as *their* book as well as mine.

Prologue

This book traces developments in child care policy over the past thirty years. In that period a new child care service was created, adapted and finally discarded with the coming of social services departments. In its lifetime it was characterized by enthusiasm and optimism. Developments were uneven and varied and practice did not always measure up to theory but generally morale was high. Legislation and practice (the latter often far in advance of the former) moved from a narrow concern with the provision of good substitute care for deprived children to a much broader commitment to prevention of deprivation and delinquency, to work with the whole family and to care for the delinquent as well as the deprived child. The consequent expansion of the service and the change in emphasis of its work had profound effects on its organizational structure, the methods of social work used and, ultimately, they brought the child care service to an end. From the point of view of children in need and the social workers concerned with them it was a generation of rapid development and change.

Yet despite all these changes and some palpable improvements in service, we are now faced with many of the same problems and failures with which the era began. The child care service was formed in a ferment of public concern about standards of practice, touched off by a scandal concerning the death of a child in public care. Now again, in the Maria Colwell inquiry, it has been demonstrated that tragedies can occur through poor communication and co-ordination (despite the efforts of professional workers in a newly integrated administrative structure) just as in the days of Denis O'Neill, and that an 'anxious and responsible spirit' is as necessary and as elusive now as it was then.

New difficulties have also arisen, some as a direct result of the progressive policies which have been pursued, others because of stalemate between conflicting principles, old and new. Intended as

1

an aid to 'preventive' family casework, the power to give financial and material aid has faced social workers with serious dilemmas over rationing resources, and the accusation that they are operating a substandard income maintenance system by 'coercive' means. The aims of fostering have been adapted, and sometimes badly strained, by the increasing emphasis on rehabilitation of children with their families. The 1969 legislation has turned intentions on their head and has resulted in more—not less—young offenders becoming involved with the police, detention centres, borstals and prisons. An historical perspective can remind us of lessons we once seemed to have learned and it can also enable us to trace the unwanted and unforeseen consequences of change, as well as its benefits. Indeed, our present situation can really only be understood in terms of an historical process of compromises between conflicting aims, in which the very oldest problems (and attempts to solve them) have a tendency to recur.

Further, policy developments in the child care setting do not stand alone, but relate to similar changes in all the personal social services. Attitudes to residential care and community alternatives, experiments in prevention, and changing relationships between the executive and the judiciary form part of the history of the probation, welfare and mental health services as well as of child care. Similarly, the movement towards an integrated 'family service', which culminated in the 1970 'Seebohm' Act can be traced to several different areas of the personal social services. Study of child care policy, where all these developments are present, and are often more sharply and strongly delineated than elsewhere, is exploration of issues that have a wider relevance.

The processes by which child care policy has developed over the past thirty years are also of more than specialist interest. They demonstrate the constraints and opportunities of a legal framework; the interaction between central and local government; the influence of practitioners as well as official 'policy-makers'; the effect—or lack of it—of research, pressure groups and scandals; the circular relationship between needs, demands and service responses; and the vital, sometimes fraught and sometimes fruitful partnerships between local government officers and their council members. How social policy evolves generally may be illuminated by looking at the way in which one small segment of social policy was shaped.

This study is also specially concerned with events at the local level and with the role of those who put policy into practice and thereby shape and develop it further. Social legislation often provides only an outline of what is intended and how this is interpreted and implemented can be of key significance. Those closest to the recipients of a service may feel most powerless, yet be most influential. There are lessons for social workers in looking to see where practice has led them. To this end two authorities—Devon and Oxfordshire—have made available their children's department records. They were chosen, not because they were in any sense 'typical' but because, together, they illustrate very clearly some of the main developments in child care policy—sometimes in its most extreme (and therefore atypical) form. But it is 'extremists', however unrepresentative, who are liable to have the most influence and, in child care, national policies have often been built upon quite small-scale, local experiments. Material from local archives helps to illustrate this. It has been used selectively to highlight general themes and, therefore, in no sense provides a comprehensive case study of child care in either authority. This means the picture given of the two departments is fragmentary, partial and idiosyncratic and this should be borne in mind and allowance made for possible distortions.

Finally, child care services are essentially *personal* and their successful provision depends on the human qualities of the social workers who offer them. A view in close-up which enables this dimension to be appreciated should be included in any account of their history. In the words of the Curtis Report, 'we have been increasingly impressed by the need for the personal element in the care of children. . . . No office staff dealing with them as case papers can do what we want done—work which is in part administrative, but also in large part fieldwork, involving many personal contacts and the solution of problems by direct methods. . . .' By describing services at the local level we can, perhaps, begin to do justice to this most vital element of all.

CHAPTER ONE

Creating a Framework

The child care service, which was created in July 1948 when the Children Act was implemented, forms the context of most of the discussion of social policy which follows and the years between 1948 and 1974 its boundaries. These limits are inevitably artificial, because developments in the care of deprived children occurred outside the service as well as within it, and because policies are no respecters of dates, but evolve continuously. That these artificial limits nevertheless focus attention upon an important area and era of social policy has been argued already, in the Prologue and elsewhere.[1]

Since a beginning must be made somewhere, it seems best to start with the administrative framework which was set up in 1948. Asked to

inquire into existing methods of providing for children who from loss of parents or from any cause whatever are deprived of a normal home life with their own parents or relatives; and to consider what further measures should be taken to ensure that these children are brought up under conditions best calculated to compensate them for the lack of parental care,

the Curtis Committee[2] supplied a blueprint for the Act which followed. One of its main aims was to achieve the right form of administration.

Past inadequacies in child care were blamed on the administrative chaos which had developed through the operation of numerous departments of central and local government, all responsible in some way for deprived children. The Curtis Committee observed that 'the problem of providing for children deprived of a normal home life has not hitherto been dealt with as a single one and ... a large part of our task is to devise the means of simplifying and unifying the exercise of public responsibility'.[3] Simplification and unification of the administrative machinery were, in fact, two of the main achievements of the new legislation. In place of the Ministry of Health, the Ministry of Education, the Ministry of Pensions and the Home Office at central government level, only the Home Office was to bear responsibility for deprived children in future. Instead of involving Health, Education and Public Assistance Committees at local government level, new *ad hoc* Children's Committees were to be set up, with responsibility for most groups of deprived children, hitherto cared for by the old departments.[4] Nor were they to be responsible for anyone *other* than deprived children, for the Curtis Committee was anxious that all their energies should be concentrated upon this neglected group, and it was for this reason that alternative solutions, such as making Education Committees responsible, were rejected. In other words, it was to be a truly 'specialist' service—a point to be explored later. The chief executive officer in the new local structure was to be the Children's Officer, supported by 'adequate staff'. The local authorities would exercise their functions 'under the general guidance of the Secretary of State'[5]—guidance in effect by statutory instruments and government circulars and by regular visits of the Home Office Child Care Inspectorate. The Secretary of State was, in turn, to have an Advisory Council on Child Care, composed of his own appointees, who were expert in child care matters, some of them having experience of local government. Financial responsibility for the new service would be shared on a fifty-fifty basis between the local rates and Exchequer grant.

The aims of simplification and unification were thus achieved by a judicious mixture of old, tried means (the Home Office, with its century-old tradition of responsibility for delinquent children, for instance) and new ones, like the *ad hoc* committees of local government, employing a new style of chief officer. The evils that the new, simplified structure was set up to avoid had been vividly illustrated in the Curtis Report and in the Monckton Inquiry of 1945.[6] The latter had followed on the scandal of the death of Denis O'Neill in his foster home and revealed how divided responsibilities —in this case between Education and Public Assistance Committees as well as between two local authorities—magnified the risks of error and neglect by the administration. The vital importance of careful selection of foster homes and regular supervision of foster children had been neglected, for want of proper concern and communication between the authorities involved. Curtis pointed out that complicated administration was also responsible for absurd anomalies in the treatment of deprived children.

Thus we often came across instances where the Education department and the Public Assistance department in the same area were
paying to foster parents in the same village different rates of
maintenance, pocket money and clothing; where one department
was employing trained visitors and the other used its office staff;
where requirements as to investigation of the foster home, the
frequency of visits and the medical care varied not only because
of the difference in the regulations laid down by different Government departments but because of the custom of the committee
concerned.[7]

Some of the poor standards of child care found in institutions were
also blamed on ineffective and overelaborate subcommittee structures, and on too great a reliance on local guardians' committees,
with old-fashioned 'poor law' attitudes.

The simple and comprehensive pattern of the new service was
therefore designed, hopefully, to avoid tragedies like the O'Neill
case, and the lesser, but more widespread scandals of poor and unimaginative care for deprived children. (The 'repressive conditions
that are generations out of date', and 'the chilly stigma of charity',
denounced by Lady Allen of Hurtwood in her famous letter to
The Times in 1944[8] were fully supported by the evidence of the
Curtis Committee, reporting two years later.) It is clear that it was
also aimed at standardizing policies and procedures within local
authorities, ironing out the anomalies to which Curtis drew attention.

But the aim of greater uniformity of practice between local
authorities can also be detected in the particular structure chosen.
It has been pointed out, for example, that the reasons for choosing
the Home Office as the Ministry responsible for the new service,
have never been disclosed,[9] but the Curtis Report, for all its careful
impartiality on this point, hints at possible reasons. The poor and
sometimes appalling standards of child care revealed in the report,
were not only an indictment of local government, but also of central
government in its role as overseer. In a section on Inspection, the
committee point out that visits by inspectors from all the Ministries
concerned were too often ineffective. They had often criticized the
selfsame faults that the Curtis Committee itself highlighted, but
little action had been taken in consequence. This resulted, either
through failure of the Ministries to put criticisms strongly enough
to the local authorities, or through apathy and passive resistance on
the part of the local authorities themselves. Only the Home Office

inspection of Approved Schools and Remand Homes seemed to the committee to approach a reasonable standard—visits being on at least an annual basis (compared with lapses of three to six years in some Ministry of Health inspections) with some reports of high quality.

> For example, in a newly established girls' school, of which we had the inspector's reports, there had been five visits from general and medical inspectors during a period of eighteen months. We were very well impressed with the thoroughness of the reports. They showed good discernment about the staff difficulties, a lively individual interest in the girls and good sense about the practical needs of the School.[10]

This tradition of more vigorous involvement on the part of the Home Office may well have recommended it to the legislature, who revealed in other clauses of the 1948 Act a complementary desire to give central government some 'teeth' in relation to the new service. If this *was* the intention behind the choice of the Home Office, then subsequent developments appear to some extent to justify that choice. In J. A. G. Griffith's study of the relationship between central departments and local authorities,[11] for example, the style of Home Office inspections of the child care service is contrasted with the Ministry of Health's interest in the mental health and welfare services. The former is characterized as 'regulatory'—'a deliberate paternalism which partakes both of firmness and kindness', which Griffith suggests may be partly because 'the Children Act was passed, if not in an atmosphere of panic, at least because it was thought that "things had gone wrong" and needed putting right'.[12] The relationship between the Ministry of Health and local authority welfare services, on the other hand, is styled '*laissez faire*', and the lack of central support for so young and weak a service is criticized by Griffith in consequence.

Apart from the choice of Ministry, there are other less ambiguous features of the 1948 legislation, which support the intention of firm central control. The requirement that each local authority should establish an *ad hoc* Children's Committee to administer the new service is one example. Local authorities have frequently argued for the right to fashion and group their own committee structures to suit local circumstances and they can often do this.[13] The fact that the Children Act denied them this right reflects a conviction on the part of the legislators that a particular pattern of administration was essential—in this case a specialist committee, subordinate to no other, which would concentrate on providing a new service at a much more acceptable and standardized level than before. A similar concern is reflected in the regulations governing the choice of the Children's Officers who were to run the new service. They were to be appointed only after the Secretary of State had seen particulars of all candidates that each local authority was considering, and he had the right to prohibit the appointment of anyone he thought unsuitable.[14] Determination to appoint the right staff in these key positions overrode concerns of local autonomy in the matter.

The significance assigned to the role of Children's Officer can hardly be exaggerated. 'We desire ... to see the responsibility for the welfare of deprived children definitely laid on a Children's Officer. *This may indeed be said to be our solution of the problem referred to us*' (my italics) was the Curtis Committee's way of expressing it.[15] The reasons for the emphasis are clear. Shocked by the unimaginative and insensitive handling of many deprived children, the committee were 'increasingly impressed by the need for the personal element in the care of children, which Sir Walter Monckton emphasized in his report on the O'Neill case'.[16] The Children's Officer was the key to providing this personal element. Curtis envisaged the ideal candidate as a graduate, with social science qualifications, experience with children and with good administrative ability. 'Her essential qualifications, however, would be on the personal side. She should be genial and friendly in manner and able to set both children and adults at their ease.'[17] It was expected that, in all but large county areas, she would know all the children in her care personally and where this was not possible she should 'aim at allocating a group of children definitely to each of her subordinates'.[18] In other words, Curtis seems to be suggesting, for most areas, a one-woman, personal *social work* service (though the term, as such, is nowhere used). The small *scale* of what was envisaged proved, in the event, grossly to underestimate the amount of work that would be involved and the number of subordinates required to carry it out. Nevertheless, the idea was enthusiastically adopted in the debates which followed. 'It is a particular source of gratification that each local authority will be obliged to appoint a Children's Officer. The work of securing for deprived children a normal home life is essentially personal and the Children's Officer will be the key person,' said a *Times* leader of 25 March 1947. Mr. Chuter Ede, in guiding the Bill through its last stages, commented that 'in the future much happiness would be created and many promising lives preserved through the skill, affection and attention of those officers'.[19] Through the Children's Officer, warmth, love and skill were to breathe life into the new, streamlined administrative machinery.

A further requirement for the new service was trained personnel.

At an early stage of our investigations into the present provision for children deprived of a normal home life, it became apparent to us that large sections of the staff caring for such children were without any special training for the task, and that this circumstance was in part responsible for unsatisfactory standards where these existed.[20]

The Curtis Committee were so concerned about this that they published an interim report, in advance of the main report, urging the setting up of a Central Training Council in Child Care, to promote and oversee new courses of training. First priority was training courses for the staff of children's homes, which would teach elements of child development, social conditions and the social services, as well as the practicalities of household management and health care. Two-year courses were envisaged located in, for example, polytechnics, technical colleges, teacher training colleges, or based on voluntary bodies like Barnardo's, which had already developed their own training. In the event, fourteen-month courses evolved, and a small band of newly qualified houseparents were ready to take up posts when the new Act was implemented.

A need for training for the Children's Officers' subordinates—the boarding-out visitors, as Curtis termed them—was also recognized. Since the turn of the century, a social science training at a university had been the recognized preparation for social work but additional, specialist courses had evolved, more recently, to equip students for particular fields of practice. By the 1940s mental health, probation and hospital almoning were served in this way and one implication of the new, specialist child care structure was that new, specialist child care training was also necessary. Curtis wanted their proposed Central Training Council to promote such courses, which would deal with child development, family life, social conditions and social services. They should be housed in universities already committed to social science training and preferably where there was a Chair of Child Health, and where the subject matter was the same as that covered by house-parent courses, it should be at 'a considerably higher academic level'—a distinction of significance which will be explored later.

Here, too, recommendations were treated with the urgency the committee desired. Ministry of Health officials, who had been concerned with evacuees, were transferred to the Home Office to help launch training and the Central Training Council was appointed in 1947. The universities of Birmingham, Leeds, Liverpool, Nottingham, Cardiff and the London School of Economics were the first to house courses and, as with houseparents, there was a small cohort of trained boarding-out officers, ready to take up positions in the new children's departments in 1948.

The effect that these first few trained workers (and their tutors) had upon the new service was probably far greater than their numbers would imply. As pioneers, they were a strongly committed and sometimes exceptional breed. One tutor recalls a candidate, who presented references from Dame Myra Curtis herself, and the Archbishop of Canterbury! She was accepted for training. The first group of students at L.S.E. were able to attend the debates on the Children's Bill in the Lords, to witness at first-hand the shaping of the legislation that they were to implement.

Problems of building in suitable practical experience as well as theoretical training were uppermost, as they always must be when the untrained equal or outnumber the trained. Local authorities had to be persuaded to take students on placement, not only in the children's homes but alongside the field officers, responsible for boarding-out (something they had never done before). They also had to be persuaded to employ the new species of social worker, once qualified. This was not always easy. Untrained personnel had for long carried out many of the duties that the new service took over, and many of the newly qualified boarding-out officers were young, having trained immediately on graduating from their first degree courses. Many local authorities were dubious about the value of youth and academic achievement as compared with age and experience, and some of the first qualified boarding-out officers spent many dispiriting months, seeking employment in the service that they had understood to be hungry for their skills. This must have underlined the fact that they were now professionals, working in a not always sympathetic bureaucracy, and hastened the formation of their own professional association, which began as early as 1949. Through the association, the qualified staff, though scattered throughout the country, were able to keep in touch with one another, maintaining and reinforcing the values and standards acquired in training, and influencing the new service in the spirit that Curtis had envisaged.

The significance of the Central Training Council was also great.

Curtis had seen that administrative reorganization was not enough, and that a powerful central impetus in training was required. Nominees (but not delegates) from central and local government bodies with an interest in child care, as well as voluntary organizations, and interested academic institutions, formed a standing council, whose role was to set standards, facilitate and encourage the provision of training, oversee curricula, but not to provide training itself. This meant that field and residential social work services for children began in a very different way from those for the elderly, the mentally subnormal and disordered, the physically handicapped and the homeless, where no such training provisions were built in to the post-war welfare legislation. That the child care service developed much more dramatically than the services for these other groups is thus no accident.

The lessons of the past thus made their mark on the new service. The Curtis Report had been full of examples of poor and uneven standards of child care. It abounded with vivid observations of children as victims of clumsy administration and at the not so tender mercy of untrained staff.

> Whatever comfort and happiness may have come to him later, the child's first introduction to the Home was often formal, cold and hurried, just at the moment when leisured kindness, warmth and affection were his main need. Some of us have a depressing recollection of seeing two small girls who had entered the Home some half-an-hour or more before sitting sadly side by side with their hats and coats still unremoved. No-one was taking any notice of them. They looked the very picture of desolation yet so far one comfort remained to them—they were together. In too many Homes they would not be together long.[21]

The remedy seemed to lie in a combination of the 'right' administrative structure infused with Monckton's 'anxious and responsible spirit', and served by high quality, trained personnel. The new service would thereby be standardized, personal and specialized.

The tasks that the new service was designed to accomplish were no less clear-cut than its administrative structure. Its central responsibility was to be the care of children who could not live in their own homes, either temporarily or permanently; children who were, according to the Curtis Committee's terms of reference, 'deprived of a normal home life'. The circumstances in which such children might become a local authority responsibility and the routes by which they could enter public care were embodied in the first section of the 1948 Children Act and in the much earlier Children and Young Persons legislation of 1933. According to the former, a local authority had a duty to receive into its care any child under seventeen who was without proper care, through parental loss, abandonment, illness, incapacity or any other circumstances. Admission to care in such cases was by voluntary agreement with the parents or relatives and was informal in the sense that no judicial procedures were involved. Under the earlier legislation, children who were found to be in need of care or protection, through neglect or cruelty on the part of parents, for example, or through being in moral danger or truanting from school and also a minority of children who had been found guilty of an offence, might be *committed* to the care of a local authority by a juvenile court. This route into care was 'formal' in the sense that it was preceded by a court hearing and marked by a 'Fit Person Order'. In effect, responsibility of the first kind was a direct inheritance from the Public Assistance Committees and their responsibilities towards 'destitute children'. Responsibility of the second kind was taken over from the local Education authorities.

In scope, however, the responsibilities of the new service were far wider than those of their predecessors. Under the 1948 Children Act, older children could be admitted to care (the upper age-limit for admission had previously been the sixteenth birthday) and they could be kept in care for longer (until they reached eighteen, instead of sixteen years). Local authorities also had a *duty* to accept children committed on Fit Person Orders, whereas previously there had been a right to refuse. These extended responsibilities clearly affected the *quantity* of children for which the new child care service had to provide—of which, more later. But of much greater significance was the qualitative extension of responsibilities, brought about by the new legislation.

Comparisons between Section 15 of the Poor Law Act of 1930 and Section 12 of the 1948 Children Act have frequently been made,[22] but they bear repetition. According to the former—the basis on which Public Assistance Committees had been expected to operate—it was a local authority duty to 'set to work and put out as apprentices all children whose parents are not, in the opinion of the council, able to keep and maintain their children'. Descent from the earlier Poor Laws of 1834, and even of 1601, is direct and explicit, uncluttered by any duties to educate, or compensate, or love and care for the children concerned. The Children Act, however, frames its responsibilities more generously.

(1) Where a child is in the care of the local authority, it shall be the duty of that authority to exercise their powers with respect to him so as to further his best interests, and to afford him opportunity for the proper development of his character and abilities. (2) In providing for a child in their care, a local authority shall make such use of facilities and services available for children in the care of their own parents, as appears to the local authority reasonable in his case.

The wording is still formal and spare but the implications are wide and fundamental. The children 'in care' were in future to be treated as individuals and not as an undifferentiated category of youngsters; and they were to have access to the same range of facilities as any other children. In other words, their situation was at last to cease to be 'less eligible', in nineteenth-century Poor Law terminology.

That the old 1834 notion of 'less eligibility' had lingered on into the mid-twentieth century and that it still characterized much of the care offered to deprived children, is argued forcibly by Nigel Middleton in his book *When Family Failed*.[23] He provides examples of institutionalized children in the 1930s and 1940s who were denied many of the experiences of the average child through lack of toys, games, radios and newspapers, outings and social contacts. He quotes instances of segregation and stigma—through the clothing worn, and through movement in 'crocodiles'. There are examples of lost educational opportunities because, 'Who do you think is going to keep you until you are sixteen? The over-taxed rate-payer!'[24]

The Curtis Committee also gathered evidence that the notion had not died, in the public's view of things, either. 'Officials of local authorities suggested that the children suffered from the attitudes of the public to children maintained under the Poor Law.'[25] Their intention to make a break from any such attitudes in the new legislation is expressed again and again. Paragraph 435 states

the broad responsibility of the central department will be to see that all deprived children have an upbringing likely to make them sound and happy citizens and that they have all the chances, educational and vocational, of making a good start in life *that are open to children in normal homes* (my italics).

Again, in paragraph 439

we find a strong impression that the stigma attached to Public Assistance even if called, as it often now is, social welfare, is so clearly ingrained that only a completely new approach will enable the authorities to keep clear of it.

In future provision for deprived children was no longer to be set at a minimal level (which, at its worst, had been no better than the conditions of the poorest and most deprived in the community at large—the essence of the 1834 principle) but at an *optimal* level. The growth and development of each deprived child in care was to receive individual attention and there was to be no question of denying him opportunities and facilities which were available to children in general. In this sense, the Children Act bears comparison with that other example of Welfare State legislation at its optimum—the Health Service Act of 1946—whose first section states:

> It shall be the duty of the Minister of Health ... to promote the establishment in England and Wales of a comprehensive health service designed to secure improvement in the physical and mental health of the people of England and Wales ...

How the new service might establish its aim of good, compensatory substitute care is also spelled out in the 1948 Act. The Curtis Committee had made the point that 'the aim of the authority must be to find something better—indeed much better—if it takes the responsibility of providing a substitute home'.[26] In the view of the committee, the ideal substitute was adoption (that had been legally sanctioned since 1926)—a complete and permanent absorption of the child into a new family situation. But this situation was clearly open only to those children without parents at all, or with parents prepared, or constrained, to make a total break with their children (generally unmarried mothers). It was also a situation confined mainly to the very young who were most readily acceptable to would-be adopters. As a form of care to be used by the Children's Service it was therefore of marginal importance. The new departments were free to place children in their care for adoption, if circumstances permitted, but it was not likely to be one of their major activities.

For the majority of children in care, the choice of substitute home would fall between some form of institution or a foster home and the Curtis Committee was unequivocal in its preference for the latter.

> The evidence is very strong that in the free conditions of ordinary family life with its opportunities for varied human contacts and

experiences, the child's nature develops and his confidence in life and ease in society are established in a way that can hardly be achieved in a larger establishment living as it must a more strictly regulated existence.[27]

This preference was embodied in the 1948 legislation, which states in Section 13,

> . . . a local authority shall discharge their duty to provide accommodation and maintenance for a child in their care—
> (a) by boarding him out on such terms as to payment by the authority and otherwise as the authority may, subject to the provisions of this Act and regulations thereunder, determine, or
> (b) where it is not practicable or desirable for the time being to make arrangements for boarding-out, by maintaining the children in a home provided under this part of the Act or by placing him in a voluntary home the managers of which are willing to receive him.

Fostering was thus to be first choice in most cases, and the emphasis was stressed by some of the first child care workers in the service, who in many areas were called 'boarding-out officers'.

Responsibility for maintaining good standards of care for children who had once been 'in care' is also expressed in several sections of the Children Act. The intention seems clear. Ground gained by the provision of good substitute homes, in childhood, should not be lost through lack of continuity or support in adolescence and early adulthood. Thus, local authorities could provide hostels for working boys and girls under twenty-one (Section 19)— an acknowledgement that young people might need special support in their living situation, when coping with the early years of employment. Local authorities could also assist in the maintenance, education and training of those over eighteen who had been in care (Section 20)—a clause inserted, perhaps, to guard against the danger, all too clearly present under the previous administration, of lost opportunities in education and employment through lack of encouragement or downright parsimony. The children's departments also had a duty to 'advise and befriend' children over school age, but under eighteen, who had, at school-leaving age, been in the care of either a local authority or a voluntary organization, 'unless the local authority are satisfied that the welfare of the child does not require it' (Section 34). Again, the implication is that once having taken on the onerous responsibility of providing a child with 'substitute care' a local authority cannot shuffle off its responsibilities, but must sustain its efforts for as long as is necessary.

Responsibilities of the new service were not solely concerned with children who were—or had been—in its care. However, responsibilities towards other groups were of a supervisory rather than a quasi-parental nature. Children who were privately placed in foster homes or independent children's homes, and children who were awaiting a court order in adoptive homes, for example, were to be under the regular, protective supervision of children's departments. (Sections 35–7.) In addition, Juvenile Courts wishing to make a supervision order on any non-offender brought before them would name the relevant local authority—a device less drastic than removal from home, and something akin to the probation order for offenders. In comparison with responsibilities towards children 'in care', however, these were peripheral duties. The focus for public concern, at the time, was the deprived child living away from his family, in public care. Through scandal, exposure and public inquiry, that care had been shown to be uneven, out of date and sometimes appalling. The major part of the Children Act was concerned to remedy this state of affairs and to ensure that 'substitute care' was no longer synonymous with 'substandard care'. The supervisory duties of children's departments were subordinate to this aim and only later began to assume a growing importance.

It is interesting to see that even legislation which imposes duties and dictates administrative frameworks as clearly as did the Children Act, is not automatically followed by uniformity of practice at the local level. Statutes cannot spell out every detail and local government guards its autonomy jealously, develops its own style and sometimes struggles hard against central control. The Oxfordshire 'Children's Care Committee' met first in October 1947, and consisted of four women and seven men. For more than six months it resisted Home Office pressures to unite with Oxford City, to make a joint appointment of a Children's Officer. (The city was equally determined to 'go it alone'.) It also tried to put the new department in the hands of an 'administrative officer' (male) with a Children's Officer (female) as his subordinate. This was vetoed by the Home Office—the intention of the Children Act being clear on this point. Finally, it tried to appoint, as the first Children's Officer, someone without what the Home Office believed to be 'the qualifications for the post'. Central government won that battle, and the first approved Children's Officer took up her duties in October 1948. In the first instance, she was responsible for approximately 135 boarded-out children and another 165 children in children's homes, and she was to be assisted by one 'boarding-out officer'. In contrast, Devon's children's service began more smoothly. The 'Committee for the Care of Children' was massive, by comparison, with 42 members, and as early as January 1948, it had appointed its first Children's Officer. Five 'children's visitors' were transferred from the welfare staff of the County's Education and Welfare departments, to assist her, and by July 1948, when the Children Act was officially implemented, their number had risen to nine. They were responsible for approximately 750 children—40 per cent of whom were boarded out.

Thus each local authority in the country, in its own way and at its own pace, constructed the framework for a new children's service, and set about implementing what had been dubbed 'the Children's Charter'. The progress made and the directions taken form the subject of the chapters which follow.

NOTES

1. See Peter Boss, *Exploration into Child Care*, Routledge and Kegan Paul, 1971.
2. *Report of the Care of Children Committee*, Cmd. 6922, H.M.S.O., 1946. Full discussion of the events leading to the establishment of the Curtis Committee is to be found in Peter Boss (op. cit.) and in Jean Heywood, *Children in Care*, Routledge and Kegan Paul, 1959.
3. Op. cit., para. 423.
4. Not all the children who were considered to come within the Curtis Committee's terms of reference were subsequently made the responsibility of Children's committees. Handicapped children in special boarding-schools remained the responsibility of the Education committees. Ineducable subnormal children and mentally disordered children became the responsibility of the hospital authorities and local health committees, under the Health Service Act. Children in approved schools maintained their direct link with the Home Office; and war orphans still maintained their connection with the Ministry of Pensions.
5. Children Act, 1948, section 42.
6. *Report by Sir Walter Monckton, K.C.M.G., K.C.V.O., M.C., K.C., on the circumstances which led to the boarding out of Denis and Terence O'Neill at Bank Farm, Minsterley, and the steps taken to supervise their welfare*, Cmd. 6636, H.M.S.O., 1945.
7. Op. cit., para. 123.

8. Lady Allen's letter published in *The Times* on 5 July 1944, strongly criticized existing methods of care for deprived children and stated that 'a Public Inquiry, with full government support, is urgently needed'. Letters of support followed and this correspondence, and the O'Neill tragedy which followed are generally credited with the eventual establishment of the Curtis Committee Inquiry in the following year.
9. See Peter Boss, op. cit.
10. Op. cit., para. 404.
11. J. A. G. Griffith, *Central Departments and Local Authorities*, Allen and Unwin, 1966.
12. Ibid., p. 520.
13. Witness the scramble by some local authorities to reorganize their personal social services, before the Seebohm Report was implemented and a standard committee structure was once more laid down.
14. Children Act, 1948.
15. Op. cit., para. 441.
16. Ibid.
17. Ibid., para. 446.
18. Ibid., para. 445.
19. Reported in *The Times*, 29 June 1948.
20. *Training in Child Care*, Interim Report of the Care of Children Committee, Cmd. 6760, para. 1.
21. Op. cit., para. 186.
22. See, for instance, Jean Heywood (op. cit.) and Clare Britton, in *Social Casework in Great Britain* ed. Cherry Morris, Faber and Faber, 1950.
23. Nigel Middleton, *When Family Failed*, Victor Gollancz, 1970.
24. Janet Hitchman, *King of the Barbareens*, Penguin, 1966.
25. Op. cit., para. 154.
26. Ibid., para. 447.
27. Ibid., para. 461.

CHAPTER TWO

Fostering—'The Ideal Method'

The Curtis Report had argued in favour of fostering as the best possible form of substitute care for deprived children (barring adoption) and the preference had been enshrined in the Children Act. But the practice of fostering was of long standing and many of the arguments in its support had been debated since at least the mid-nineteenth century. Poor law guardians had experimented with boarding-out, both inside and outside the boundaries of their unions, and many of the big nineteenth-century voluntary foundations for children, like Dr. Barnardo's Homes, the National Children's Home, and the Waifs and Strays (the Church of England Children's Society), had also used fostering as one method of child care. More recently, the 1933 Children and Young Persons Act had required Education authorities to board-out any children committed to their care by the juvenile court.

Many of the reasons given for choosing foster care in preference to institutional care, in the century before the Children Act, are remarkably similar to those offered by the Curtis Committee. Victor George[1] quotes the Mundella Report of 1896—

> where children are brought up in large institutions the standard of health is lower than that of children living under ordinary conditions . . . there is a consensus of opinion that the children have a tendency to become dull, sullen and mechanical.

In contrast, upbringing in an ordinary family was thought to be natural and beneficial especially in the development of personal affections and 'the children, almost without exception, looked strong and thriving and happy'.[2] Thus, also, Curtis observed

> the contrast between the children in the Homes and the boarded-

20

out children was most marked. The boarded-out children suffered less from segregation, starvation for affection and lack of independence. They bore a different stamp of developing personality, and despite occasional misfits were manifestly more independent. For example, they were much more indifferent to visitors, were much better satisfied by their environment (by which we mean the special features of security and love). There was, we thought, much greater happiness for the child integrated by boarding-out into a family of normal size in a normal home.[3]

In some ways, therefore, the Curtis inquiry reiterated old truths, rather than revealing new ones.

The new children's departments were building on old foundations and they began with an inheritance of foster children who were transferred from public assistance departments (nearly 5,000 according to Curtis), from education departments (6,000) and from health departments, who were responsible for three thousand 'homeless evacuees', left stranded in foster homes at the end of the war. The significance of this last group is perhaps greater than their numbers imply. Boarding-out was more than a century old (in some forms it stretched back as far as the Tudors) and for that reason, in some areas, and for some families, it must have been a familiar form of community care—a tradition handed down from one generation to the next. Evacuation, in contrast, was a new phenomenon, but one which appears to have had a profound effect on the children who were moved from industrial centres to 'safe areas', on the families they left behind and on the families on whom they were 'billeted'. More than a million children changed homes in the first months of the war and this meant that close on a million households had their first taste of other people's children. Richard Titmuss[4] has traced the effects this had on social policy—the rude shock to complacency, caused by the poor physical and educational state of many urban children; the miles of rubber sheeting that had to be found and issued, to stem the tide of bedwetting that swept the reception areas; the special residential facilities that had to be developed to house the 'unbilletable'; and the legacy of homeless children whose families were lost to them, when the war came to an end.

Evacuation clearly added to the number of deprived children for whom children's departments were responsible (in addition to the 3,000 in foster homes, another 2,000 evacuees were in children's homes at the time of the Curtis inquiry) but it must also have made many more members of the public aware of the strains and rewards of fostering. Some, no doubt, like the unfortunate folk in Evelyn Waugh's novel *Put Out More Flags*[5] would do anything not to look after such children again, though there were presumably few evacuees to rival the dreaded Connolly's! Others, with happier memories, or made of sterner stuff, might be prepared to try again. In either case, fostering as a fact of child care must have been a great deal more familiar after evacuation, than before.

Reinforcement for the concept of fostering came from other directions as well—most notably from the child care experts of the period. Among key witnesses to the Curtis inquiry were the children's psychiatrist Dr. D. W. Winnicott, Dr. Susan Isaacs, who had written of the problems of evacuees in Cambridge, Miss Clare Britton, who subsequently founded the first child care training course at L.S.E. and—most significantly—Lt.-Col. John Bowlby. Dr. Bowlby's monograph for the World Health Organization on the deprivation of maternal care, was published in 1951.[6] The popular version appeared in a Pelican edition in 1953. Thus, in the very early years of children's departments, theories of child development which stressed the prime significance of a child's earliest ties to his mother, were widely debated and publicized. *Child Care and the Growth of Love* was written very much as a manual of good child care practice, with the new children's service in mind. The emphasis was on maintaining a child's place in his family, wherever and whenever possible, and particularly during his earliest years. Evidence of damage to a child's educational, social and emotional development if such ties were broken, was amassed from studies made over a generation and more, in Europe and the United States. They ranged from direct studies of the development of deprived children in different settings, through retrospective studies which investigated the early histories of adults and young people suffering psychological disturbance to follow-up studies of children who had been deprived in their early years. The value placed on 'a warm, intimate and continuous relationship with his mother (or permanent mother substitute—one person who steadily "mothers" him)' meant that if a child *had* to be separated from his parents, the best remedy was not an institution, but an adoptive or foster home, where the optimum conditions for his mental health would prevail. Bowlby wrote of the advantages of using familiar people as foster parents—relatives and neighbours of the child, for instance. He also recommended the use of temporary foster-parents, for short-term, emergency admissions of infants and young children, and praised the East Suffolk Children's Department for its practice of keeping a register of such homes. He argued for the development of semi-professional status for foster parents; that they should be regarded as colleagues, paid for the job, and should be partners in an enterprise which stresses the child's links with his natural family, and seeks to restore him, wherever possible.

There is no doubt that Bowlby exerted a profound influence on the new service. His work was standard reading both for the students on the few child care training courses at this period and for the larger number of social administration students, from whose ranks many of the early child care workers were recruited. Much of what he wrote was directed specifically at the new service, and as early as 1951 he addressed the annual conference of the Association of Children's Officers. Devon's Children's Officer, the secretary of that Association, makes mention of this 'most important address' in his report to committee that year. Indeed, the service as a whole responded with respect and enthusiasm. His message appealed to the heart as well as the head and was readily translated into layman's language—perhaps *too* readily, leading to over-simplification and misunderstanding in some instances. Fortuitously, it was also perfectly timed and thus had a significant influence on social policy. The World Health Organization had asked for his help in 1948, when the United Nations were understandably concerned for the plight of homeless children after the war. Publication, at a time when Britain had just framed new legislation for deprived children, gave him both a ready-made audience and an administrative structure within which his theories could be put into practice, and tested further. Few research studies can have had such a favourable launching, nor such a profound impact.

One more factor ensured that foster care was seen as the most desirable means of caring for deprived children in the years immediately following the Children Act—economy. Since the scandals of baby-farming in the late nineteenth century, it had been the practice to pay foster parents enough to maintain the children in their care, but no more. That they should receive a 'wage', or that there should be any margin of profit in their allowance, was considered dangerous, and liable to encourage people with the 'wrong' motives. This issue was discussed in the Curtis Report, as some witnesses were in favour of an 'element of remuneration', particularly as a means to finding more foster homes. However,

some of us feel that the acceptance of payment for the work cuts at the root of the relation between foster mother and child which we wish to create ... we are sure that it should not be an important motive where the child is received into an established household and we recommend that the basis of payment shall not be changed so as to include remuneration.[7]

In consequence, the cost of maintaining a child in a foster home has always been far less than the costs of residential care, where the capital outlay, maintenance, staff salaries and running costs, whether beds are occupied or not, all contribute to a high cost per child. Roy Parker[8] has pointed out that the average cost of institutional care in 1952/3 was 2·9 times that of the boarded out child and the gap widened as time went on. In 1961/2 children in Homes cost 3·7 times as much as foster children. In Devon, in 1952, the cost per child per week in Children's Homes was £2 15s. 10d. and in nurseries £6 10s. 0d. compared with weekly boarding-out allowances (including clothing grants) which ranged from £1 5s. 0d. for babies to £2 4s. 6d. for teenagers at grammar school.

The virtues of pursuing a policy which cut costs, while contributing to the best interests of deprived children, were obvious at all levels of government. The 1951/52 Select Committee on Estimates, which concerned itself with child care costs, drew the attention of the Home Office and the local authorities to this mode of economy and in November, 1952, the Home Office duly circularized the children's departments.

Finally, boarding out is the least expensive method of child care both in money and manpower and in the present financial condition of the country it is imperative to exercise the strictest economy consistent with a proper regard for the interests of the children.[9]

Some local authorities were already alert to the situation. In January 1952, for instance, the Devon Children's Officer, in response to a Finance Committee request for a reduction of £6,650 in his estimates, offered to meet half that reduction 'by reducing estimated expenditure on Voluntary Homes and other local authority Homes. This is made on the assumption that the new posts of Children's Visitors will be advertised immediately and that we shall be able to get the children boarded-out from the Homes early in the financial year.'

The pressure on the children's service to save money was all the greater because, in addition to the gloomy economic climate at the start of the fifties, the service itself was proving far more expensive than had been anticipated. Curtis had urged an improvement in the quality of care, but the new departments also found they were dealing with a greater quantity of cases. The number of children in care in England and Wales rose by 10,000 from 55,000 in 1949, to 65,000 in 1953. Even these figures conceal some of the pressures on the service, for many admissions to care were of short duration and these scarcely show in the total figures. The wider scope of the new legislation accounts, in part, for the rise, but from the alarm expressed it seems the financial implications had not been worked out in advance. Faced with the task of providing good substitute care for more and more children, it was inevitable that fostering, which was legally sanctioned, and which had the blessings of Curtis, Bowlby, *and* the Treasury, should play a key role in the early years of the service.

The first means by which most children's departments sought to expand fostering was to review the children in institutions, to see how many could be boarded-out, and their early efforts were often directed to emptying the Homes of as many children as possible. From its inception, Oxfordshire's 'Boarding-out subcommittee' —an offshoot of the Children's Care Committee—was obliged to 'consider the circumstances of each child admitted to a children's home or nursery . . . and to give directions with regard to boarding-out. The facts relating to any child who shall not have been boarded-out within three months from the date of its admission shall be reported to the main Committee.' This was an explicit implementation of Section 13 of the Children Act, but it is interesting to see a committee taking such a strong, directive line with its officers. The early minutes record progress in this direction. The solitary boarding-out officer had investigated fifteen new foster homes in her first month of office and had approved fourteen of them. By May 1950, ninety-eight children had been boarded-out and 'all but a very small percentage of the children in the Children's Homes who were ready for boarding out had been found foster homes'. Perhaps not surprisingly the boarding-out officer's health was said to be failing from strain and overwork! Later, in 1956, when field staff had grown to number eight, three additional fieldworkers (now 'children's welfare officers') were appointed 'to help bring about the closure of first Oakfield Nursery and later Wise House and finally Ashurst House' (the remaining pair of a group of cottage homes).

In the same way, Devon set about transferring children from

C

institutions to foster homes. A report of November 1953, entitled 'What Happens when Homes Close' shows that between August 1952, and July 1953, two large institutions and one nursery were closed and another institution reduced its capacity from 40 to 20 beds. In all, this meant 113 fewer places for children and 40 of those affected went to foster homes—the rest to their families, to employment, to adoptive homes and to other forms of residential care.

Transferring children who were already in Homes to new foster homes was, of course, only the first step. Many of these children had been in care when the 1948 Act came into force, or were received soon after, and the campaign to 'rescue' them from the institutions that had been so severely criticized by Curtis had a marked effect. The proportion of children in care who were boarded-out was 29 per cent in 1946 (at the time of Curtis), rose to 35 per cent by 1949 and to 37 per cent by 1950. The zeal and single-mindedness of the first child care workers must have contributed much to this change. With a novelist's eye, John Stroud describes those early years—

> There was a tremendous crusading atmosphere about the new service. Our impression at the University was that the country outside was dotted with castle-like institutions in which hundreds of children dressed in blue serge were drilled to the sound of whistles. We were going to tear down the mouldering bastions. We were going to replace or re-educate the squat and brutal custodians. I had a dream of myself letting up a blind so that sunshine flooded into a darkened room as I turned, with a frank and friendly smile, to the little upturned faces within.[10]

But to maintain the crusade, once many of the existing residents of Homes had been dispersed, meant an extension of the range of foster care. Many of those first placements, after the Children Act, had been long term ones—permanent substitute homes for children who had lost contact with parents or relatives. However, Bowlby had suggested that foster parents must be found who would act in emergencies, taking children for temporary periods, direct from their own homes, without recourse to residential care. To clear and close nurseries for very young children, for example, as many local authorities did, meant recruiting and maintaining a pool of short term foster parents who would stand by to receive any tiny children who might be admitted to care in future. In addition, the pool had constantly to be replenished, as foster parents withdrew, moved or as short term cases grew into long term ones, and blocked the temporary homes.[11] If departments were to go on raising the proportion of children fostered, they had to prevent many more children from ever entering residential care, and reduce the time spent in Homes of those whose admission could not be prevented. The fact that proportions boarded-out went on rising steadily till the early 60s, when over half the children in care were fostered, is some measure of their success.

Progress at a national level concealed local variations, however, and while central government was praising the departments for their vigour in promoting foster care, it was also quick to point out that some authorities were more successful than others. At a conference of Children's Officers, their Committee Chairmen, and Home Office personnel, held in April 1951, the Assistant Under-Secretary of State drew attention to the fact that in one county, 73 per cent of the children in care were fostered, whereas in one unfortunate borough the figure was only 9 per cent. He quoted the figures 'with reserve' and said that a high proportion of children boarded-out was not necessarily a reliable index of good child care, but went on to say that 'authorities with a proportion under, say, 30% might do well to regard measures for expansion of boarding-out as calling for immediate review'. Attention continued to be drawn to these local variations throughout the life of children's departments. In the returns of children in care, which the Home Office published each year, the proportion of children boarded-out in each authority, and in England and Wales as a whole, was a prominent item, and comparisons could readily be made. Some Children's Officers complained bitterly of these 'league tables' and were defensive about the implications that might be drawn about the standard of their work. Clearly they had a point. They had started with very different handicaps. Some had inherited a situation where the proportion boarded-out was already well above the national average. Devon and Oxfordshire both seem to have been in this position—approximately 40 per cent of the children in their care in 1948 being in foster homes. Perhaps the fact that both were rural areas (counties always tend to achieve a higher boarding-out rate than boroughs) and both had been evacuation reception areas had some bearing on this. With something of a headstart, both were able to maintain a rate well above the average, even as the average itself climbed steadily. In the event, however, Devon drew well ahead and, by 1963, when the national figure was at its peak of 52 per cent, Devon had 83 per cent of its children in foster homes while Oxfordshire's figure was 63 per cent—a reflection of different policies that will be explored later. Authorities which inherited few foster homes obviously had much further to go and local housing difficulties, women's employment opportunities, and the pressure of needs were all plausible reasons for continuing difficulties in some areas.

The debate over the variations in rates of fostering was, in fact, one of the ways in which the *quality* of foster care, as well as its quantity, was discussed. Authorities that felt themselves under pressure to expand sometimes called into question the standards of their more successful neighbours. Were all foster homes selected carefully enough? Were the individual needs of so many children *necessarily* best met in a domestic setting? The published statistics offered no clues about this, as they did not even show how many foster placements 'failed' in the crudest sense of breaking down, with the removal of the child. Though no national data were collected, individual authorities were, of course, aware of the hazards. In her report on the first year of the department's work in Dudley, the Children's Officer (later the Children's Officer in Oxfordshire) showed that of seventy-one children in foster homes, twenty-six had experienced more than one foster-home placing— fourteen of them having had three or more homes. She comments 'it is a depressing table in the unhappiness and disturbance to the children which it represents' and goes on to note 'the main cause for these figures is the lack of accommodation in institutions, particularly reception accommodation'. In some instances, therefore, boarding-out was not the *preferred* mode of care, but the only one available, and as departments closed more of their old children's homes, this risk must have increased.

In fairness, however, the stress on fostering was always seen in more than purely expansionist terms. The wartime scandal that had caused so much public concern had, after all, been about the death of Denis O'Neill in his foster home and the ensuing Monckton Report had severely criticized the casual and inefficient selection and supervision of foster homes that had been a contributory cause. The care with which foster parents ought to be selected, the regularity with which they should be visited and inspected and the training and experience that were required of staff engaged in these activities were all stressed by Monckton and Curtis. National standards of practice were laid down in the Boarding Out Rules of 1946 and were subsequently modified in the Boarding Out of Children Regulations of 1955.

The latter repay study, both for the standards laid down and for the light they shed on changing relationships between central and local government. Authorities are required to pay attention to the sleeping, living and other domestic conditions of prospective foster homes and to make confidential inquiries about the suitability of applicants. They must pay special regard to the number, sex and age of members of the family and—an illuminating glimpse of the way in which foster care was regarded as a simulation of a natural unit—they must remember 'that the ages of the children in any household should be such as to give the appearance of a natural family'. Amongst other regulations, minimum frequencies for visits are laid down and the child, as well as the foster parents, must be seen. Records are to be kept of visits, in which the child's health, welfare, conduct and progress and any complaints are noted and regular six-monthly reviews by 'persons who do not usually act as visitors' must be undertaken. In any placing, 'the selection of a suitable foster home cannot be an exercise on paper: to "match" the child and the foster parents requires personal knowledge'.

Despite the number of regulations to which the authorities were required to adhere and upon which much of the Home Office Inspectors' time was spent when visiting, there are clear indications that central government had begun to loosen its hold on the local authorities. There is no longer any statutory limitation on the number of children in any one foster home because 'the Secretary of State is confident that local authorities... can be relied on to exercise a proper discretion'. Again, 'local authorities are usually required to "secure the performance" of duties, rather than to "perform them". This phrase... is intended to facilitate the adoption of arrangements suited to local circumstances.' Further, 'the Regulations prescribe what are considered to be essentials. There is nothing in the Regulations to prevent the local authority ... from doing more than is prescribed, according to the need.' Interestingly, too, after six years of experience the child care workers appear to have gained some status, *vis-à-vis* other professions, for although a doctor must give a written report on a child's physical health and mental condition, before boarding-out, 'he is not required, as he was by the former Rules, to express an opinion as to the child's suitability for boarding-out; that is a matter for the authority... to decide'.[12] By 1955, in fact, children's departments and their staff are acknowledged to have acquired some expertise of their own.

Foster care, at its best, followed exactly the Curtis theme of a 'personal' service, which would meet each child's needs on an individual basis. Where homes were selected with care, and where there was sufficient choice to make the 'matching' of child and foster parents a reality, there was at least a basis for the realization of Section 12 of the Children Act—'to further his best interests, and to afford him opportunity for the proper development of his character and abilities'. The ways in which departments built upon this and tried to put these ideals into practice can be seen, even in committee minutes. The members were clearly deeply involved in the detail from the start—sanctioning special expenditure, hearing of particular difficulties, and inevitably getting the 'feel' of the new service, for which they were responsible, in the process.

In November 1948, Oxfordshire's committee, having considered the Home Office circulars on boarding-out allowances, resolved to pay the maximum rates and, in addition, to make grants of up to £3 per year, per child, for holidays, and up to £5 for 'exceptional expenditure' on, amongst other things, 'the provision of facilities to develop special ability or aptitude of the child'. Thereafter reports of grants to individual children sprinkle the minutes. We learn of two girls who are 'to have piano lessons for a trial period of one term and then, at the end of the term, the Boarding-Out Officer should report the progress to the Committee'. (Presumably with a view to stopping the lessons if they showed too little aptitude or enthusiasm!) In 1950, the chairman of the committee wrote to a foster child, congratulating him on obtaining a grammar school place and, in the same minutes, one boy's scout camp expenses were authorized and 25/- was granted for the restringing of a girl's tennis racket. At Christmas, 1951, it was resolved that foster children should receive gifts, together with letters from their officer and the committee, in place of the postal orders of the past. 'It is worthwhile for the greater personal pleasure of the children involved.' Incidentally, it also added to the personal pleasure of the fieldworkers, most of whom delighted in selecting Christmas presents for the children in their charge.

From these beginnings the range of items of special expenditure grew over the years, reflecting, in part, the rising standards of living and expectations of the world of 'ordinary' children, from which the deprived children were not excluded and partly, perhaps, the greater experience and flexibility of the officers and representatives. By 1965, authority was being given for foreign holidays, travel to music competitions, the cost of sheet music, dancing lessons, driving lessons, a football coaching course and a tractor driving course. Only riding lessons seem to have given the committee pause—seen as an 'out of the ordinary' luxury perhaps—but they, too, were subsidized soon after. The committee minutes also reveal something of the personal endeavours of the fieldworkers, in getting to know their foster children as people, not cases. An evening party at the office, for children in employment, was arranged in 1950 and, a little later, a day out on the Isle of Wight. Much later, child care officers were to take parties of youngsters camping and climbing in the Welsh mountains.

Devon's main committee records are less detailed (area committees dealt with most of the case-detail) but even in these there are indications of an expanding notion of personal care. The rather frugal 'initial outfits' for boarding-out children in 1948 included only two of most items (among them, liberty bodices and aprons for girls). Later, they were enlarged, and items came in threes—(one on, one spare and one in the wash?)—and there were no more aprons or liberty bodices!

That such details reached committee level was later to be strongly criticized by the first Maud report on local government.[13] In pure management terms it was probably right. The elected representatives obviously spent a great deal of time on minutiae, and ratified very small items of expenditure. In an established service, the officers would rightly demand the power to determine most of the detail themselves—to act as a true 'executive', thus freeing the committee for broader considerations of policy. Even the first child care workers must have found some of the endless putting-in of requests and reporting back a time-consuming irritant. But this was a *new* service—small and weak in comparison with some other local government departments, employing untrained, or newly-qualified, but generally very young staff—yet committed to change and a sharp break with past policies and standards. To succeed, the members needed to be as informed and engaged as the pioneering staff, both to give the latter moral support, and to press their cause within the councils as a whole. As one lifelong member of Oxfordshire's Children's Committee put it—

I, myself, was almost new to local government and had no idea that as members of a committee we were replacing old Poor Law standards and people who thought these standards were good enough for 'those' kinds of children . . . (the) staff have always involved committee members so deeply in their work that they have come to regard themselves as having a real part to play and to feel wholly committed.[14]

The presentation of a mass of case detail was, in fact, a way of enabling members to consider children in care as individuals, with personal needs and problems, upon whom policies reacted in an individual and personal way. Not only Children's Officers and their staff, but council members as well, thus had the opportunity to take to heart the Curtis dictum that child care must be a truly 'personal' service.

The ramifications of putting foster care high on the list of priorities spread beyond committee involvement, to the structure and processes of the departments themselves. The first requisite for the implementation of such a policy was obviously field staff. Staff had to be employed under whatever title—boarding-out officers, children's visitors, child welfare officers—to find, vet, match and supervise foster homes and to forge the vital link between the child, his family, the Children's Home and the foster family. Numbers of field staff rose sharply after 1948, as the magnitude of the expanding task began to be appreciated. Oxfordshire, having begun with one boarding-out officer, had eleven by 1956. Devon already had that number in 1951—but with a far larger area to cover and more than twice the number of children in care. There are no national figures for the early years of the service, but membership of the professional Association of Child Care Officers (A.C.C.O.), gives some indication of growth. In 1950 there were 241 members, in 1959, 845.[15] What proportion these formed of all field staff is not certain, though it was probably high, since we know from the Association of Children's Officers that in 1960 there were eleven hundred child care officers in post in England and Wales.[16]

Growth in the size of departments was one dimension. Increases in the number of qualified staff was another. Both Monckton and Curtis had stressed the need for trained staff to deal with fostering and we have seen how some child care courses were set up in advance of the 1948 Act. By April 1951, the Chairman of the Central Training Council in Child Care was able to report that 216 people had so far qualified—211 of them women.[17] They joined untrained staff who had often transferred from other departments of local government, which had previously been responsible for deprived children. That they were regarded as a mixed blessing by some authorities is hinted at by the C.T.C. Chairman, who notes 'there had been some comment by appointing authorities about the immaturity of some of those who had qualified'[18] and this is supported by the personal reminiscences of some of the first qualified officers, who had initial difficulty in getting jobs. Nevertheless, by 1960, 28 per cent of field staff were fully qualified. Perhaps the predominance of young women in the first decade of child care contributed something to the development of an organizational model that Etzioni would term 'semi-professional'; that is, one where professional work is subject to a good deal of control by higher ranks, and which contains a significant administrative component.

> The typical semi-professional is a female. Despite the effects of emancipation, women on the average are more amenable to administrative control than men. . . . It is difficult to determine if the semi-professional organisations have taken the form they have because of the high percentage of female employees, or if they recruit females because of organisational reasons; in all likelihood these factors support each other.[19]

Other factors, besides the sex of the workers, influenced the structure of emerging children's departments. In order to expand foster care and improve its quality at the same time, there had to be teamwork amongst fieldworkers and between field and residential staff. It was not a policy that could readily be pursued by individual fieldworkers, acting autonomously. 'Matching' a child with suitable foster parents, who appeared best equipped to meet his particular needs might entail lengthy consultation between colleagues. One fieldworker might know a family who would suit a child on another's caseload. Similarly residential staff might be in the best position to describe how a child behaved and what he might be like in a substitute family. They would also be vital in preparing the child for a move, and perhaps accompanying him on introductory visits. On their side, the fieldworkers would more usually know what he had been like in his natural family and what his parents' reactions would be to foster care. Communications between staff had to be regular and good and personnel needed to be designated to co-ordinate and facilitate this if the policy was to work. There also needed to be ways of reinforcing the initial zeal and enthusiasm of all concerned.

Devon's system provides a good example of the kind of strategy which developed. A report of 1953 stresses that, in addition to 'appointing enough Visitors with the right ideas . . . it is impossible to over-rate the importance of morale among field staff. Each member must be convinced of the rightness of the policy and must feel she was making a personal contribution to the endeavours of the whole group.' Each child in care had a 'planning officer' and there were regular conferences (known as 'callover') at all the Homes, when the future of every child in residence had to be considered. 'It is important at the callover, as in the whole business of planning for children, to be *decisive*.' Each review had, therefore, to conclude with an 'action paragraph', which could be referred to and checked up on subsequently. Finally, every two months there was a 'baby show', at which fieldworkers went through every child on their lists, to report progress, or seek for help in making plans. This insistence on planning and regular review would delight recent critics of long-term care for children who deplore the lack of decisiveness and tendency to 'drift' in much current child care practice.[20] It also underlines the particular emphasis that Devon laid on fostering. It is interesting, too, in the importance ascribed to staff morale—something which some recent observers of social work organization see as a vital ingredient, that requires specific structures for its nurture.[21]

The Boarding Out Regulations also played a part in developing organizations that were not simply collections of autonomous professionals, housed under the same roof (like the cherished view of the old Probation Service), but complex teams, differentiated by task and rank. The regular reviews of the progress of boarded-out children, for example, had to be made by 'persons who do not usually act as visitors' and it was left open whether these should be subcommittees or departmental officials. Similarly, where an officer wished to remove a child from a dubious foster home—a power that required no judicial backing—it was 'assumed that, in practice, the officer would consult . . . the Children's Officer'. In other words, some responsibilities in relation to foster children were considered too important to fall on the shoulders of one social worker alone. Being *in loco parentis* meant departments were open to severe public criticism if any harm came to the children in their care (as the O'Neill case had shown and as recent scandals have again highlighted) and structures of shared responsibility and hierarchies of decision-making were one understandable response.

A final consequence of the pursuit of foster care in the first decade of the service leads us into the following chapter. The 1948 Act, by stating that fostering was the preferred method of child care, had reinforced the opinions of Curtis and others that residential care was an inferior substitute. Departments gained prestige as their boarding-out rates climbed and their Homes closed. Though recognized training for fieldwork was as new as for residential child care, fieldworkers were university trained, but trained residential workers needed to have no formal educational qualifications. As the morale and status of fieldworkers was enhanced, so that of the residential workers declined.

NOTES

1. Victor George, *Foster Care*, Routledge and Kegan Paul, 1970, p. 17.
2. Mrs. Nassau Senior, quoted in Victor George, op. cit.
3. Curtis Report, op. cit., para. 370.
4. Richard Titmuss, 'Problems of Social Policy', *History of the Second World War*, Longmans Green, 1950.
5. Evelyn Waugh, *Put Out More Flags*, Penguin, 1943.
6. John Bowlby, *Maternal Care and Mental Health*, W.H.O., 1951.
7. Curtis Report, op. cit., para. 470.
8. Roy Parker, *Decision in Child Care*, Allen and Unwin, 1966, p. 19 n.
9. H.O. Circular 258/52, November 1952, para. 2.
10. John Stroud, *The Shorn Lamb*, Longmans, 1960, p. 8.
11. See Josephine Ball's account of closing Northumberland's nurseries, in *Where Love Is*, Gollancz, 1958.
12. All quotations from the Home Office *Memorandum on the Boarding Out of Children Regulations 1955*, H.M.S.O., 1955.
13. *Committee on the Management of Local Government*, H.M.S.O., 1967 —especially Chapter 12, in volume 5.
14. Mrs. MacDougall, in '21 years of Child Care in Oxfordshire: a programme of fact and comment, reminiscences and anticipation', produced and circulated within the authority in 1969.
15. From Alan Jacka, *The ACCO Story*, The Society for promotion of Education and Research in Social Work, 1974.
16. Jean Packman, *Child Care: Needs and Numbers*, Allen and Unwin, 1968, p. 176.
17. Proceedings of a Conference of Chairmen of Children's Committees and Children's Officers, Church House, Westminster, 4th./5th. April 1951.
18. Ibid.
19. Amitai Etzioni, *Modern Organisations*, Prentice Hall, 1964, p. 89.
20. See, for instance, Roy Parker, *Planning for Deprived Children*, National Children's Home, 1971, and Jane Rowe and Lydia Lambert, *Children Who Wait*, Association of British Adoption Agencies, 1973.
21. See, for instance, Claudine Spencer, 'Seebohm: organisational problems and policy proposals', *Social and Economic Administration*, Vol. 4, No. 3 and 4, 1970.

CHAPTER THREE

'The Mouldering Bastions'

The reasons why the Curtis Committee favoured a massive extension of fostering were, in large part, the reasons why they were
so critical of much residential care for children. Pursuit of the
positive benefits of personal care in a domestic setting was retreat
from the worst features of institutionalization—the other side of
the coin. In some instances it was the sheer scale of the Homes
that depressed the committee, often compounded by the age and
decrepitude of the buildings. 'Barrack' type buildings that housed
up to two hundred or more children were a relic of the nineteenth
century and besides constituting 'a dead loss to the ratepayers
unless they can be used or converted', there was often 'nothing
cheerful or homely about them'. Grouped cottage homes were often
no better, 'unhomely in appearance and set out in grounds that were
often formal and forbidding, with large main gates of institutional
type, asphalt drive ways and a lack of opportunity for variety and
privacy in the gardens'.[1] Years of use and neglect of maintenance,
exacerbated by wartime conditions, meant that their physical state
was often extremely poor, with damp, cracked structures, broken
furniture, dark and badly ventilated lavatories.

Shortage of accommodation also meant that many Homes were
badly overcrowded. One home with a listed capacity for forty-
three, was housing seventy-five children. Cottages built for sixteen
children, harboured between twenty-five and thirty. Overcrowding
meant lack of play space, crowded sleeping and bathing facilities,
more likely spread of infection. Clearly, it also led to depressed and
frustrated staff and children. Shortage of accommodation was also
blamed for the fact that some children were still housed in workhouses, alongside adult inmates. Emergency admissions of children,
which were supposed to last no more than six weeks, sometimes
resulted in much longer stays, for lack of any alternative. Sometimes
such children were segregated, sometimes not, so that 'children

were being minded by aged inmates and by cleaners or were simply placed in a ward with senile old men or women to be looked after by the nurse on duty'. It was in workhouses that the committee found some of the very worst conditions of child care.

> In the children's ward was an eight year old mentally defective girl, who sat most of the day on a chair commode because, the nurses said, 'she was happy that way'. She could not use her arms or legs. There were two babies with rickets clothed in cotton frocks, cotton vests and dilapidated napkins, no more than discoloured cotton rags. The smell in this room was dreadful ... The healthy children were housed in the ground floor corrugated hutment which had once been the old union casual ward. The day room was large and bare and empty of all toys. The children fed, played and used their pots in this room. They ate from cracked enamel plates, using the same mug for milk and soup. They slept in another corrugated hutment in old broken black iron cots, some of which had their sides tied up with cord. The mattresses were fouled and stained.[2]

That such Dickensian conditions could exist in the mid-twentieth century was a powerful and shaming argument for change.

It was clearly not only the deficiencies of bricks and mortar that were to blame for poor child care standards, however. The inadequacies of overworked, untrained staff were also very apparent to the committee. This showed in the 'emotional hunger' of many of the children visited—their intense desire for individual attention from any visitor who called. It was revealed, too, in the uncertainty with which some of the staff tried to deal with problems like bedwetting, destructiveness and pilfering and in their lack of understanding of underlying causes. The advice of a psychiatrist or psychologist would often have been welcome, yet was rarely available and there was 'very little evidence that the child guidance service had begun to play a part in helping the staff of homes with difficult children'.[3] The importance of play to children—space in which to play, toys and equipment to experiment with, interested adults to listen, suggest or unobtrusively to supervise—were all sadly lacking in many Homes, so that 'life has to develop more from the circumference to the centre than by any growth of the children's own powers operating from the centre outwards'.[4]

The upbringing received by children in the Homes was therefore often more satisfactory at a physical level (though in the worst institutions it was poor on this count, also) than at an emotional level. Too often children were cut off from the world outside, and grew up to have little idea how ordinary households functioned—how they budgeted, for instance, so 'the problems of ways and means never came their way'. Many children had few personal possessions and there was 'either a distressing dearth of pictures or, what was worse, a collection of ugly, uninteresting pictures which appeared to have been thrown out as valueless from other houses'.[5] To emotional deprivation was added cultural deprivation.

Curtis chronicled evidence for the existence of institutionalization. Bowlby underlined its effects. European and American research, synthesized in his famous W.H.O. Monograph, stressed the links between the 'affectionless character', the intractable delinquent and a cold, institutional upbringing. The conditions in Homes, described by Curtis, were too often the antithesis of the 'warm, intimate and continuous relationship' that Bowlby had declared vital for the child's successful upbringing and subsequent mental health. Hence, the commitment of the new child care service to avoidance of institutional care, wherever possible, and, where *not* possible, to sweeping changes in the *nature* of residential care.

Curtis made several suggestions for improving residential care for the committee were convinced that, however successful the new measures of social insurance and family allowances might be in preserving family life, and however vigorous the expansion of foster care in the new departments, the need for institutional care would persist and 'we doubt whether the next 10 or 15 years will bring us to the stage at which institutions can be dispensed with, or even in sight of that stage'.[6] A key proposal was the abandonment of the large institution in favour of small group homes, containing not more than twelve boys and girls of various ages. In an environment on this scale, run ideally by a married couple, the woman would 'play the part of a mother to the children', whilst the man 'must play the father ... (pursuing) out of door and recreational activities rather than physical care of the child'.[7] (There was little recognition of joint conjugal roles in the 1940s!) Such a pattern was clearly an attempt to simulate ordinary family life—to reproduce, in the institution, a near-replica of the foster home that had found such favour with the committee.

No such specifications as to size and composition were embodied in the general duty 'to provide, equip and maintain ... homes for the accommodation of children in their care', under Section 15 of the Children Act, perhaps because the cost of the rapid and wholesale pursuit of such a policy would be enormous. Children's departments inherited a huge legacy of large institutions, that would be hard to sell, and expensive to replace. Nevertheless, reduction in the size of children's homes and the gradual closure, or adaptation of old institutions was attempted by many authorities, and encouraged by the Home Office. Periodic reports from the Children's Department of the Home Office plot the declining numbers of children accommodated in Homes, as compared with those boarded-out, and in the numbers in large institutions as opposed to those in small ones. Between November 1954, and March 1960, for instance, children in residential care fell from twenty-three thousand to nineteen thousand and the Home Office reported an increase of 277 small homes (for not more than twelve children) and a decrease of 75 large homes (for more than twelve children) in the same period.[8] The Curtis ideal that all children in residential care (apart from those in specialist reception homes and nurseries) should eventually be accommodated in this optimal environment was never achieved, however. By 1970 there were slightly more in small homes (eight thousand) than large (seven thousand) but by then notions about residential care had developed and changed.

In Oxfordshire, the very small children's home was never adopted, though several old institutions were closed in the early years of the service and new properties purchased. The inherited cottage homes, which were thought unsuitable and isolated, were finally disposed of in 1956—to the welfare department, for the care of the elderly! Instead of very small units, children's homes for twenty or thirty children were adapted to house small 'family groups', where children had their own special rooms and their own special members of staff attached. The County was hesitant to commit itself to the Curtis model, seeing the difficulties in placing some large families together in the smaller homes, and anticipating greater staffing difficulties. The small size of family group homes made it difficult to pay high enough salaries to attract qualified staff (the level of remuneration was tied to the number of beds) and, where the burden of care rested on only two or three people, turnover could result in considerable disruption for the children.

Devon showed a similar concern with closing down unsuitable homes, but went further than Oxfordshire and replaced far fewer than it closed. In 1948 it was proposing to replace seven out of its eleven children's homes, but economic constraints in 1950 slowed down the pace of change. Gradually, however, the amount of residential accommodation in the County diminished, and the small 'group home' achieved some prominence. (Three homes for

eight children each, are listed in 1951.) By 1961 the proportions in
residential care in both authorities were well below the national
average, but the details differed. Only 47 Devon children, out of
400 in care (12 per cent) were housed in children's homes, 18 of
them in small group homes, compared with Oxfordshire's 83 out of
589 (14 per cent), of whom none were in homes for fewer than 12
children. This reflects not only the differing developments in policies
about residential care, which will be expanded later, but differences
in the total number of children to be accommodated.

A second recommendation for improvement, made by Curtis,
was for greater differentiation and specialization amongst children's
establishments. The committee were convinced (largely by the experience of evacuation) that special reception homes which would
assess the needs of children on first admission to care were a vital
resource that must replace the facilities previously available in the
workhouse. Their purpose was to be both medical (checking and,
if necessary, treating the child for any infection, before transfer to
another home) and observational. It was felt that careful assessment
would improve subsequent placing and ensure that the child's
individual needs were properly met. It was recommended that each
local authority should have at least one reception home, and that
children ought to spend a maximum of a few weeks in residence.

Many children's departments did in fact open reception homes
(they were required to do so or to make use of other authorities'
reception homes, in the 1948 Act) though progress was slower
than had been anticipated and even by 1970, by no means all local
authorities possessed their own facilities. Both Devon and Oxfordshire were among those that did, and had done so from their early
years. Oxfordshire purchased a large country vicarage for the purpose, in 1950. It was extended and adapted several times, in the
ensuing years and replaced, finally, in 1967, by a purpose-built
home for thirty children. Devon's new reception home was under
discussion in 1951, when the Children's Officer and two of his
committee toured several neighbouring authorities to learn from
their experience. Impressed with some of the homes they saw, they
nevertheless foresaw difficulties if special short-stay homes were not
also provided, because 'lack of accommodation of this nature was
slowing up the transfer of completed assessment cases from reception homes'. It was in this respect, in fact, that the Curtis blue
print failed badly in practice. Most authorities discovered that,
though 'assessment' might take as little as a few weeks, 'placement' took far longer. Careful selection and introduction of foster

parents might be a lengthy business, causing a stay of several months. In many cases there was delay through lack of appropriate resources—of their own, in the form of children's homes, hostels, or suitable foster parents; or of resources belonging to other departments, special boarding school places, for instance, or hospital beds. Most reception homes came to serve an uneasy dual purpose—that of assessment, and that of short-term, or even indefinite care. In addition, because they were already geared to turnover and disruption, they often specialized in emergency admissions as well. The tidy ideal of Curtis was replaced by an untidy, and sometimes unsatisfactory compromise.

Another type of specialized institution, recommended by Curtis, was the residential nursery for babies and infants of not more than two and a half years. The demands made by young children were thought to be too great to be easily met in family group homes and their special health care needs were stressed. Here the committee were at odds with many child care experts of the period. John Bowlby, in particular, was adamant; 'it cannot be too strongly emphasised that with the best will in the world a residential nursery cannot provide a satisfactory emotional environment for infants and young children' and he regretted the Curtis recommendation as 'a most serious shortcoming in an otherwise progressive report'.[9] The new service was thus faced with a large practical problem, in the shape of many young children in care, living in an inheritance of poor facilities, and with contradictory advice about how to proceed. In general it appears to have reacted in two distinct phases. First, old, inadequate, nursery accommodation in workhouses and elsewhere, was replaced or refurbished; later, as alternative care in children's homes or, more often, foster homes was explored and expanded, many of the new nurseries were closed down. The Home Office noted a decline in numbers in residential nurseries, from nearly 5,000 to 3,500, between 1954 and 1960.[10] By 1970 numbers shrank to 2,500 out of a total 13,500 in care under school age.[11]

In both Oxfordshire and Devon these trends were also apparent. Concern with standards of nursery care and the effects on the children in residence pepper the earliest records of both children's departments. Devon, struggling with overcrowding and poor sanitary conditions in several institutions in 1948, responded to goads and guidance from the Home Office. 'This would seem to have the makings of a very nice nursery . . . (but) . . . many plans have been submitted to the Ministry and turned down.' Oxfordshire had

D

a similar inheritance of remote and unsatisfactory homes for infants, which it replaced with two new nurseries in 1949 and 1952. The disadvantages of poor nursery care emerge vividly from the Devon committee records of 1948.

> Some of the nursery school children are two years mentally behind ordinary children. Some could not walk on rough ground or upstairs because they had never been for cross country walks and they lived always on the ground floor. They did not recognise their reflections in the mirror, were terrified of animals and vehicles.

Ultimately, Devon's response was to close all its nurseries, in favour of foster care. Oxfordshire retained just one nursery, for the handicapped, damaged, and those who had already suffered foster breakdowns. It sought to avoid further damage by, amongst many measures, 'vertical' family grouping (covering all ages), high staff ratios, continuity of staff, extensive and reliable outside contacts and—coincidentally—by the use of large mirrors, set at toddler height. Small children were often to be seen gravely—or delightedly —examining their images in the glass.

At the other end of the age-scale, Curtis reluctantly agreed that hostel accommodation for working boys and girls would be necessary; reluctantly, because 'we regard that as a last resort and should much prefer placing the young people in suitable lodgings, or using existing hostels for working boys run by voluntary bodies'.[12] Section 19 of the Children Act gave permissive power to local authorities to make such provision, but it was used sparingly in the early years of the service and by 1960, only twenty-nine hostels for boys and thirty-one for girls existed in the whole of England and Wales.[13] In Oxfordshire the impetus came later, when the department was heavily committed to caring for delinquent teenagers—something Curtis had not foreseen. It opened a girls', and then a boys' hostel in 1961 and 1964 respectively. Devon, in contrast, considered the pros and cons in 1960, when magistrates were pressing for alternatives to approved school committal for girls. The Devon Children's Officer actually paid an exploratory visit to Oxfordshire, at the time, but he and his staff decided against such provision, because of the practical difficulties of staffing and because 'a child care officer is more ready to give up trying to maintain a child in lodgings or in a foster home in the community, because the alternative of a hostel exists'. The fear of residential care as an 'easy answer' is explicit. In general, even in the last years of the child care service, this particular form of specialized care played only a small part. Only 700 young people were accommodated in children's department hostels in 1970, with a further 500 in hostels run by voluntary bodies, out of a total of 14,000 children of working age in care.[14]

Residential establishments on a smaller scale and with more clear-cut functions were part of the Curtis Committee's answer to the poor conditions they had found. Training was another vital ingredient and we have seen, already, that special courses for houseparents were launched, in advance of the 1948 legislation. By the end of 1950, the Chairman of the Central Training Council was able to report the award of 355 residential child care certificates—300 of them to women, a figure that Curtis had thought would meet annual replacement needs.[15] Despite this optimistic start, the ideal of a fully-qualified residential service for children was never in sight of achievement. The output of trained workers continued steady but small, and rapid staff turnover widened the gap between demand and supply. When the Williams Committee looked at all kinds of residential care in 1963, only 15 per cent of the staff in local authority children's establishments had a Home Office child care qualification.[16]

More interesting, perhaps, than the failure to provide qualified residential staff in sufficient quantities, is the quality of training that was originally envisaged. The interim report was anxious that trained residential workers should 'be definitely above the level of domestic workers', but the emphasis was nevertheless on household skills, and where theoretical subjects were included, it was in terms of 'non-technical instruction in child development' and 'elementary lectures in social conditions and the social services' (my italics).[17] This is in sharp contrast to the university-based training thought to be necessary for boarding-out visitors. In a laudable reaction against the chilly impersonality of institutionalization training for residential work was conceived in homely (and largely female) terms. The residential task as something more sophisticated, requiring relationship and therapeutic skills of a high order, equal to or even exceeding those needed in the field, only gradually came to be recognized and articulated as the service developed. At its inception training merely underlined the second-class status of residential care, which was already spelled out in the statutory preference for fostering. It thus contributed to an uneasy split between the two main branches of the child care service—a split still apparent, in some degree, today.

The 'right' kind of establishments and trained personnel were not goals in themselves, but means to an end—the end of personal care for deprived children, that would meet each child's individual needs and would approximate to the 'normal' family life they had lost, or never known. Published statistics tell us how far the new service made progress in terms of staff and buildings, but it is only from the local authority records that changes in outlook and atmosphere can be glimpsed.

There seems no doubt that changing the image of residential care —laying the Poor Law ghost—was a first priority in both Devon and Oxfordshire. Both had inherited their share of unsatisfactory establishments which required immediate attention. The first Oxfordshire Children's Officer spent much time, in the early months, at the cottage homes.

> We went in by the back entrance as the puddles prohibited the use of the front door. The smell on entry was very bad from the lavatories in the outhouse ... There was no carpet or linoleum of any sort on the stairs, the house had been painted unfortunately, making use of institutional paint and the usual dark colours.

And on a later, evening visit,

> The back door and the windows of the sitting room were wide open, the boys were playing wildly in the grounds in the wet and dark. ... There was a fire in the grate in the sitting room and three of them were doing nothing in particular. The light was very dim and they had nothing to do and no-one with them.

It was discovered that several children got up at 6.0 a.m. to light fires, carry coal, get breakfast and do other household chores. Not surprisingly, in such conditions, 'many had spots and places on their faces which they picked. This is a sure sign of boredom and lack of individual attention in children.' Light paint was subsequently applied, an extra £20 spent on toys, children were allowed to go shopping to choose their own clothes and were relieved from many household chores. The Children's Officer took it upon herself to spend as much time as she could at the Homes 'until the children are well cared for physically and mentally by people whom I can trust'. At that stage, the chief officer was far from being a deskbound administrator.

In Devon, the first Children's Officer toured establishments with her chairman, reporting on what she found. At one home 'the

Master and Matron are elderly and very regimental in their ideas —the staff are always spoken of as "officers". We attended a Children's Committee meeting here and were shocked at the practice of interviewing each child before the full committee—serving no apparently useful purpose of any sort.' Early Children's Committee minutes were full of suggestions for improving such bleak conditions. 'Aunt and uncle' schemes were proposed 'to help the child develop its emotions in a normal way'. Punishments were looked at carefully and deprivation of food, sending to Coventry, punishment dress, shutting in dark cupboards and sending to bed in the daytime were all 'to be rigorously avoided'. There was a lively memorandum on 'playfriends', who would introduce cultural activities to the Homes and much time (including a trip to a London art gallery) was spent by the committee chairman, selecting suitable pictures to brighten the Homes. The task of choosing a religious picture for each Home was delegated to the committee's clerical member.

From across the border, Dorset's Children's Officer wrote in 1949, describing how he had used his field staff to help with staff shortages in the Homes and what the benefits had been. Carrying out both residential and field duties had involved 'a fifteen hour day at least and I am proud that we have such a loyal team'. Not only was this new perspective 'very salutory for the welfare officers' it also brought to light 'many instances of arrangements for meals, bathing, changing of laundry, household tasks done by children etc. which have become fixed more as a matter of convenience for staff than in the real interests of the children. Although in themselves these factors may not be serious, out of such things comes institutionalization.' In the true spirit of Curtis, he concluded 'I believe in taking a dose of my own medicine and have been carrying out residential duties, with the very great assistance of my wife, for the past month'.

What emerges from all the records is the personal involvement and commitment of chief officers and their committees, in the task of improving residential care. Lay members and the chief executive (admittedly, a chief executive who might have a staff of only a handful of helpers) were deeply enmeshed in day to day detail, in a manner that would have shocked later management pundits. The Curtis revelations had hit home, and everyone seemed eager to do his personal bit to bring about improvement. Indeed, the Homes themselves must sometimes have felt very much at the receiving end —'being done good to' in a fashion that cannot always have been welcome. New paint and pictures, chosen by others, were just some aspects of change. Redeployment or removal of staff, through closure of Homes, or because of their personal unsuitability, were others.

For all their eagerness for change, there were also severe limits to what a local authority could and would do. Not all residential staff were Victorian workhouse masters, ripe for conversion. Some had ideas in advance of their employers and then it was the latter who applied the brakes. One ruefully remembers his brief stay in Oxfordshire's ubiquitous cottage homes, in 1954, where his alleged extravagance and novel ideas of child management led to his swift departure. Having scandalized all, by putting up tents in the garden, made of council sheets and blankets (secured by council forks), by evolving a form of children's self-government and by ordering tinned duck for Christmas, he then attempted to improve the heating system, and received the following letter—'The recent meeting of the Children's Care Committee considered, among other requests, the eight hot water bottles you recently bought. The purchase was approved, subject to their being available in the other two homes, should the occasion arise.'

A new look for residential care meant, also, new regulations and new procedures for the administration of the Homes. The benevolent free-for-all which seems to have characterized the earliest months of the service, gave way to more formalized administrative structures and relationships. By 1951, the Secretary of State had published his 'Administration of Children's Homes Regulations'. These required local authorities to arrange for monthly visits to be paid to each Home, either by a committee member or by an officer of the department. Records of admissions and discharges, punishments, important events, fire drills and menus must be kept and inspected by the monthly visitors. Each Home had to have its own medical officer, who would take a general interest in the health and hygiene of the establishment as well as making regular inspections of each child. Fire authorities had to be consulted about precautions, fire drills undertaken, and children had to receive regular dental care and religious instruction. The exact limits of any corporal punishments were spelled out; none for girls over ten, or boys over school-leaving age, for instance; 'caning of the posterior' for big boys only, and no more than six strokes 'with a cane of a type approved by the Secretary of State'. The child's parents or guardians, and the Secretary of State himself, were to be informed of the death or serious illness of any child in a Home.

Within this framework, different authorities developed their own particular patterns and elaborations. Oxfordshire favoured a House Committee structure, each Home having a committee made up of some Children's Committee members and additional, co-opted members from the locality. Each member would carry out the monthly visiting duties in turn, on a rota basis, and the committee were responsible for the appointment of all staff, other than the Heads of the Home. These committees reported, in turn, to the Finance and General Purposes subcommittee of the main Children's Committee and the degree of detail that they considered comes through in the main committee minutes. There are notes on architectural minutiae, for improvement of buildings; the style of tableware (even the Home Office became involved on this issue and were asked for, and eventually gave approval to the purchase of plastic cups and plates); problems with the vicar who thought the Homes children should attend church more regularly and behave better; difficulties in obtaining pasteurized milk—could Matron herself boil and cool it for the children—and so on. Devon had a slightly different structure of management subcommittees, which dealt with the Homes and the boarding-out which occurred in a particular area, but there is a similar attention to detail, which confirms the impression that residential care in the 1950s was under very close scrutiny. Public outrage and guilt had been followed by a sense of public responsibility that gave limited scope for any professional freedom of action for residential child care workers.

Children's Homes were subject, too, to Home Office inspection, but they were also visited regularly by various officials of the children's departments. We have seen how much the first Children's Officers became involved and they or their deputies seem to have kept a close personal eye on residential care for some years. Early in their history many departments also created an administrative role or section at central office—some person or persons who would oversee things like the bulk buying, budgeting and general maintenance of the Homes, checking on costs and standards and ensuring a rough uniformity. Sometimes (as in Oxfordshire) the Homes Administrator became much more—a trouble-shooter and general support—a prototype for the 'Homes Advisors' who developed much later in the history of the service. In some authorities specialists were also drawn in to advise on the needs and handling of the children in care. Devon children's department employed its own psychologist, and one of the first things the Oxfordshire Children's

Officer did was to invite the local children's psychiatrist to advise her residential staff.

Finally, there were the boarding-out officers. They were under no statutory obligation to visit, for the Children's Homes Regulations required only the *Home* to be visited regularly, and this was normally undertaken by committee members. Unlike the Boarding Out Regulations, there was no parallel duty to visit each individual *child*, and this led to a variety of practices in different authorities. Some eventually designated a fieldworker to have special responsibility for all the children in a particular Home. Others, like Oxfordshire, preferred to give each child in a Home his 'own' welfare officer, who was expected to visit him in much the same way as he would a child in a foster home. Whatever formula was adopted, however, fieldworkers were bound, by the nature of their work, to move in and out of the Homes. Children had to be admitted and discharged. Foster care had to be arranged and—often in this connection—case conferences attended. In some authorities (not only in Dorset) fieldworkers had to help out in times of staff shortage. Some visited for the sheer enjoyment of being with the children.

Relationships between field and residential workers were thus varied and complicated. Curtis and the Children Act had decreed that most children should be rescued from institutional care. The fieldworkers were thus cast as crusaders, and residential workers as an unfortunate necessity. Such unequal status emphasized by different educational backgrounds and training, created one kind of tension. Shortage of resources, which turned crusading fieldworkers into supplicants for Children's Home places, created another. Resolution of these tensions became one of the major preoccupations of the service as a whole.

The new child care service was thus faced with a formidable, yet coherent and understandable task. It had been shown that public care for deprived children was often poor, sometimes disgraceful, and it had to be improved. All were agreed that children need personal care and attention, continuity of affection, nurture and stimulation. Normally a child receives such care in his own family. If, for any reason, he is deprived of his natural family's care, strenuous efforts must be made to find him a substitute family—an adoptive or foster home. If this is impossible, then residential care must be available—but residential care that is as *un*institutional as possible—small scale, 'homely', offering warm relationships, a range of 'normal' activities and outside contacts, and flexible enough to meet his individual needs; and the material standards of such Homes must not be a Poor Law minimum, but something comfortable and respectable, with no taint of 'less eligibility'.

The challenge to central and local government was great; in terms of capital expenditure; in terms of staff training, recruitment and deployment; in terms of developing administrative structures that would facilitate the task. There is evidence of the expenditure of tremendous effort and energy to this end, and a high degree of personal involvement by both members and officers. No 'ideal' state is attainable, and it should not be surprising that the service fell short of the targets it had been set. We have already seen that the expansion of foster care reached its peak after about ten years, and that, nationally, no more than half the deprived children in care were ever accommodated in this way. Residential care therefore continued to play a significant role and continued to be beset by some of the problems discussed by Curtis. Greatest of these was staffing. At the time of the Williams Committee census, 70 per cent of staff were without *any* formal qualifications for their work. Perhaps even more significantly, an average of a third of Homes' staff changed each year, so both competence and continuity of care must be in question. Men remained in a minority—80 per cent of care staff were women, according to Williams, and two-thirds were *single* women, so even if 'family care' was successfully simulated, it must usually have been on the one-parent model.[18] We have seen, too, that not all large Homes were closed (though only 2 per cent of local authority Homes were still housing more than fifty children, by the 1960s); that some residential nurseries continued to exist and that reception homes had their own difficulties.

To record the shortfall cannot detract from the very substantial achievements, however, and it is by turning to spheres of child care, untouched by the children's departments, that their successes can be better appreciated. One group of deprived children, who were discussed by the Curtis Committee, but not included in the responsibilities of the new service, were the severely subnormal who could not live at home. Most of these children had been, and continued to be, cared for in hospitals and thus became the responsibility of the National Health Service. Descriptions of many hospitals for subnormal children today (the children's wards described in the Ely Hospital inquiry are an extreme, but not isolated example)[19] are reminiscent of the Curtis descriptions of some of the worst Homes in 1946.

In the same sphere, research offers another yardstick. Between

1963 and 1968, King, Raynes and Tizard[20] investigated patterns of residential care for mentally handicapped children, using measures of institutionalization and of its opposite—child-orientated practice (personal care, in Curtis terms)—to describe different styles of child management. Broadly, hospitals were institutional in approach, while local authority hostels were not, and the latter took their tone from the Heads of establishment. The Heads of hostels carried a high degree of responsibility and enjoyed a fair measure of autonomy —both apparently conducive to a child-centred approach. Also— most significantly—they generally had a child care training. 'We found considerable support for our hypothesis that high rates of interaction with children are associated with training in child care whereas low rates of interaction were associated with nursing training.'[21]

This finding supports and partly explains the fact that the transformation of residential care by the children's departments was concerned with much more than externals—smaller buildings, better equipment, pastel paint and pictures. Training in child care fostered different attitudes to children amongst residential workers, and though the proportion of trained staff in children's homes has remained low, the qualified are generally in senior posts and thus in a position to have a significant influence on how the Home is run. Residential care is, on average, a lot more sensitive and child-centred now, than it was a generation ago, and where this is not the case, or where it has developed in ways not envisaged by Curtis, this has been partly because of expansion and redefinition of the initial task. Children's departments were given a tough, but fairly narrow brief. Their efforts to broaden their responsibilities and shift their emphasis had repercussions on both fostering and residential care. It is these processes of redefinition, and its repercussions, which form the subject of the chapters which follow.

NOTES

1. Op. cit., para. 167.
2. Ibid., para. 144.
3. Ibid., para. 220.
4. Ibid., para. 211.
5. Ibid., para. 209.
6. Ibid., para. 476.
7. *Training in Child Care*, Interim Report of the Care of Children Committee, Cmd. 6760, para. 10.

8. *Eighth Report on the Work of the Children's Department*, Home Office, 1961.
9. John Bowlby, *Child Care and the Growth of Love*, Penguin, 1953, p. 154.
10. *Eighth Report on the Work of the Children's Department*, op. cit.
11. Summary of Local Authorities' Returns of Children in Care at 31 March 1970. Home Office Statistical Division.
12. Op. cit., para. 506.
13. *Eighth Report*, op. cit.
14. Returns of Children in Care, 1970, op. cit.
15. Report of the Proceedings of a Conference of Chairmen of Children's Committees and Children's Officers, April 1951.
16. *Caring for People*, Report of a Committee of Inquiry set up by the National Council of Social Service. Chairman: Professor Lady Williams, C.B.E., Allen and Unwin, 1967.
17. *Training in Child Care*, op. cit., para. 14.
18. *Caring for People*, op. cit.
19. *Report of the Committee of Inquiry into Allegations of Ill-Treatment of Patients and other irregularities at the Ely Hospital, Cardiff*, Cmnd. 3975, March 1969.
20. Roy D. King, Norma V. Raynes and Jack Tizard, *Patterns of Residential Care*, Routledge and Kegan Paul, 1971.
21. Ibid., p. 197.

CHAPTER FOUR

'An Even Better and Even Cheaper Way'

The 1948 Children Act provided a new administrative structure and a new sense of purpose in dealing with deprived children, but it had little to say about the families they came from or about ways in which their deprivation might be prevented. Local authorities had to be convinced that admission to care was 'in the interests of the welfare of the child', the implication being that this should not be undertaken lightly. They also had to endeavour to return the child to the care of parents, guardians or relatives—again, only where it was 'consistent with the welfare of the child'. Nothing more precise, in the form of preventive or rehabilitative duties or powers was spelled out in legislation, though the Home Office circular which accompanied it stressed the importance of keeping families together.[1] In this the Act merely echoed the Curtis Committee which had felt unable to deal with these issues.

> The consideration of the welfare of children deprived of home life has inevitably raised in our minds and in those of many of our witnesses the question whether this deprivation might not have been prevented. This a question which we regard as of the utmost importance and we hope that serious consideration will be given to it; but it is not the problem with which we have been asked to deal.[2]

Concern that this seriously limited the legislation was evident, even before it became law. A *Times* article in June 1947, suggested that the Bill was not a children's charter at all, but a competent statute that dealt with only one aspect of the problem; 'a transitional measure pending a more enlightened conception. It was a good deed in a naughty world.'[3] The Women's Group on Public Welfare were clearly also of this opinion for, responding to the Curtis challenge, they set up a subcommittee in 1946, to look at the problem of '*The Neglected Child and his Family*'. In his introduction to their published report,[4] J. B. Priestley describes it as 'a kind of sequel-cum-preface to the famous Curtis report' and its analysis of the problems of child neglect and its prevention still have a fresh-ness and relevance today. The Group were sure that 'the removal of the child provides an easy answer to the problems of the un-satisfactory home, but not a psychologically sound one' and they examined many ways of helping such families stay together. Material aid, domestic help, training and guidance in home manage-ment and child welfare, and residential care for whole families, were all considered relevant. They believed that the first priority was 'an intensive family casework service' and they recommended that 'local authorities should be made responsible for providing a comprehensive service for all children living in their care ... exer-cised through a children's committee'. This was a radical suggestion at that time for 'family casework' of the period was seen as the province of voluntary organizations. Researchers, like Bowlby, added their voices to the 'preventive' lobby and the training courses for boarding-out officers began with a strong emphasis on the child in his family context. Even as the child care service was set up, therefore, there was a growing sense that the task set had been too narrow and that there was work to be done for which there was no legislative sanction.

The need for further legal or administrative powers to forestall child neglect and where possible also prevent the admission of children to care (not necessarily one and the same aim) found expression in parliamentary debates in 1949 and in the setting up of a Home Office working party. An administrative solution was pro-posed in July 1950, with the issue of a joint circular to local authorities by the Home Office, the Ministry of Health and the Ministry of Education.[5] The assumption was that, spread amongst several departments of local government, there were significant powers to help children and their families and that better co-ordination of the services involved would improve the help given. It suggested that local authorities should designate a Co-ordinating Officer to secure the co-operation of all local statutory and volun-tary agencies concerned with the welfare of children and that he should call regular meetings of their representatives to discuss 'significant cases of child neglect and all cases of ill-treatment'. Improved co-operation ought to lead to improved service for 'if the right help is not given in time children who might otherwise have remained with their parents may have to be removed from home'.

The law was amended two years later, by the 1952 Children and Young Persons (Amendment) Act. This placed on children's departments the clear duty to 'cause enquiries to be made' into any case where information was received 'suggesting' a child was 'in need of care or protection'—a clear lead to departments to follow up mild as well as grave complaints. It also followed an earlier suggestion of the Women's Group on Public Welfare, by widening that definition to include cases of neglect that were not in any sense 'wilful'. This at least gave children's departments a right of entry into the homes of *some* of the families of children who were likely to come into care. Immediate action was expected on receipt of any complaint and the process of inquiry itself implied some diagnosis of the alleged problem and decisions about whether or not court proceedings were justified. There was still no explicit power to offer *alternatives* to court proceedings—intensive family casework, for example—but at least child care workers now had a legal foot in the door.

There were pragmatic as well as idealistic reasons why the notion of 'prevention' gained ground. The rising costs of the new service have already been mentioned and these were in part due to the steadily mounting numbers of children in care. In 1949, 55,000 children were in care in England and Wales; and the figure rose to 62,500 in 1951 and 64,500 in 1952.[6] Part of the rise was due to the fact that children's departments had wider responsibilities than their predecessors, covering a greater age range and more categories of deprived children. Part was doubtless due to the publicity that the new service had received, causing a natural public response and the presentation of hitherto unmet needs. Certainly an immense pressure of applications for *temporary* reception into care was one result—a trend deplored by the Schaffers in their study of short-term admissions.[7] Part was also accounted for by a steady movement from the voluntary to the statutory sector. As numbers of children in voluntary homes declined, numbers in local authority care rose. The effect on costs was considerable. The Select Committee on Estimates (1951/1952), which had noted the economies that could be effected through foster care, was also alive to the potential savings through 'prevention'. 'Much frustration and suffering (would be) avoided if more attention were directed towards the means whereby situations that end in domestic upheaval and disaster might be dealt with and remedied before the actual break-up of the home occurs.' At the grassroots level, John Stroud had a less polite way of describing this encouragement from central government.

> When I first came galloping out of the University, in shining armour and with all pennants flying, it was to the Rescue of the Deprived Child. Light and air were going to be flooded into the dark places, all those miserable public waifs were going to have a new square deal. And indeed over the years this had happened, we had brought a measure of increased happiness to the children in care. What we hadn't stopped to consider was how they managed to get there in the first place. . . . But we'd only taken a few cautious steps in this direction when Whitehall seized upon the development with glee: here was an even better and even *cheaper* way of caring for children, so cheap it didn't cost anything! Don't care for them at all![8]

The few cautious steps (and some not so cautious) that the local authorities had taken are well illustrated by events in Oxfordshire. The County's response to the Joint Circular was to set up co-ordinating machinery, with the Clerk as the designated officer, but delegating to the Children's Officer. With the 1952 Act pending, it also began to have discussions with the N.S.P.C.C., to consider whether it should make a grant to enable the voluntary body to undertake duties on its behalf. This was, in fact, what Devon chose to do but Oxfordshire eventually decided that the children's department should make its own investigations, but should liaise with the local N.S.P.C.C. inspector on a regular, monthly basis. The department therefore became deeply involved with most complaints of neglect in the area, and this became a part of all fieldworkers' normal duties.

By May 1951, the Children's Officer was also arguing the case for employing a special worker, who would concentrate on working with families whose children were at risk of coming into care. Such a worker would use casework methods, preferably on the Family Service Unit model, and would justify his employment because he would 'have to keep only one family of three children out of care to have saved the Committee the cost of his salary'. Her report to committee had special force, because she was able to use the findings of a Rural Casework Research Group, which had been working in the county and which had produced evidence to show that this approach would be feasible in a rural area. The task of the specialist worker would fall into three parts—prevention, rehabilitation and after-care—and he would concentrate on a small caseload of families that were the most costly to help, if they broke down— large and disorganized families, whose children were often 'unboardable'. By September 1951, the committee had agreed to the proposal and the new officer arrived in January 1952.

The preventive work envisaged was very much influenced by the pioneer work of the Family Service Units. It was aimed at 'hard core problem families', often known to the department over a long period of time and usually beset by a whole host of problems. Such families formed only a minority of any department's total caseload, but the repercussions of their episodic or total collapse were disproportionate. The help given was long-term, painstaking and immensely practical. The new officer was equipped with boiler suit, distemper brush, trowel and scrapers, tablecloths and pots and pans, second-hand clothes, toys and books and substantial supplies of rubber sheeting. 'It is not suggested that sums of money should be given to these families to spend unsupervised . . . what is needed is someone who will bolster up self-respect through gradual stages of achievement in which the worker helps the family to help itself.'

Looking back after three years, a report on his work mentions twelve families where eviction was prevented most effectively by visiting 'on the evening of pay day to take the rent before it can be spent'. Bedding and clothing were sold to families at a weekly charge and 'when the last contribution has been paid the article is handed over. The advantage of this method, apart from the incentive to improvement, is that it encourages the idea of paying for articles before they are worn out.' Octavia Hill might have uttered similar sentiments, and with the same emphasis on a longstanding and trusting relationship between the worker and his families. In sum, by 1955 it was estimated that his efforts had kept fifty children from thirteen families out of care.

The appointment was the first of its kind in the child care service and other local authorities watched with interest. In 1953, Oxford city followed suit and employed a family caseworker and in the summer of 1954 an officer and the Chairman of the L.C.C. Children's Committee came down to discussions in the county, and subsequently employed two special, experimental workers. One forum for the exchange of ideas between local authorities was the professional associations and a sign of the times is the Association of Children's Officers' decision at its annual conference in 1952, to amend its stated objectives. To its aim 'to further the welfare of children deprived of a normal home life' was added 'and to encourage and assist in the preservation of the family'. Training bodies also helped reinforce a commitment to prevention and a tutor at the time stated that 'students assess a department's professional standing by its interest and work in prevention of neglect in problem families and rehabilitation of the parents of children in care'.

There is thus plenty of evidence that people within and outside the child care service were chafing against the constraints of the Children Act almost as soon as it had become law. Providing good substitute homes for deprived children might be the primary task of the service, but it was not the only one and, in a phrase which became familiar throughout child care, 'a fence at the top of the cliff is better than an ambulance at the bottom'. 'Prevention' was more complex than such vivid imagery implied, however, and it is worth looking more closely at what it meant in theory and practice.

At its root lay the conviction that a child's own family was, in most cases, the 'right' place for him to be. Research studies of the period stressed the importance of the mother-child relationship and the damaging effects on a child's mental, emotional and even physical development, if the relationship were inadequate, disturbed or broken. Most studies examined the latter—deprivation by separation—the phenomenon in its most readily observable form. The emphasis therefore tended to rest on the temporary, or even irreversible damage caused to children by removing them from home. To these studies were added the observations of the child care workers themselves. Seeing, at first hand, the unhappiness and distress of many children in care, they were naturally spurred to seek ways of avoiding admissions. Depressingly, too, they saw that many deprived children themselves grew up to be inadequate parents whose children were, in turn, deprived. A 'cycle of deprivation' was acknowledged long before it became a political catchphrase.

To this central concern to avoid separating children from their parents, was added the complicating factor that some families were clearly incapable of providing even a minimum of physical or emotional care and stability for their children. Social workers were therefore faced with decisions about whether or not the deprivations suffered by a child within his family were worse and more hazardous than those he would suffer by removal from home. Such decisions were also affected by estimates of their own skills and the resources available to them, to intervene and *improve* the family

E

situation, to the child's benefit; and by the standards of substitute care that might offset and compensate the child for the effects of separation.

Prevention thus came to be a two-pronged concept; prevention of admission to care; and prevention of neglect and cruelty in the family. A variety of methods of working towards each of these ends can be seen emerging, in response to the differing circumstances of the families concerned. With some families the work was clearly directed to their weaknesses, whether these were problems of poor home management and low standards of hygiene, or of disturbed and volatile relationships. Specialist workers, like the one in Oxfordshire, or ordinary boarding-out officers with such families on their caseloads, tried to improve the family functioning by regular and frequent visiting, practical aid and advice, persuasion, example and consistent support. Sometimes a further degree of specialization arose spontaneously as social workers found they could cope best, either with the physically disorganized and their smells, or with the mentally disordered and their fantasies. This process of intensive casework could, at best, preserve the families intact and improve the children's care within them and, at the very least, would ensure that if the children had to be removed, it was not to complete strangers, by a hostile organization.

In other situations more stress was laid on family and community strengths. Child care workers were aware that many children came into care at a time of family crisis, for lack of any alternative. It was their task to explore and encourage links with kin or with neighbours who could offer care for the children in a familiar environment. If this could not be done without financial aid from the department, then this was preferable to removal to a strange foster home or children's home. Fostering with friends or relatives was no cheaper, but it *was* preventive of much child distress. A further extension of this approach developed in Oxfordshire, where there was concern for two depressing estates of temporary dwellings, where many 'problem families' lived. A conference was convened by the Rural Community Council in 1955 and 'one proposal resulting from the meeting was that consideration should be given to the appointment of a social worker to be resident on the site and to do rehabilitative work, particularly of a community type'. Eventually such a worker was appointed, financed jointly by the Diocesan Council for Moral Welfare, the Education Committee and the Children's Committee. Part of her brief was to build up a sense of community on the estates and the staff of the children's department were drawn into the entertainments and outings that flourished in consequence.

A third dimension to preventive work grew from the knowledge that some families collapsed through external pressures which were beyond their control, yet were within the power of children's departments to influence. A prime example lies in the field of housing. As early as 1951 concern was expressed at the effects on children, separated from their parents because of homelessness. Housing departments were sometimes responsible for evicting families or for failing to house those who were made homeless by other landlords or in other ways. Welfare departments had the responsibility of providing temporary accommodation but this was often insufficient or inadequate and some children had thus to come into care. On behalf of central government, the Under Secretary of State at the Home Office stated 'Housing authorities should realise the consequences to children of eviction, and both they and the welfare authorities should recognise the importance of keeping families together till they could be rehoused.'[9]

Different local authorities took different initiatives on the question. Devon's Children's Officer stated categorically that 'the duty to provide for homeless families rests primarily with the Housing Authority and failing that, with the Welfare Department' and he refused to countenance admissions for homelessness unless the children involved were problems in their own right. As a complement to that attitude, the Devon welfare department developed a family casework service of its own, undertaking work that was the province of children's departments in many other authorities. Oxfordshire, with a less developed welfare department, sought to stave off evictions by the rent-collecting and debt-clearing activities already described. When this was not possible, or when it failed, children had to come into care. As the housing situation worsened, numbers rose till, at their peak, they represented 20 per cent of the total in care. The Children's Committee organized two conferences with housing committee representatives in the late fifties and early sixties and as a result asked the County Council to allow them to pay arrears of rent to avoid eviction in certain cases. Permission was refused and the department had to await new legislation before they could check the dramatic rise of numbers in care, by this means.

Prevention could thus involve members and officers of a children's department at many different levels, in a variety of activities and to a variable degree. At one extreme it could be expressed in a strictly defensive posture towards applications for admission (caricatured as the 'goalkeeping' method of child care, by David Donnison). Authorities varied a great deal in their propensity to admit children to care, some rejecting 70 per cent of all applications and others only 20 per cent.[10] At the other extreme it might involve positive engagement in work with families, their community environment and with other agencies whose influence impinged upon them. At all events, it created a number of problems with which departments wrestled, and to which they responded in different ways. One was the degree to which a children's department ought to engage in preventive work at all. Since the statutes gave no sanction to the activity, some authorities took the view that it was outside their brief. Devon's Children's Officer believed that the service only had such responsibilities when an application for care had been made. 'Preventive work should be done by Health Visitors for children under five and school welfare officers for those of school age.' We have seen, too, that Devon's Welfare Department took on responsibility for work with the homeless, so the children's department's preventive work was within narrowly defined limits. Oxfordshire lay at the other extreme, its Children's Officer arguing that it was a proper part of the department's work because

> the Children's Committee has the greatest incentive to make it possible for children to stay at home, since they have to bear the cost of maintaining them away from home. The staff of the department have more direct experience than any other social workers of the bad effects attendant upon the separation of parents and children.

Preventive work also brought child care officers (the title gradually superseded the original 'boarding-out officer' as the scope of the work widened, not least through prevention) face to face with problems about material and financial aid. They experienced the frustration of recognizing many family situations where cash or help in kind would greatly assist their preventive and rehabilitative efforts, yet there were no funds available for them to use. Some one-parent families would manage more comfortably if money could be given to them to make good day-care arrangements for their children while they worked. Re-establishing homeless families would get off to a better start if they moved to a house equipped with reasonable furniture and sufficient bedding, crockery and pots and pans. There was no sanction for such direct help to families under the Children Act, however, so departments had to exercise their ingenuity by indirect means. They could act as persuasive go-betweens to the National Assistance Board for emergency or exceptional needs grants for families where the parent was not in work. For the poor wage-earning family there were charities and voluntary organizations with resources to be tapped. Dr. Barnardo's, for instance, was developing a valuable 'auxiliary boarding-out' scheme, which helped unsupported mothers financially, instead of taking the children into care. Sometimes a charity could be persuaded to clear debts, to help a family make a fresh start. The W.V.S. was a valuable source of second-hand clothing and household equipment. Alternatively, departments like Oxfordshire built up their own stores, persuading church congregations, local traders and their own foster parents to hand on discarded cots and prams, clothing, toys and household goods and even food, at Christmas, to be given to families who were known to be needy. In this they acted very much as the voluntary family casework agencies had always done, having few resources beyond social work manpower, but using that manpower to beg, borrow or persuade material goods and money from others, on their clients' behalf.

Many of the families that children's departments helped were, in fact, poor, with little or no margin for making an extra effort or for recovering from crisis or the effects of mismanagement. This created for child care workers the dilemma, not only of where to find the necessary money and goods to help them, but of knowing in what circumstances it would be beneficial or perhaps harmful to do so. Engagement in preventive and rehabilitative work revived all the old nineteenth-century problems of whether 'giving', in a material sense, saps initiative, erodes self-respect and 'pauperizes' the receiver. We have seen already how carefully Oxfordshire spelled out the limits of its material assistance to 'problem families'. In this it echoed the Women's Group on Public Welfare, which, though it recommended 'an extension of assistance in kind available for certain cases', thought that it should be closely linked with supervision. While the giving or withholding of material assistance lay outside the full control of child care officers, because their sources of aid lay outside their own department, the dilemma was, perhaps, only faintly perceived and they were better able to identify the cases where they would have wished to assist than those where they would have hesitated to do so. When they subsequently acquired the funds themselves, the dilemma became much more acute.

Thus, by the mid 1950s, most children's departments were actively engaged in preventing the admission of children to care and in working towards the rehabilitation of those in care with their families. In an effort to bolster the child care officers' resistance to 'unnecessary' separations, in fact, some authorities required the Chief Officer or even the Committee to sanction each admission. In other authorities, a careful check was kept on progress in rehabilitation. In Devon, for instance, regular and detailed reports on children in care because of homelessness were made between 1952 and 1955, plotting the gradual decline in their number, through restoration to their families. The results of these policies seemed encouraging in terms of total numbers in care. Both in actual numbers and in the proportion these represented of the child population, figures declined slowly after the peak year of 1953. From 65,309, or 5·6 per 1000 of the population under 18 years, they dropped to 62,347 (5·3 per 1,000) in 1956 and were down to 61,580 (5·1 per 1,000) by 1959.[11] Prevention of the neglect of children in their own homes was more difficult to measure, however, and no published statistics existed to show the extent of work in this sphere.

We have seen that all children's departments had a duty to ensure that inquiries were made into suspected cases of child neglect and that some had carried this further and become deeply involved in a more fundamental aspect of prevention. There was nevertheless a strong sense of frustration and dissatisfaction and this stemmed from two main causes. One was the lack of any clear legal responsibility to undertake this work and hence of funds to support it. The other was the limitations of the 'co-ordinating' solution that had so far been advocated. Following the original Joint Circular of 1950, another in 1956 required up-to-date information on progress made in co-ordinating arrangements. From the replies it was calculated that more than 90 per cent of local authorities had responded by creating formal co-ordinating machinery and over 50 per cent of designated co-ordinating officers were Children's Officers. The *need* to co-ordinate and to co-operate for the benefit of the client was very plain. Parallel with the greater involvement in prevention on the part of children's departments, were complementary developments in other services. A Health Ministry circular of 1954, for instance, had stressed the role of Health departments in preventing family breakdown and there had been expansion of the home help service and the appointment of some specialist Health Visitors in response. Education welfare services were focusing more clearly on the causes of school refusal and some were regarding truancy as a sign of family problems that required more than superficial attention. The N.S.P.C.C. had begun to appoint special female inspectors, to emphasize that preservation of the family was a key aspect of the society's role.

The number of different visitors to families in difficulty was probably no greater than before, since each service had their respective duties to perform. But the role of each one was now less distinct, so that several might call, each with the aim of preventing breakdown or child neglect. It is in this period that tales, true and apocryphal, of processions of do-gooders arriving on the doorsteps of unfortunate families, belong. The mother who tossed her front door key to the latest caller, suggesting it might be of more use if it were kept at the Town Hall, summed up the discomfiture of clients and workers alike. Yet the discomfiture was not adequately resolved by the co-ordinating arrangements that had been made. Departments were jealous of their own territory and were not always keen to refer cases to others. Workers were ignorant or suspicious of each others skill and capacities. Time spent in co-ordinating often seemed time wasted.

Pressure for a clearer statement and demarcation of responsibilities in the preventive field led, at length, to the inclusion of a significant clause in the terms of reference of the Ingleby Committee.[12] This was a Home Office Departmental Committee, set up in 1956 to investigate the powers and procedures of juvenile courts, residential treatment facilities for children who had come before the courts and the prevention of cruelty and exposure to moral and physical danger of juveniles. In a final clause, which Donnison describes as an 'afterthought'[13] the committee were to consider 'whether local authorities responsible for child care under the Children Act, 1948, in England and Wales should, taking into account action by voluntary organisations and the responsibilities of existing statutory services, be given new powers and duties to prevent or forestall the suffering of children through neglect in their own homes'. To children's departments it seemed that, at last, legislation might catch up with and even overtake current practice, and their original task be redefined in a more comprehensive way.

In the event the committee's deliberations took four years and the Report was not published until October 1960. It devoted only ten pages to consideration of new powers for children's services and failed to recommend that they should be imposed. Instead, it urged that a 'general duty' be laid upon local authorities to prevent and forestall the suffering of children through neglect in their own homes; that local authorities (but no specific department) should have power to do preventive casework and 'to provide material needs that cannot be met from other sources'; that there was a need for widespread *detection* of neglect and for 'impartiality in and a measure of independence for those responsible for diagnosis'; that local authorities should be required to submit their schemes for prevention, for Ministerial approval (though Ingleby was not saying *which* Minister); and finally that there should be 'further study by the Government and the local interests concerned of the reorganisation of the various services concerned with the family'. The reaction of spokesmen for the child care service and of some academic observers was one of exasperation and disappointment. David Donnison, who had made a special study of the neglected child and the social services in the early 1950s,[14] summed up the Report as 'respectable and cautious, lacking all sense of urgency and offering no vision of the future structure of the social services— in fact, conservative'.[15]

The Ingleby Committee had, in fact, stumbled into the 'jungle' of the personal social services—'a jungle haunted by primitive prejudices and infested with professional and political pressure groups of the most ferocious kind'.[16] In its own milder terms, it makes this clear in the Report. 'Not unnaturally there still exists a certain amount of inter-departmental rivalry in this field; it was apparent from some of the evidence we received and its existence is common knowledge. . . . We are of the opinion that much of the difficulty which at present exists . . . is due to inter-service rivalries . . .'[17] Its reaction was to retreat. Asked to consider giving new powers to only one of three rival organizations, it fell back on the idea of 'general duties' and 'independent' diagnostic units, perhaps situated in the neutral atmosphere of Clerks' departments, where cases would be sorted out for referral to the appropriate specialist services. Far-reaching solutions needed 'further study'. Understandably, perhaps, a committee that was not inter-departmental and which was composed, very largely, of magistrates and lawyers with no experience of the personal social services, failed to respond in the way these services wished. The reasons why co-ordination had failed were the very reasons why the committee felt unable to propose a radical alternative.

Despite its shortcomings, the Ingleby Report did make some important observations which both reflected and amplified the debate on prevention. One was the link between child neglect and juvenile delinquency. The inclusion of the preventive clause in terms of reference that were concerned with delinquency and the juvenile court system assumed a connection between the two and Ingleby was the first of a whole series of reports and white papers in the 1960s, which explored this connection. An important influence on the committee's deliberations was the rising graph of juvenile delinquency. At the time it was appointed, delinquency rates had shown a reassuring downward trend after a post-war peak in 1951. By 1958 the picture had changed dramatically and rates for the 14 to 17 year age group were double those in 1938 and 47 per cent higher than in 1954.[18] Explanations of delinquency which blamed wartime upheaval and separations now seemed inappropriate and, while 'detailed consideration of the causes of such misbehaviour and neglect is not within our province' the committee nevertheless suggested that 'it is the situation and relationships within the family which seem to be responsible for many being in trouble . . . and it is therefore with family problems that any preventive measures will be largely concerned'.[19] Ingleby had interpreted 'neglect' widely, to include not only the 'inadequate or substandard family' but also the family in which there was 'maladjustment of personal relationships'.[20] It had then suggested that the neglected child was in danger of becoming delinquent and that prevention of distress would also be prevention of deviance. Finally it had assumed that family casework would be of major importance in any preventive programme. This chain of reasoning was to be reiterated and elaborated over the next decade and led, eventually, to major changes in legislation and the whole direction of child care policy.

A second significant thread in the Ingleby Report is its insistence on positive rather than negative prevention. 'Everything within reason must be done to ensure not only that children are not neglected but that they get the best upbringing possible. . . . It is the duty of the community to provide through its social and welfare services the advice and support which such parents and children need' and 'such help should always be directed towards building up the responsibility of the parents whenever this is at all possible'.[21] This seems to imply a reaching out to a wide spectrum of families, and promotion of an optimum level of child care rather than the maintenance of a bare minimum; an extension, in fact, of Curtis standards for children living *away* from their parents to those living in the community *with* their parents. It also relates to the committee's notion of a well-publicized family advice service, which families in need, who might otherwise remain undetected, could feel confident to approach, 'Some door on which they can knock, knowing that their knock will be answered by people with the knowledge and capacity and with the willingness to help them.'[22]

Despite its failure to suggest radical legislative or administrative measures for the extension of prevention, the whole tone of the Report did, in effect, favour tremendous developments in this field, and practitioners were quick to seize on this. The Association of Children's Officers Conference in 1961 had, as its theme, the Ingleby Report and in a remarkable address[23] Mrs. Kahan, the Oxfordshire Children's Officer, rallied her colleagues by emphasizing the positive challenge in the Report and by arguing that the child care service was the only logical place from which to meet the major part of that challenge.

> In no other department, except the Children's Department, are functions in relation to the neglected and the delinquent child combined, nor does any other department have the intimate care of children from birth to 18 years old. No other department is charged with the legal obligation to investigate suggestions of neglect and take legal action, if necessary, and no other service has more than 50% of its officers already carrying out the duties of co-ordinating the social services in the interests of neglected children.

She concluded with a quotation from J. B. Priestley's introduction to 'The Neglected Child and his Family', the report by the Women's Group on Public Welfare, published in 1948, when children's departments were born.

> We are building up an immense structure of health and social services, together with an increasingly complex array of services and organisations that deal with delinquency and crime; but while there are neglected children, who may easily grow up to hate society, we are locking stable doors after vanished horses. If we can rescue the child from his feelings of isolation and despair we can not only give that child some security and a chance of happiness ... but we can also begin to free the community from the strain of trying to turn into good citizens great numbers of men and women who were thoroughly warped long ago in infancy. We can in fact begin at the beginning.

The child care service was thus determined to make the best of a bad job. It urged that Ingleby's general recommendations for an extension of preventive effort should be made more specific. New duties should rest squarely upon the child care service itself, and there should be provision for material help, and even assistance in cash, to families. There followed a period of considerable tension in the local authority jungle. Medical Officers of Health were equally convinced that any new preventive powers should go to them and it was unclear whose view would be accepted, or whether these bitter rivalries would end in deadlock. Eventually, three years after Ingleby, the hoped-for legislation reached the statute book. Considering the struggles that had taken place outside Parliament, the Bill had a relatively calm passage and the political parties were united in its support. Debate was about detail. As Charles Royle, a member of the Labour opposition put it, 'on occasions like this it is very refreshing to get away from party fights'.

The Children and Young Persons Act, 1963, like Ingleby, dealt mainly with aspects of delinquency and the juvenile court system, but section I gave local authorities the preventive powers that had been sought for so long.

> It shall be the duty of every local authority to make available such advice, guidance and assistance as may promote the welfare of children by diminishing the need to receive children into or keep them in care . . . or to bring children before a juvenile court; and any provisions made by a local authority under this subsection may, if the local authority thinks fit, include provision for giving assistance in kind or, in exceptional circumstances, in cash.

There are strong echoes of Ingleby in the *positive* stance implied by the phrase 'promote the welfare'; and in the linking of prevention of admissions to care with prevention of appearances before a juvenile court (not, as some Children's Officers pointed out, necessarily always compatible aims, for prevention of delinquency might sometimes be achieved by admitting disturbed youngsters to care). Making available advice and assistance is also suggestive of the greater publicity and accessibility that Ingleby thought essential for good preventive services.

Children's departments had also won the case for giving material and even monetary assistance to families. The Association of Children's Officers had, in fact, prepared a detailed memorandum on the Bill, while it was being debated in 1962, in which 100 cases were analysed where acute material need had been assessed, and met, by children's departments or voluntary resources. Debts accounted for a quarter of the cases, food and clothing 22 per cent, fares 9 per cent and household necessities 43 per cent. In no case had the National Assistance Board been able to help, because of its own rules or inflexibility. Children's departments had therefore used ingenious means to give help themselves, ranging from using powers of persuasion to atttract 'anonymous benefactors', to 'the device of condemning bedding in children's homes somewhat earlier than would have been done'. Reluctance to go on operating in this devious way made them press for change 'without delay'.

The law, like Ingleby, was sensitive to local authority autonomy and to the rivalries between interested departments, so the duty was imposed on the local authority in general, though it 'stood referred' to the Children's Committee. An explanatory memorandum from the Home Office in September, 1963,[24] was a masterpiece of tact, making it clear that all departments would have a continuing role to play in preventive work and that 'existing arrangements which are working satisfactorily' would not be disturbed, 'nor will it confer a monopoly of preventive work upon children's committees and their staff'. Precise arrangements for implementation were left to local authorities to determine and the variety of practice that had grown up over the years was perpetuated after the Act. In Devon, for instance, the welfare department continued its long tradition of family casework and, together with the children's department, drew on section I monies for its support. In Oxfordshire, where there was no such tradition, the children's department took a dominant role.

Many children's departments had made notable efforts to engage in and expand preventive work, since the earliest years of their existence and their achievements and, perhaps even more, their potential had impressed Ingleby and the architects of the Act. The experiments in Oxfordshire, for instance, were amongst examples mentioned in the parliamentary debates that preceded its passing. How far these efforts had nevertheless been hampered by the absence of any legislative basis was made clear once the Act came into force. The growth in referrals and in work with families in their own homes was startling. In Oxfordshire in July 1964, 655 children were being assisted under section I and new referrals were being received at the rate of nine per week. In May 1965, 722 children were under supervision in their own homes, 'a number considerably greater than in the number in care'. In May 1966, 831 children were supervised, and 517 children had been referred for various kinds of help in only thirteen weeks. Devon's referrals also climbed, but the full impact of the Act can best be appreciated by looking at statistics for the whole of England and Wales. In the year ending March 1967, 234,000 children were referred to children's departments, of whom 46,000 were admitted to care and 133,000 were helped under section I of the 1963 Act. In the year ending March, 1970, 350,000 were referred, 42,000 admitted and 220,000 helped in their own homes.[25] Thus, by the end of the decade, a third of a million children per year were being brought to the attention of the child care service, of whom only a minority (12 per cent) actually came into care, while a substantial majority (63 per cent) received help in their own homes (the remaining 25 per cent were either unhelped or still under investigation). Not only had the workload of the service grown out of all recognition but its whole composition and balance had altered in the process.

The effects on the structure and staffing of the service were considerable, particularly on the fieldwork side. In 1956 there had been just over a thousand child care officer posts in England and Wales and by 1962 this had risen by 50 per cent, to fifteen hundred.[26] This expansion was undoubtedly accelerated by the demands of the 1963 legislation, and by 1970 the figure was 3,741 with an anticipated further increase to 4,400 in 1971.[27] Though it had scarcely reached big business proportions, the service had moved out of the cottage industry stage and only in the smallest local authorities was the Curtis model of a Children's Officer who knew every child in her charge personally, still to be found. (In 1962 there was still one Welsh department which boasted a Children's Officer assisted by one part-time clerk.) With increased size of establishment came more sophisticated methods of communication (memos, tape recorders and inter-com instead of word of mouth messages and consultations on the stairs) and more elaborate divisions of responsibility, with more steps in the internal hierarchy. Authorities were appointing senior social workers, to manage and supervise junior staff, since Children's Officers could no longer do so themselves. Attempts to fulfil the Ingleby ideal of providing 'a door on which people could knock' often meant greater decentralization of services, and consequent delegation of responsibility to area offices, each with their own small hierarchies. More Children's Officers now had Deputies and Assistants. 'Middle management' had arrived.

The increased volume of work, unleashed by the legislation, was matched by growing diversity of approach. Family casework remained a key resource, as witnessed by the increase of field staff,

sometimes in the form of specialist family caseworkers, but departments experimented with many other forms of assistance to
families. A Home Office summary in 1965 of local authority reports
on the first two years' working of the Act, makes this very clear.
Some followed Ingleby's recommendation and set up or financed
family advice centres in urban areas. Cornwall pioneered 'flying
angels'—foster mothers, equipped with Dormobiles, who went to
the family instead of having the children moved to them. Holidays
were arranged or financed to provide the kind of break that many
overwrought mothers and children needed. Tentative experiments
in group work emerged—a Friendship Club for isolated mothers,
for instance, and a day training centre for mothers who had difficulty in child rearing and household management. There were
also attempts to involve the wider community. More than one
authority appointed village representatives who could be called
upon to rally help in an emergency. Another was compiling a list of
sympathetic landlords, willing to admit evicted families as a means
of preventing further family breakdown. The Home Office circular
accompanying the Act, had made the point that 'reception into
care of one or more children for a period may enable a family to
cope better with its other children and thus preserve a home to
which the former child or children may eventually return'.[28]
Oxfordshire sometimes used boarding schools in this way, preserving a fragile family situation by limiting the child's presence in the
home to holiday times—a variation on a well-known middle-class
theme.

Perhaps the most fundamental development, however, was the
increased use of material and financial aid. A wall had been erected
in 1948 between income maintenance services and personal social
services, whereby social workers no longer had any public assistance functions and money and 'welfare' were kept firmly apart.
Children's departments had chafed at the limits this put upon
their powers to help and had met many family situations where
the National Assistance Board were unable or unwilling to assist
and where they were hard-pressed to meet need themselves. The
1963 Act breached that wall, though the gap was small. 'It is not
intended that the power to give material assistance under section I
of the Act should be used to provide an alternative to National
Assistance or a child care supplement to National Assistance
payments.'[29] Local authorities were generally cautious, but differed
in its use. Heywood and Allen found variations in expenditure from
£18 to £0·7 per 1,000 population under 16 years in their study.[30]

Nationally, expenditure under section I increased from £88,000 in 1966 to £202,900 in 1969 and individual authorities reflect this trend. Devon children's department, for example, records a figure of £1,882 in 1966 and of £2,249 in 1967. Much assistance was given in kind or indirectly (to council landlords or public utilities, in payment of arrears and debts, for instance).

The operation of the new power had some very important consequences. One was the increased involvement of children's departments in negotiations with other public bodies. It had been urged upon them that careful discussion and demarcation of boundaries with the National Assistance Board would be necessary. Oxfordshire records a joint meeting in 1965, when complaints were made that the children's department's habit of paying off debts, when the Board had refused to do so, damaged the latter's relationships with their clients. It was concluded that the 'disparity of policy at government level' should be taken up nationally. The child care service also found itself more heavily engaged than ever in negotiations with housing departments over rent arrears and threatened evictions and many developed a system of rent guarantees—paying to one arm of local government from the purse of another. Debts to public utilities were also presented to children's departments for solution. Families threatened with disconnection of gas or electricity supplies obviously faced hardship, especially in winter, and the child care service sometimes felt obliged to pay off arrears to ensure that children were not being kept in cold, dark houses, with no cooking facilities. Work under the 1963 Act meant that involvement with other agencies was now on a much greater scale and on a new and sometimes uncomfortable basis. Cast in the role of Fairy Godmother to families in difficulties, the service found itself under considerable pressure to square the accounts of other public bodies, by drawing on its own funds. For fear of being overwhelmed, it argued and bargained, offering part-payments, requesting the instalment of pre-payment meters, suggesting more frequent rent collections and more efficient presentation of accounts, promising supervision of families in return for concessions from creditors, and so on. Some departments developed standing orders, or regular referral procedures to committee level, to cope with some of these problems. Others proceeded on an *ad hoc* basis. By 1969, Oxfordshire decided that a specialist with expertise was necessary and appointed Tony Lynes (sometime secretary of the Child Poverty Action Group and subsequently a personal adviser to the Secretary of State for Health and Social Security) as 'family casework organizer' to undertake many of these negotiations on the department's behalf.

The pressures and dilemmas for the service as a whole were also experienced at grassroots level, by individual child care officers. They were exposed to a much wider range of families in difficulty, some of whom suffered from no other problem but poverty. Limited financial help combined with supervision seemed inadequate and inappropriate for these families and help with budgeting on so little 'an insult'.[31] The discretionary nature of section I meant, also, the power to withhold as well as the power to give and the choice might be difficult, painful or invidious. According to Heywood and Allen, the new legislation achieved some success in averting short-term crises but was of less obvious benefit in pursuing the long-term goal of better care for children in their own homes.[32] Once again, the service seemed caught up in first-aid and emergency work, when it had aspired to prevention of a more fundamental and lasting kind. The new powers, which had been sought for so long, were soon regarded as a mixed blessing.

The earliest struggles to prevent child deprivation rather than merely dealing with it on a more generous and sensitive level had led, within the space of two decades, to an important shift in the focus of the whole service and to great increases in its scale. By the 1960s, children supervised in their own homes far outnumbered those 'in care' and departments were involved, not only with a significant minority of all families with children (one-third of a million children, referred in one year, represents roughly 3 per cent of the total child population) but with a whole range of other services on their behalf. With increased size came increased complexity and specialization of the service's internal organization and a greater diversity of working methods. New problems emerged and old ones were revived. Not least of these was the most crucial problem in child care—judging the lesser evil. Prevention meant workers had, time and again, to weigh the likely damage caused by separation against that caused by physical, material or emotional deprivation within the home. As standards of substitute care rose these had to be balanced against the sometimes tragically inadequate standards within natural families. The effect of all this upon the child care task, as it was originally defined in 1948, were considerable and will be examined more fully in later chapters.

NOTES

1. Home Office Circular No. 160/1948 states 'To keep the family together must be the first aim, and the separation of a child from its parents can only be justified when there is no possibility of securing adequate care of a child in his own home.'
2. Curtis Report, op. cit., para. 7.
3. *The Times*, 29 June 1947. Article by K. Lindsay.
4. *The Neglected Child and his Family*, O.U.P. 1948.
5. Joint circular from the Home Office (No. 157/50), the Ministry of Health (No. 78/50) and the Ministry of Education (No. 225/50), 31 July 1950.
6. Local Authorities' Returns of Children in Care.
7. H. R. Schaffer and Evelyn B. Shaffer, 'Child Care and the Family', *Occasional Papers in Social Administration* No. 25, G. Bell and Sons, 1968.
8. John Stroud, *The Shorn Lamb*. Longmans, 1960, pp. 242–3.
9. Mr. Ross, Assistant Under-Secretary of State, Home Office, at a Conference of Chairmen of Children's Committees and Children's Officers in April 1951.
10. Jean Packman, *Child Care: Needs and Numbers*, Allen and Unwin, 1968, p. 199.
11. Local Authorities' Returns of Children in Care.
12. Committee on Children and Young Persons, under the Chairmanship of Viscount Ingleby, which reported in 1960 (Cmnd. 1191).
13. In 'Social Services for the Family' one of three critical essays on the Ingleby Report, *Fabian Research Series* 231, December 1962.
14. David Donnison, *The Neglected Child and the Social Services*, Manchester University Press, 1954.
15. 'Social Services for the family', op. cit.
16. Ibid.
17. Ingleby Report, op. cit., Chap. 2.
18. Ibid., Chap. 1.
19. Ibid.
20. Ibid.
21. Ibid.
22. Ibid.
23. B. J. Kahan, 'Prevention and Rehabilitation', published in the *Approved Schools Gazette*, December 1961.
24. Home Office Circular No. 204/1963.
25. Local Authorities' Returns of Children in Care.
26. Sylvia Watson, 'Manpower in the Child Care Service', in *Social Work*, January 1964.
27. Summary of Returns of Child Care Staff at 31 March 1970., D.H.S.S.
28. Circular No. 204/1963, op. cit.
29. Ibid.

F

30. Jean S. Heywood and Barbara K. Allen, *Financial help in social work*, Manchester University Press, 1971.
31. Ibid.
32. Ibid.

CHAPTER FIVE

Miscellaneous and Pending

Insistence on the importance to the child of his own family had led some children's departments to break the bounds of the 1948 legislation very early in their careers. Not all were so bold, but 'prevention' made sufficient psychological and economic sense to produce a broad consensus on its desirability. Early experimentation gained momentum and won approval and led, ultimately, to significant changes in the law and a marked shift in the emphasis of the whole service. In some other spheres of children's department activity, however, there was much more ambivalence and attempts to widen the scope of the service were less successful. One such area was that of private fostering.

Amongst the many deprived children who had been considered by the Curtis Committee, was a group of some fourteen thousand children who were under the supervision of welfare authorities in accordance with the Child Life Protection provisions of the 1936 Public Health Act. Roughly eleven thousand of these children were in foster homes, having been placed privately and directly by their parents or guardians, without the intervention of any public or voluntary body. The rest were in private, profit-seeking Homes or nurseries. Curtis had been concerned at the precarious situation of many of these children and regarded the then upper age limit for supervision, of nine years, as far too low and wanted this raised to school-leaving age. It also recommended that the definition of foster children should be widened to include not only children maintained 'for reward' by non-relatives, but also those who were so maintained without any reward—'*de facto*' adoptions, in effect. The committee did not, however, recommend either the abolition or the strict control of private child care arrangements, though it was clearly uneasy. Having 'considered whether the private boarding-out or "fostering" now arranged direct between the parent of the child (generally illegitimate) and the foster mother could be brought under the full control of the children's committee and children's officer', it drew back, but 'concluded with regret that this is as far as public control can be carried'. It feared that further intervention, by requiring parents to consult children's departments before any placing, for example, would merely drive private fostering underground, concealing it from the supervising authorities. Presumably it was also felt to be an unwarrantable infringement of parental rights to ban the practice altogether.

The 1948 Act raised the age limit for the supervision of privately placed children, as Curtis had requested, but failed to include children for whom no payment of any kind was made. The duty to supervise passed, with that Act, from local authority health departments to the new child care service. It was a very general duty, however, and no regulations comparable to those governing the visiting of officially boarded-out children were made. It was expected that child care staff would visit the foster homes to satisfy themselves about the welfare of the children, but the frequency of visits was not stipulated, there was no obligation to work towards restoration with parents and no power to help financially or materially or to require medical examinations or regular reviews. This was in sharp contrast to children in care. People who fostered children privately were required to notify the children's department no less than a week in advance of any placing (unless it was an emergency) and on its part, the department was obliged to 'make enquiry whether there are any persons residing in the area who undertake the nursing and maintenance of foster children' for reward. Children found living in unsatisfactory circumstances might be removed by means of a court order, but not on the visiting officer's initiative alone—again in contrast to the position of officially boarded-out children.

The law thus emphasized the peripheral nature of the child care service's responsibilities to this particular group of children. If departments undertook their own fostering they first had to select and approve the foster parents and then supervise and support them with considerable care. If parents made their own fostering arrangements, departments merely had to *know* about these arrangements and keep a weather-eye on the children involved. Only if there were problems serious enough to warrant bringing a court case were they encouraged to intervene.

Evidence is slender, but it suggests that most children's departments accepted the status quo and regarded the supervision of privately placed children as a necessary but minor part of their work. There seems to have been no large scale attempt to take over the private market, for example, except perhaps in the very first year of the service. The 11,000 children in private foster homes, recorded by Curtis in 1946, had shrunk to 7,411 by 1949, which might mean that a substantial number of placements were terminated after the war or were made official by taking the children into care under the Children Act. Thereafter, the figures declined only slowly and were at their lowest in 1960, at a little under six thousand.[1] More dramatic reductions had taken place in the private nurseries and children's homes which were also supervised under child life protection legislation so that, by 1960, only a few hundred children were left in such accommodation. By comparison, the private fosterings had remained fairly static.

Local authority records are more illuminating but even here the privately placed child is mentioned only occasionally. A minute in one of the Devon Area records for 1952 resolves 'that the action of the Children's Officer, declining to receive this London child into care from a private nursing home be confirmed and that the Children's Officer be instructed to deal with similar cases in the same way'. This gives a clue to why many children's departments were content to let private arrangements alone. A continuing feature of such children has been their uneven distribution throughout the country. In the 1950s, country areas, especially in the south, supervised the bulk of private placements and many of the children concerned came from urban areas, sometimes a considerable distance away.[2] This must have made useful work with parents by supervising authorities very difficult but it seems also to have produced resistance to becoming involved with 'other people's problems'. Services financed by local taxes have always been inclined to pass back problems to the area from which they came— with or without the sanction of laws of settlement. In child care, the belief that links between children and their parents ought to be encouraged, not severed, may have reinforced this tendency. The costs to a local authority of *not* operating in this way could be high. In Oxfordshire, where concern for privately placed children seems to have been unusually vigorous, half of the children in private foster homes in the county in 1959 came from the London area and more than half of these were subsequently admitted to Oxfordshire's care, because the placements were unsatisfactory.[3]

Some children's departments may have colluded with the weaknesses of the legislation, but in 1958 a new Children Act revised local authority powers. In the words of a Home Office Report, 'the new legislation is substantially on the same lines as the old, but is rather more positive'.[4] Section I of the new Act outlined overall responsibilities.

> It shall be the duty of every local authority to secure that children within their area who are foster children within the meaning of this part of the Act are visited from time to time by officers of the authority, who shall satisfy themselves as to the wellbeing of the children and give such advice as to their care and maintenance as may appear to be needed.

Private foster parents were required to give more advance notice of placing (fourteen days instead of seven days); local authorities could prohibit placements with unsuitable people—amongst others, those whose own children had been removed by a court or who had been convicted for offences against children. They could also prohibit on the grounds of unsuitable premises and impose various requirements on those who habitually fostered children, specifying maximum numbers, adequate staff and facilities, records to be kept and so on. Failure to comply with such regulations or refusal to allow child or premises to be visited or inspected was sufficient grounds for a warrant to be issued to remove the children. Juvenile courts took over responsibility for hearing such cases from magistrates courts.

Though the object of the new legislation was to strengthen local authority powers, it appears that supervision of private placings remained on a largely *laissez-faire* basis and, despite expressions of alarm at the low standards of some private foster homes, there were few cases of intervention to forbid placings or to remove the children concerned. Robert Holman's interesting study of private fostering, made in 1968[5] (the only piece of research so far done on this topic) showed that in the two Midland authorities studied, a consistently lower standard of supervision of privately placed children prevailed, when compared with foster children in care. The former were visited less often, their parents were rarely seen, the foster parents were given much less support materially and in terms of discussion of problems and the records kept were more limited. The child care officer's role in relation to private foster homes seemed predominantly inspectorial and no attempt to remove any child from a home had been made in either authority, despite the fact that workers considered about half of the placements to be unsuitable—some of them seriously so.

It is impossible to know how typical these findings are, though Holman's authorities were selected as 'average' on a number of criteria. In Devon, an elaborate analysis of work done in 1953 shows the average time spent per visit to private foster homes to be seven minutes less than visits to official foster homes, but averages may conceal wide variations and there is no analysis of the *content* and therefore *quality* of visits, nor of the number of visits per year to children in the different categories. The marked national growth in numbers of private placings after 1960 can also be interpreted in different ways. From 5,833 in 1960, numbers grew to 10,907 in 1969—as high as in 1946. Children's departments may have contributed to a reduction in the private fostering market in the first decade of their existence, but certainly failed to do so in the second. Part of this expansion may have been due to more effective notification procedures after 1958, though Holman's work casts doubt on this, since only 5·6 per cent in his sample were notified to local authorities in advance. A lot was undoubtedly due to new problems of immigrant parents seeking foster care for their children while one or both of them studied. Over half of Holman's cases fell into this category.

If a rather negative view of the child care service's involvement with private foster homes is accepted, it is worth considering why this should be so. One obvious reason is the law itself. The 1958 legislation made only marginal changes and departmental obligations were loosely drawn. The child care officer's duty to visit private foster homes 'from time to time' contrasted with the regularity and frequency of visits that was spelled out in the boarding-out regulations. Since advance notification procedures were rarely observed—perhaps through ignorance more than intent to deceive—children's departments had little chance of prohibiting placements before they occurred. They also felt hamstrung by the necessity to prove a case for removal of children in a juvenile court. General unease about a placement, or a feeling that it was 'not good enough' would not make a case and even in more extreme circumstances a lot of time, energy and skill was required to assemble evidence that would stand up to judicial scrutiny. Oxfordshire's records reveal years of work and the involvement of officers and committee members in a single case of unsatisfactory foster care.

Frustration with the law and its limitations led, in fact, to further changes in the 1969 Children and Young Persons Act, but, again, these are marginal and, paradoxically, in some respects they even weaken local authority powers. Children placed for no 'reward' whatever are at last included in the definition of 'foster child', as Curtis had wanted, but regular foster parents no longer need to notify the comings and goings of individual children in their care. Similarly, local authorities have more discretion and need only visit where they think it 'appropriate'. Thus the ambivalence of the law remains to reinforce that of its administrators.

This ambivalence seems to stem from a variety of causes. One is probably economy or expediency. Most children's departments were under heavy pressure to admit children to care and many had great difficulty in finding foster homes. Refusal to allow the use of a private home, or a decision to remove children from it, inevitably involve finding alternatives. If the parents themselves are unable or unwilling to have their children back, the department must provide its own substitute home. In a situation of shortage the temptation is to leave well alone. As with local authority powers to declare houses unfit or overcrowded, the consequences of action rather than the incapacity to act, may be the determining factor.

Belief in the importance of preserving parental choice and upholding parental rights may also be influential, and accords with the law. The 1948 Children Act is concerned essentially with providing substitute care for children whose parents *request* it. True, there is also provision under section 2 of that Act for a local authority to assume parental rights over children whose home circumstances appear disabling enough to warrant it, but this is a power that can only be exercised *after* the child has been admitted to care. *Removing* a child from parental care against their will has always been, and still remains, a court's prerogative. In the same way, the right of parents to make their own arrangements for the care of their children, with the minimum of interference from public bodies, is enshrined in all child protection legislation. In this respect, the law takes into account the thousands of satisfactory holiday and emergency arrangements that are made between friends. But it must also take into account the exceptions—the extreme cases, where babies are handed over to complete strangers or children entrusted to unsuitable people. The element of protection for the child is thus balanced against and in some senses competes with parental rights. Understandably, perhaps, a service that had become convinced through the evidence of research and from its own experience that the well-being of children was inextricably linked with that of their natural parents, would favour the encouragement of private enterprise in this sphere. Holman's study certainly showed that the parents who had made their own fostering arrangements had more contact with the home and therefore with their own children than those who had entrusted their children to local authority care.[6] To set against this rather generous interpretation of service motivation, however, it must be remembered that, again according to Holman, child care officers did little positively to *encourage* parental involvement with private foster homes (they rarely had contact with the parents) nor to help resolve conflicts between natural and foster parents or deal with the difficulties of the children. '*Laissez-faire*' may more often have been a form of neglect than a positive policy.

Further confusion is caused by the dual standards that social workers apply when attempting to assess the welfare of a child. Child care literature stresses the central importance of the emotional ties that a child makes with the adults who care for him. Providing these are basically sound and loving, material deprivation or lack of mental stimulus may be regarded as lesser evils, to be tackled *in situ*, without disrupting the emotional bonds by removing the child. Where removal has occurred, however, the substitute home must then be much *better* than the original, to make up for the vital ingredient of emotional continuity. In the words of Curtis 'the aim of the authority must be to find something better—indeed much better—if it takes the responsibility of providing a substitute home'.[7] Thus conditions of poverty, disorganization or squalor may be tolerated in a 'natural' family that would cause a department to reject it outright, should it apply to foster. It may be that child care workers have been uncertain about which standards they are applying when assessing private foster homes. Should they be equated with official foster homes and judged according to that yardstick? Or is it imagined that, by some alchemy, direct parental choice and commitment to a substitute home turn it into a 'natural' unit, to be judged accordingly? To be fair, the fact that workers only become acquainted with most private homes *after* the child has arrived, makes further difficulties. It is far easier to reject would-be foster parents before a child is placed, than to risk upsetting and harming the child by removing him, once he has settled.

A final factor affecting a large part of the private market, at least since the 1960s, is the emergence of new needs for which legislation has not provided. A high proportion of private fosterings concern children of immigrants—especially West Africans—who seek temporary substitute care while they study or support each other in the quest for qualifications that will be highly prized at home.[8] But the child care service has not usually interpreted the 1948 legislation to cover admissions of children, because of the educational or financial aspirations of their parents. Indeed, child care workers would argue that emotional stability for the child is of paramount importance and should take precedence over such aspirations. Nor, during its lifetime, did the child care service have any control over alternatives to full-time substitute care for such children—day nurseries, for instance, or registered daily minders—which might have provided an acceptable compromise. If intervention in unsatisfactory arrangements meant taking the child into care against established principles there may have been reason—though no excuse—for turning a blind eye.

For all these reasons, the child care service in general, with some exceptions, seems to have missed an opportunity to extend its influence and to apply the improved standards of the post-1948 era to the private child care sector. Aware of this, the professional associations have pressed for improved legislation, and met with only partial success. The Association of Children's Officers, for instance, wanted stricter controls of visiting, comparable with the boarding-out regulations for children in care—an interesting indication that professional discretion was thought to be ineffective. They failed, and the 1969 legislation remains vague on this point. Perhaps a crucial factor, amidst all the complexity, is that improvements in supervision and control over private foster care would mean more expense, not less. The seductive arguments for 'prevention' do not apply.

Another group of deprived children, linked with the local authority system, are those cared for by voluntary organizations. Following a Beveridge, rather than a Bevanite model of the welfare state, the Curtis Report recommended that these organizations (many of them dating from the nineteenth century) should remain in existence alongside the newly created child care service. Indeed, if nationalization or, more properly, municipalization had been contemplated, the expense would have been tremendous, since no less than 33,000 children were cared for by voluntary bodies in 1945—considerably more than were maintained under the Poor Law. In any case, there was no evidence that voluntary bodies, in general, were caring for children any less adequately than the public bodies of the period, and in some instances their standards were among the best. They ranged in size from big organizations with London headquarters and a national network of facilities, like Dr. Barnardo's, the Church of England Children's Society and the National Children's Home, to small, single Homes run by local committees. Among features that disturbed Curtis most were the legacy of big, barrack-type buildings, which were often unadapted, for lack of adequate funds; the isolation of the children and the old-fashioned quality of care experienced in some Homes—especially those with a strong religious bias; and the stigmatizing trappings of special clothing, or unfortunate house-names that were occasionally used. Two hundred little girls in identical velvet dresses, made from the surplus window material of a big store; children who bobbed up and down curtseying and saying 'Yes, Ma'am, No, Ma'am'; Homes with notice boards proclaiming 'Home for Destitute Children' and the 'Magdalen Home'; and establishments where children were involved in day-long routines of work, prayer and little free leisure time were examples of some of the things that most troubled the committee.

To improve these standards whilst allowing voluntary bodies the freedom to go on operating and encouraging their best efforts, the 1948 Act extended direct central government controls, already in existence under the 1933 Children and Young Persons Act. All voluntary homes for children supported wholly or partly by voluntary subscription, or by endowments, were to be registered with the Secretary of State, who had power to refuse registration and, in effect therefore, to have the home closed. Like children's departments, they were subject to Home Office inspection and the Secretary of State could make regulations governing the conduct of voluntary homes. These regulations could take into account such things as numbers, staffing, records, facilities for parental visits and—an interesting inclusion, in the light of Curtis—prohibition of 'clothing of any description' that seemed inappropriate to the Secretary of State. In effect, the regulations that were subsequently applied to local authority homes also applied (with some additions) to the voluntary sphere. In the same way, the boarding-out regulations for local authorities applied equally to voluntary bodies, who practised fostering. Not all the links were regulative or inspectorial, for the Secretary of State was empowered to make grants for improvements to voluntary homes.

Links with local authorities were on a different basis. Children in care could be placed in voluntary homes, and this often happened where a voluntary home seemed more appropriate, or where local authority accommodation was in short supply. Such children had to be visited by officers of the children's department. If a voluntary home was closed, through the Secretary of State's intervention, the local authority in whose area it was had to take the children concerned into care—whatever their home circumstances and even if they were over seventeen years old. Children's departments also had to 'advise and befriend' young people between school-leaving age and eighteen who had been discharged from the care of voluntary agencies, unless they were satisfied that the organization itself was providing an adequate service. This was a direct result of criticism in Curtis of the poor after-care arrangements for some working children who had been in voluntary care, and were unsupported and 'adrift' at a crucial period of their lives. Finally, under section 54(3) of the Children Act, it was a local authority duty to visit all children in voluntary homes in their area 'from time to time ... in the interests of the wellbeing of the children'. This was presumably an attempt to draw the two arms of the child care service together and to counteract any tendency to isolation on the voluntary bodies' part. The Home Office circular accompanying the Act was careful to point out, however, that the section 'provides for the visiting of homes, not for their inspection'. Suggestions of local authority superiority were to be avoided and if 'a local authority have reason to think that there is need to examine the conduct of a voluntary home, or that there is any matter in regard to the home which should be brought to notice, the authority should report the circumstances to the Secretary of State, on whom the responsibility for the inspection rests'. Like the Secretary of State, local authorities also had power to make grants to voluntary bodies concerned with promoting the welfare of children.

Predictably the creation of a statutory child care service led to a decline in the scale of voluntary care. The Home Office statistics chart the falling number of children cared for by voluntary organizations, from 25,000 in 1954, to 19,000 in 1960 and 11,500 in 1971. Many voluntary homes ceased to be registered, some because their function changed (some became boarding-schools, for instance), others being 'obliged to close' through 'the absence of demand for places in the home, staffing difficulties and sometimes lack of funds'.[9] In due course many large voluntary homes were closed and replaced by smaller units. Adaptations and improvements were aided by central government grants.[10] Nevertheless, local authorities continued to use voluntary homes to accommodate some of the children in their care. Indeed, though these numbers also fell at first from 6,500 in 1951 to under 4,000 in 1960, they climbed again in the 1960s and had reached 5,500 by 1971—or nearly half of all children in voluntary care. To this extent the dividing line between the two systems of child care became much more indistinct.

One reason for this must lie in the complementary roles that the two branches of child care were encouraged to adopt. The Home Office frequently stressed that voluntary organizations should not merely replicate the statutory system. Their explicit religious commitment offered parents of the same persuasion a real alternative to local authority care and, in addition, they were urged to meet the needs for 'specialist provision, for continued experimental work in the care of children and also in preventing a breakdown of family life'.[11] Successive Home Office reports draw attention to the way the voluntary organizations responded to this— offering special residential care for physically and mentally handicapped children; developing hostels for working adolescents and young adults; expanding family assistance schemes to keep children and parents together, and so on. Barnardo's, celebrating its centenary in 1966, laid emphasis on the task of seeking out new needs and pioneering new methods and in the 1970s it reorganized itself completely and ceased to attempt national coverage, concentrating instead on seven urban areas of acute child care need, and developing new forms of help, including day-care and community work. Foster-care never assumed the importance that it did in the local authority sphere—roughly 20 per cent of voluntary society children were boarded out compared with the 50 per cent that children's departments achieved. This clearly worried the Home Office in the 1950s, but only a few voluntary organizations employed sufficient social workers to support such developments. In the 1960s, what was seen as a handicap seems to have been turned to an advantage, for the voluntary bodies advertised their experience and expertise in residential care and local authorities were often glad to use them for this reason. A decade of decline and withdrawal was followed, for some voluntary bodies at least, by one of experiment and rejuvenation.

The pattern at local level is, however, much harder to discern. Voluntary bodies have never been evenly spread throughout the country and their influence is much more deep-rooted and directly felt in some parts than in others. Children's departments themselves also adopted a variety of attitudes—some eager to refer cases to voluntary society care and others reluctant to do so. Interpretations of the Children Act varied, so that one authority might admit children in certain circumstances to care, while another would claim it had no power to do so, and might suggest voluntary care instead. The balance between statutory and voluntary care is therefore subject to significant local variations.[12]

Other links between the two child care systems apparently remained tenuous. No space is given in any of the Home Office Children's Department Reports to discussion of 'advising and befriending' activities on the part of local authorities in relation to ex-voluntary society children, and the numbers involved appear always to have been small. By 1969, a mere twenty-two children in the whole of England and Wales were recorded as receiving this form of supervision, though whether because of improved after-care by the voluntary bodies themselves, or ignorance and apathy on the part of local authorities is not revealed. The extent to which local authorities took an interest in voluntary homes in their area is also unclear. The first Home Office Report following the Children Act notes that visits have been taking place and 'have had the good effect, among others, of enabling the officers of the children's departments of local authorities to improve their knowledge of the work of voluntary homes'.[13] No subsequent reports make any further mention of the subject. At the local level, a letter from the Superintending Inspector to the Children's Officer for Oxfordshire, in 1957, refers to a recent departmental inspection and makes special mention of the visits paid by a social worker to a large voluntary establishment in the county, 'where your interest and help in the care of the boys there seems to have been greatly appreciated'. This partnership led to the attachment of a special worker from the children's department, who could offer social work support to boys, many of whom came from far away and were only rarely in touch with their own local authorities. Local authority fieldwork resources were thus added to voluntary residential facilities, for the greater well-being of the children concerned. How far this was typical, however, or to what extent such experiments were sustained elsewhere, is not easy to judge. No published local authority records concerning this kind of development exist, but the absence of references in reports of central government suggests that this was not a widespread trend. Coexistence rather than active collaboration was probably the norm.

Children placed for adoption form one more important group with whom local authorities and voluntary bodies have been concerned since before the Curtis Committee reported. Before 1926 it was possible for parents to place their children permanently in the care of relatives, friends or strangers, but their parental rights and obligations were not thereby extinguished and the children had no legal status *vis-à-vis* their foster parents. Natural parents were entitled to remove such children whenever they wished. The insecurity and instability that this caused for all parties—parents, foster parents and, not least, the children—was recognized and led, eventually, to the Adoption of Children Act, 1926, which for the first time made possible the irrevocable transfer of parental rights from natural parents to foster parents by means of a court order. Adoption became increasingly popular and, in due course, the law came to be used in three main ways. In the majority of cases it involved the transfer of children to non-relatives, who thus provided them with a permanent substitute home, in place of their own families. In some cases it concerned the transfer of children from natural parents to the care of relatives and adoption was then a device for providing a child with a new status and security within his own family network. Finally, in a substantial minority of cases (estimated at over 30 per cent in the 1950s) an illegitimate child's status was made more 'respectable' by adoption by his natural mother or father, either in his or her own right or—more usually—in conjunction with a spouse who might or might not be the natural parent of the child. Most children who were adopted were born illegitimate (approximately 80 per cent). The rest had generally been victims of parental death, abandonment or broken homes.

Before and after Curtis, it was legally possible to place children for adoption with *non*-relatives in any one of four ways. Parents could, themselves, choose and effect a placement—'direct placings'. Individuals (but not corporate 'bodies') could act as intermediaries, putting would-be adopters in touch with available babies. Doctors, midwives and other members of the medical profession were sometimes in a position to do this when they had contact with both unwanted children and childless couples. Placements arranged in this manner were known as 'third-party placings'. Voluntary bodies, having the status of 'adoption agencies', could also make arrangements. Some of the big voluntary organizations for children, that have already been mentioned, had this status and their adoption work formed part of a wide range of facilities for deprived children. Other voluntary bodies concentrated solely on arranging adoptions. Finally, local authorities could themselves arrange to discharge children from their care, by means of adoption.

After Curtis, children's departments had additional duties with regard to adoption, besides their important right to arrange placements for children in care. One concerned the *supervision* of all children placed for adoption within their boundaries. Whether such children were placed with natural parents, relatives or non-relatives and whether placements had been arranged directly, by third-parties or by adoption agencies, children's departments became involved. The law stipulated that adoptive parents must have had continuous care of the child for a minimum of three months, before an order could be granted and during this 'probationary period' the child had 'protected' status and was subject to supervision by the relevant children's department. The terms of supervision were similar to those affecting children in private foster homes. At a later stage in the proceedings, when a date for an adoption hearing had been fixed, the court had to appoint a '*Guardian ad Litem*' to act as an independent agent on its behalf, His duties were to investigate all the circumstances of the placing, to see all the parties involved, to check that the law had been complied with (consents properly given, no payments made in respect of the adoption and so on) and to give a full and confidential report to the court. Children's departments were usually chosen to fulfil this function, so that in most cases child care officers would first come to know adopters in their capacity as supervisors, concerned to safeguard the welfare of the protected child and then, changing hats, would act as agents of the court, reporting on all aspects of the case and having a potentially significant influence on its eventual outcome. The benefits and tensions inherent in combining these two roles will be explored later. Where children's departments had themselves been concerned in placement arrangements, an independent outsider had to act as *Guardian ad Litem*. Sometimes this was a probation officer and sometimes a member of another children's department. Finally, voluntary adoption agencies had to register with the local authority in whose area their headquarters were situated. This gave children's departments the power to call for information about their activities and gave them a right to withhold or cancel registration if their management or staffing was unsuitable or inadequate. In this respect their relationship to adoption agencies had similarities with that between the Secretary of State and voluntary homes.

During the years following Curtis developments in law and in practice in relation to adoption and the contribution of the child care service, in particular, are uneven and often hard to follow. The law was frequently under review. Curtis had included adopted children in its brief and amendments to pre-war legislation were made in 1949 and consolidated in 1950 but even then a further review was promised at a later date. The Hurst committee of inquiry[14] duly sat from 1953 to 1954 and, in consequence, further amendments were made in the 1958 Adoption Act. At the end of the 1960s another departmental committee of inquiry (Houghton)[15] was set up, which made more sweeping proposals for change, which are currently being enacted. Throughout all these changes and the varied responses of the statutory and voluntary administrators who influenced, or were influenced by them, three distinct but inter-related themes can be seen emerging. One concerns the balance between the rights of natural parents and the rights of adopters. A second relates to the quality of service to be offered to all parties to adoption which, in turn, affects some of the legal processes involved. The third concerns the appropriateness of adoption for children in a variety of circumstances. For whom is it the ideal 'solution' and for whom would other forms of care or legal status be more suitable? Linking all three is the constant, but steadily more articulate concern to achieve what is in the best interests of the welfare of children.

The permanent relinquishment of a child by his parents to the care of other people is no simple exchange relationship. Few, if any, parents come to a final decision to abdicate their role without doubts, depression and anguish. Similarly, the emotional investment in the exchange by couples who seek to add to or to create a family by means of adoption is enormous. The law and those who administer it try to hold the balance, seeking, on the one hand, to ensure that natural parents reach their decision freely, unhurriedly and with full understanding and, on the other, that adopters are protected from avoidable delays, vacillations or uncertainty that might endanger both their own emotional and mental well-being and that of the child in their charge. Changes in the adoption law in the 1950s reflect the attempts made to poise on this emotionally-charged seesaw. Most, but not all, amendments moved gradually in the direction of the adopters. The 1958 Act, for example, did away with the need to obtain consents to adoption from anyone 'liable by virtue of an order or agreement to contribute to the maintenance of the infant'. In effect this removed previously held rights from putative fathers who were maintaining or helping to support their illegitimate children. The same Act also increased the grounds for dispensing with parental consent altogether, adding to neglect, ill-treatment, abandonment, incapacity and 'unreasonable withholding', the new clause of persistent failure 'without reason-able cause to discharge the obligations of a parent or guardian'. *De*

G

facto abdication of parental responsibilities could therefore be legally ratified, against a parent's will. Growing safeguards of the anonymity of adopters were also a feature of the period. Adopters could protect themselves by use of a serial number in all the pre-court and court proceedings, so that natural parents need never know who they were or where they lived. (This obviously could not apply where parents had arranged the placing themselves.) By the 1958 Act, withdrawal of consent on the grounds that the parents were in ignorance of the adopters' identity could be held to be 'unreasonable'. Severance from a child 'blindfold' not only protected adopters from parental interference but was, perhaps, also more bearable to some natural parents. More unequivocal concern for the natural parents was expressed in the prohibition of consents to adoption in the first six weeks of a child's life. The period immediately after a baby's birth was known to be one of intense emotion and potential instability for any mother and considered decisions about the future ought therefore to be delayed. For this reason, too, adopters who received babies soon after birth were not allowed to count the first six weeks of care as part of their 'probationary period'. They, too, were slowed down. In the interests of all, including the child, hasty decisions were prohibited.

The quality and nature of the service to be offered in cases of adoption was also the subject of debate and exploration. Curtis regarded adoption as the best substitute for children who could never be restored to their parents and Hurst went further and claimed 'there can be no doubt that adoption is generally a much more satisfactory solution than any form of institutional care or even fostering'.[16] Because it was also a final solution, extreme care in selecting and supervising adopters, so that children should not be brought up by unsuitable people, was also advocated. Curtis thought the skills of boarding-out officers, whose main task included vetting foster parents and introducing children to them, were specially suited to adoption work. Considering the importance it was given and the responsibilities involved—in no other work does an 'arranger' so nearly play God—it is ironic that the child care service was not given a more instrumental role in the first instance. Though it had supervisory and/or *Guardian ad Litem* duties to perform in respect of most adoptions, its role in arranging placements—and therefore in the vital processes of selection and matching—was a relatively minor one. In the 1950s, between 13,000 and 15,000 children were adopted each year, 8,000 were under children's departments' protective supervision at any one time and over 80 per cent of *Guardian ad Litem* duties were performed by members of the child care service. Yet only about a thousand children each year were actually discharged from local authority care by means of adoption. A further irony was that adoption work was not subject to the same Home Office inspection as were other aspects of children's department work.

Not all departments were content with this situation. Some made attempts to discourage private and third-party placings. Goodacre's study[17] describes how the children's departments concerned had been at pains to make known to parents the benefits of carefully arranged agency placements and had made special efforts to discourage doctors and other intermediaries who were known to arrange adoptions. A major drawback of many private adoptions was the proximity of parents and adopters and their consequent anxieties about discovery and confrontation. In extremis, one G.P. was 'eventually . . . confronted with chapter and verse evidence of the unhappiness and anxiety that had resulted from his actions'.[18] In Oxfordshire, positive co-ordinating activities, which included monthly meetings between the Children's Officer and moral welfare worker, also helped to reduce the incidence of private placements. Discouraging ineffective voluntary societies was a different matter. Despite local authority powers over registration, Goodacre concluded that some Children's Officers were generally reluctant to inspect or penalize their voluntary colleagues and the limited grounds on which they could do so were also inhibiting. The legislation was rarely used to improve standards, yet some of the smaller agencies, struggling with tiny, untrained staffs and no facilities for children if things went wrong, were clearly at a disadvantage compared with organizations with trained staff and a whole range of alternative care facilities.

In view of this situation, perhaps the most significant clause in the 1958 Adoption Act (section 28) was that which empowered local authorities to 'make and participate in arrangements for the adoption of children'. Whereas, before, it had been possible to arrange adoptions for children already in care, the new Act gave children's departments freedom to place children for adoption who were *not* in care—to act, in fact, like any other adoption agency. As with prevention, it seems that some departments were ahead of the law, for according to Pugh, 'some were in fact placing children other than those in care before this date'.[19] But legal sanction presented the possibility of an extension of responsibilities and a significant shift in the balance of *who* should provide adoption services. The number of local authority adoptions duly rose from about a thousand a year in the 1950s to over three thousand by the mid-1960s, and the proportion this represented of all adoptions climbed from 7 to 19 per cent.[20] That the growth was not greater, nor the proportion higher is, in part, due to the permissive nature of the legislation which empowers but does not oblige a local authority to arrange adoptions. True to form, the children's departments responded in different ways. By the end of the 1960s more than half were doing so (96 out of 172, according to Houghton). Reasons given by the Children's Officers for *not* doing so were various. Some small authorities felt restricted by their size and lacked the resources to range far outside their boundaries. Following the principle that children would be best placed at a distance from natural parents, they felt unable to act. Over-stretched resources, unrelated to the size of authority, was another reason given. Some simply felt they were unable to encompass one more time-consuming function. Others again (like Devon) claimed that voluntary agencies in their area were vigorous and competent and local authority participation would merely duplicate existing services.[21]

The voluntary adoption agencies had certainly expanded steadily since Curtis and had played a significant part in reducing the proportion of private placements. Whereas they were responsible for about a quarter of all adoptions in 1946, twenty years later the figure was 40 per cent, and private placements with non-relatives had taken a complementary turn downwards, from about 33 to 7 per cent.[22] Thus, by the 1960s, statutory and voluntary services were clearly in partnership but, in terms at least of the scale of adoption arrangements, the latter was still the senior partner.

Developments affected not only *who* should be the providers of an adoption service, but also the extent and nature of the service given. In the interests of the child, for whom adoption involves a permanent severance of blood relationships and their replacement by a new family (transplantation in effect), the obligation to select adopters with extreme care is obvious. It is equally important to the adopters themselves who 'must be protected from undertaking responsibilities for which they are not fitted or which they have not appreciated'.[23] The law laid down guidelines. Applicants must be interviewed, their homes seen, references taken up and medical examinations conducted. Within this framework, statutory and voluntary agencies developed their own procedures. In the 1950s when Goodacre was investigating, the children's departments that she studied seemed generally to spend more time on selection than their voluntary counterparts. They paid more visits, took up references personally, discussed more searching issues and rejected more applicants. In this they were helped by richer resources of skilled and experienced staff, time, transport and clerical assistance. The traditional chain of responsibility meant that investigations were carried out by a child care officer who would discuss her findings with a senior and decisions would then be taken, following reference to the Children's Officer. Sometimes the committee was also involved in more than a simple ratification procedure.

As departments increased their adoption work in the sixties, these processes were sometimes modified or elaborated. In Oxfordshire, for example, once its adoption agency work began to grow, a specialist Adoption Officer was appointed to take a share of the work herself and to co-ordinate the adoption work of other social workers. A panel of senior members of the department was formed to consider each application with the investigating officer. Decisions were then made jointly. Shared decisions were thought to promise a greater degree of experience and expertise and some of the burden of such far-reaching decision-making was also lifted from individual shoulders. Fresh methods of interviewing were also introduced. Two social workers would independently interview a couple—one of either sex, so that viewpoints could be compared. Greater efforts to interview applicants both separately and together were made. Experimental group interviews for new would-be adopters were also held—an economical way of imparting information about agency requirements and procedures, and about adoption itself, before proceeding to individual interviews with those still interested. In the mid-1960s the department also initiated an 'adoption group' of interested local authorities and voluntary agencies, which met at quarterly intervals in order to share, improve and standardize procedures. Some other departments arranged their work differently, creating a specialist section which dealt only with adoptions, but whatever the particular pattern chosen, engagement in adoption work was liable to have implications both for a department's administration and for its methods of work.

Developments in the supervisory duties connected with adoption were less marked. Child care workers often complained that their role was unclear and that beyond ascertaining that the child looked well cared for, there was little they could do, especially if a reputable agency had arranged the placement. Unless a home was privately chosen and grossly inadequate, there was no question of removing the child and recommendations on the suitability of the adoption were the duty of the *Guardian ad Litem*. When a supervising officer was also appointed *Guardian ad Litem*, however, there was the advantage of having additional time to arrive at an informed opinion and the supervisory visits could be well-spent considering whether adoption really *was* in the best interests of the child concerned. But social workers were sometimes conscious of other work that might be done. The early months of caring for a new baby could be very stressful and worrying ones for adopters and support and advice could be valuable. There was also scope for discussing with adopters the problems that might arise in the future —particularly the difficulty of telling children of their adopted status in a kindly and appropriate way. Discussions held during selection interviews might be reinforced, with more meaning, once the child had arrived. However, the ambiguities of the social worker's role often interfered with such work. Adopters felt too much 'on trial' and were too nervous of the outcome of court proceedings to admit to difficulties. Social workers were unsure how far they might be duplicating or cutting across the work of placement agencies. Provision of a continuing social work service to the adopters (who would have no automatic access to services at all once the order was made) was hampered in its execution by the nature of the judicial process and by the number of different agencies involved.

At the other end of the see-saw local authority social workers were often in a good position to provide a proper service for the natural parents. Giving consent 'freely' should mean not only without pressure from other persons but with some degree of real choice as well. The range of facilities that children's departments had developed or had access to, including foster and residential homes and various preventive strategies, meant that adoption could be considered as one among a number of solutions, though not all Children's Officers were convinced of the value of this. Devon's Children's Officer, for example, thought illegitimate children should either remain with their parents or be adopted, and other forms of substitute care were regarded as partial and unsatisfactory solutions. Nevertheless, it was the absence of such facilities in single-purpose adoption agencies that was one of the reasons why many local authorities were critical of them. The child care service's commitment to prevention and its growing consciousness of the environmental disadvantages of many of its clients may also have persuaded child care officers to give more sympathetic service to parents than some of their voluntary counterparts.

The 'appropriateness' of adoption is a theme which recurs throughout the whole period. Disquiet is expressed that, for some categories of children, it is a clumsy and possibly damaging device —a legal blunt instrument, in effect. The other side of the coin is the concern expressed about the numbers of children who might benefit from adoption but who have been debarred through blinkered views about who is, or is not 'suitable'.

Several categories of children have always fitted rather uncomfortably into the framework of legal adoption. One is the small group of illegitimate children, adopted by a single parent. No transfer of parental rights occurs and the only effect of adoption is to obscure the illegitimacy. Before 1959 it was even possible for natural parents to adopt their illegitimate offspring *jointly*, for there was no automatic legitimation of a bastard on the marriage of his parents, unless both had been unmarried and therefore 'free to marry' at the time of his birth. This barrier was removed by the 1959 Legitimacy Act and parents no longer had to use the device of adoption. One small group of 'inappropriate' children was thus taken out of reach of adoption law. Another group consists of illegitimate and, increasingly, of legitimate children who are adopted by one natural parent and one step-parent. Though transfer and a new sharing of parental rights is involved, the presence of a natural parent sets these adoptions apart from the majority and poses difficulties for any social workers involved. In the 1950s, supervision of such cases was regarded as difficult and ambiguous. Applicants looked on procedures as a 'mere formality', since orders were rarely refused and the supervisor's role was obscure.[24] It is probably for these reasons that the 1958 Adoption Act abolished statutory supervision in such cases, but the question of the suitability of the whole adoption process remained unresolved. Finally, there is a small group of children who are adopted by relatives. Social workers have been particularly concerned by this group, for the complications that are created when artificial, adoptive relationships are superimposed upon existing blood-relationships—grandparents becoming parents, mothers becoming sisters, for instance—seem to create more problems than they solve. It is significant that, among the small number of these adoptions that were investigated by Goodacre, no less than a quarter were either opposed, or described with strong reservations, by the *Guardian ad Litem* concerned. The fact that orders had, nevertheless, been granted suggests another category where the law is a 'mere formality'.

In contrast, denial of adoption to some children who might very well benefit is not a question of law, but of practice. Traditionally it has been regarded as an appropriate form of substitute care only for babies and very young children. Parents tend to be prepared to relinquish their children more readily when they are very young, and before they have formed strong bonds with them. In addition, research has stressed the significance of the earliest attachments of infancy and has warned against disturbing these. Effective transplantation would seem to be best assured if the child can form his first relationships with his adoptive parents. Adoption statistics reflect this, as at least 70 per cent of adoptions granted each year are in relation to children under school age and most of the remainder concern adoptions by parents or relatives. Nevertheless, agencies have begun to place a few older children, sometimes after a protracted period of fostering. In 1970, five hundred children of school age and above were adopted by non-relatives. There have been recent assertions, backed by American research, that this number could be further expanded and that agencies are still too timid in this respect.[25] How far this will lead to any large-scale increases remains to be seen. Consciousness of the difficulties that many older deprived children present, reluctance to extinguish parental ties and nervousness about the finality of adoption all suggest that developments will be slow and cautious.

In the past there has also been a tendency to assume that children with mental or physical handicaps and children of different race or colour were 'unadoptable' because most would-be adopters desire to create a 'normal' or even 'ideal' family. That this is still the case, despite the dwindling supply of available babies, would be attested by many social workers. Yet special efforts to find permanent homes for such children have met with some success. In 1965, for example, the British Adoption Project was set up specifically to promote adoptions of 'non-white' children. Besides its own success in placing more than fifty children, it ascertained that 445 adoptions of non-white children had been concluded in the United Kingdom in 1966, though as many again were in need of homes but without them. Arising from the Project, the Adoption Resource Exchange now attempts to co-ordinate agency resources in efforts to find placements for such children.[26]

All these issues are discussed and brought together in the Houghton Committee Report of 1972[27] and most have been incorporated in new legislation. The committee, aware no doubt of the emotive nature of the whole subject of adoption, made the interesting experiment of publishing an Interim Report a year after it began its deliberations and invited 'comment and criticism'. Reactions were too strong and varied to allow an acceptable compromise on every issue and some of its final recommendations are still fiercely debated. On one point, however, there was total agreement. The welfare of the child should be 'the first and paramount consideration' and this principle, already articulated in the 1958 Act (under Section 7 the court must be satisfied 'that the order if made will be for the welfare of the infant') should be reinforced at every stage of the adoption procedure.

With this in mind, Houghton made numerous recommendations for the improvement of adoption services. It wished to ban independent placements altogether, whether made by parents themselves or by 'third-parties'. Research has produced no firm evidence that these placements turn out any less well than others, but the observations of social workers and courts suggest that some very bad arrangements *are* made in this way and 'adoption is a matter of such vital importance to a child (who is usually too young to have any say in the matter) that society has a duty to ensure that the most satisfactory placements are made'.[28] In future, those who make such arrangements and those who benefit by them, will be liable to prosecution. In an attempt to counteract evasion—placing for 'fostering' with the covert intention of adoption—a child placed independently will have to have been at least a year with foster parents before adoption can be considered.

To complement these recommendations the committee made various proposals for strengthening agency services. A local authority's permissive power to provide an adoption service will be replaced by a statutory obligation and it will also be required, in co-operation with voluntary societies, to ensure that a comprehensive service exists in its area. The regional variations, caused by differing local authority practice and the patchy coverage of voluntary agencies might thus be overcome. The committee also interpreted 'comprehensive' to mean a whole range of alternative forms of care for children and families, of which adoption would be one, and hoped that all parties to adoption would receive equally extensive help and support.

To improve standards of practice central government registration of voluntary agencies was favoured (a comment upon the ineffectiveness of local authority controls in the past) and the criteria for registration will be broadened to take account of 'the programme, resources and organisation of voluntary societies'.[29] An extension of the professional advisory and consultancy services (once upon a time the central government 'inspectorate') to voluntary as well as statutory adoption agencies was also recommended. As an interesting counterbalance to the increased amount of central government responsibility, the agencies will be allowed more discretion in practice. The information to be obtained about prospective adopters will no longer be prescribed in law but should be 'a matter for guidance rather than legal prescription'.[30] For local authorities, the freedom not to provide a service at all will be replaced, to some degree, by the freedom to provide it in the way they think best.

Other proposals for improved service include the replacement of supervision by local authorities during the 'probationary period' with supervision by the placing agency. The adopters will thereby receive some continuity of service and social work resources will be less wastefully deployed. The adopters will also see the supervisor in a more helpful light, since she will be identified with the agency which has approved the placement and not with the court which might or might not grant the order. Useful work in helping adopters to adapt to 'new family roles and changed relationships' might more easily be done as a result. Again, in the interests of continuity and agency responsibility, the placing agency will be required to make a full report to the court and be represented at the hearing. A by-product of these new requirements will undoubtedly be that very small, understaffed voluntary agencies will go out of business, unable to cope with these demands.

The best use of adoption and its appropriateness in different circumstances also exercised the committee. It was persuaded by arguments against its use by single parents to obscure a child's illegitimacy, for 'it is important for a child to know the truth about its origins'. It therefore recommended that adoption in such cases should be an exceptional rather than an accepted procedure and that the court should be satisfied that 'special circumstances' justified its use. Arguments against adoption by natural and step-parents jointly, and by relatives of a child, also carried weight with the committee and in these cases it favoured 'guardianship'. It was specially perturbed by the number of legitimate children who, after the break-up of a marriage, were adopted by the new partners. To Houghton it seemed 'desirable to recognise openly the fact and consequences of divorce and death . . . (and) the legal extinguishment by adoption of a legitimate child's links with one half of his own family was inappropriate and could be damaging'. Similarly, it disliked the distortion of existing relationships within a family, when relatives adopted. Eventually it concluded that neither category should be debarred from adopting but that the court should consider guardianship first, to determine whether it would be more appropriate, 'first consideration being given to the long-term welfare of the child'.

'Guardianship' ('Custodianship' in the clumsy terminology of the new Act), is distinguishable from adoption in several ways. It does not extinguish parental rights but suspends them and parental consents are not essential; it is not irrevocable but subject to review at any time; and a child's relationships with members of his natural family remain unaltered by it. For all these reasons it seemed to Houghton preferable to adoption where relatives or step-parents were concerned. The committee thought that applicants for guardianship, like adopters, should be subject to a three month probationary period and that the local authority should investigate all the circumstances of the case during that period and make a full report to the court.

When Houghton's recommendations are implemented, substantial numbers of children will be taken outside the range of adoption law and the legislation confined more narrowly to the permanent transfer of children to non-relatives. Moves in the opposite direction —to confer the benefits of adoption upon a wider range of children than is currently possible—are inextricably linked with the vexed subject of the rights of natural, foster and adoptive parents and the right balance to be struck between them and it is in this area that most controversy has arisen. These proposals and the arguments surrounding them in fact stretch beyond adoption to the status of all children in care and their families, to the particular problems of ill-treated children and to the role of foster care. As such they belong to a later chapter, but for the present it is worth just noting the major changes that are pending. First, parents will be allowed to 'relinquish' their parental rights to an adoption agency even before their child has been placed with adopters. This may help parents and adopters alike by allowing an early final break and thus reducing uncertainty. Secondly, foster parents who have cared for a child for at least five years may apply for an adoption order, irrespective of the parents' wishes or those of the placing agency. This gives foster parents, for the first time, the right to challenge the overriding rights of parents or agencies and asserts that a person who has loved and cared for a child for many years deserves to be recognized as a parent in law, as well as in fact. (The committee's logic founders at this point, since this makes possible the extinction of existing relationships—albeit tenuous—thus contradicting its conclusions about the value of *maintaining* the original family ties of the children of divorce. Use of guardianship for long-term foster parents would be more consistent and there is provision for this in the new legislation.) Thirdly, there will be more grounds on which a court can dispense with a parent's consent to adoption; and lastly, local authorities will have greater power to assume parental rights over children in care. All these measures, taken together, might release a considerable number of children—some of them older children—for adoption or guardianship. The committee's belief that this would be in their interests is in line with some encouraging research findings on the outcome of adoption, even for older children. In Britain, the cohort studies of the National Children's Bureau suggest that illegitimate children who are adopted fare better socially and educationally than their counterparts who remain with their families and better, even, than legitimate children in their own homes.[32] In America, follow-up studies of older children who have been adopted are also encouraging.[33]

The Houghton Report has received official approval and legislation is now formulated, so that adoption is about to be integrated into the mainstream of child care, a generation after Curtis. In consequence the parties to adoption ought to benefit from an improved service and adoption may more often be considered as one possible solution for children in care. In future it will be a little easier to break the legal ties between children and their parents and to replace them with new, permanent bonds. Long-term planning will be that much easier and fewer deprived children may suffer from prevarication or the absence of any plans at all. Despite the benefits, the controversial issues will remain alive because deciding what is in the best interests of the 'welfare of the child' sometimes requires the wisdom of Solomon; and because adoption underlines the fact that a child's interests are not always compatible with the laudable aim of preventing family breakdown. Child care workers will continue to struggle with imponderables and the heartening knowledge that their interventions to provide substitute care are often highly successful will still be offset by the sadness that this is at the cost of failure to preserve some unfortunate families.

NOTES

1. Local authority returns of children in care.
2. *Child Care: Needs and Numbers*, op. cit., pp. 129–31.
3. Ibid., p. 131.
4. *Eighth Report of the work of the Children's Department*, Home Office, 1961.
5. Robert Holman, *Trading in Children*, Routledge and Kegan Paul, 1973.
6. Ibid., p. 193.
7. Curtis Report, op. cit., para. 447.
8. Holman, op. cit. Over half of his sample of privately fostered children were born of West African students.
9. *Seventh Report of the work of the Children's Department*, Home Office, November 1955. p. 25.
10. £45,000 was granted between 1951 and 1955; £70,000 between 1955 and 1960; £127,000 between 1960 and 1963 and £122,000 between 1963 and 1966.
11. Ibid.
12. *Child Care: Needs and Numbers*, op. cit., Chap. 6.
13. *Seventh Report*, op. cit.
14. *Report of the Departmental Committee on the Adoption of Children* (Hurst), Cmnd. 9248.
15. *Report of the Departmental Committee on the Adoption of Children* (Houghton) 1972, Cmnd. 5107.
16. Ibid., p. 4.
17. Iris Goodacre, *Adoption Policy and Practice*, Allen and Unwin, 1966.
18. Ibid., p. 125.
19. Elisabeth Pugh, *Social Work in Child Care*, Routledge and Kegan Paul, 1968. p. 84.
20. Data from local authorities' returns of children in care and the Houghton Report.
21. See Chapter 13, *Child Care: Needs and Numbers*, op. cit.
22. Data from Curtis and Houghton, op. cit.
23. Hurst Report, op. cit., p. 4.
24. See Goodacre, op. cit., Chap. 10.
25. See, for instance, Jane Rowe and Lydia Lambert, *Children Who Wait*, Association of British Adoption Agencies, 1973.
26. See Lois Raynor, *Adoption of Non-White Children*, Allen and Unwin, 1970.
27. Cmnd. 5107, op. cit.
28. Houghton Committee, para. 88.
29. Ibid., para. 61.
30. Ibid., para. 79.
31. A study commissioned by the Houghton Committee showed that over 2,000 children boarded-out by a sample of twenty-five statutory and voluntary organizations had been in their foster homes for more than five years, though there is no indication of how many of these foster

parents would wish to adopt. (See Appendix D.) Research published in 1973 (*Children Who Wait*, op. cit.) estimated that approximately 7,000 children in Britain were in need of permanent, substitute families but were currently cared for in institutions or temporary foster homes.

32. Eileen Crellin, M. L. Kellmer Pringle, Patrick West, *Born Illegitimate*, National Foundation for Educational Research, 1971.
33. Alfred Kadushin, *Adopting Older Children*, Columbia University Press, 1970.

CHAPTER SIX

Deprived or Depraved?

The child care service as established in 1948 was designed primarily for deprived children rather than delinquents. Young offenders had always been regarded as a special problem, requiring punishment, training or re-education, rather than substitute 'care' and separate services had developed as offshoots and adaptations of the adult penal system. The juvenile courts, as part of the judiciary, tried and sentenced young offenders. The probation service (court-based and outside local government) supervised delinquents who were thought to be in need of guidance in their own homes and there were a few probation homes and hostels which housed young probationers who had been required to fulfil a 'condition of residence'. For offenders for whom more prolonged removal from home was judged essential there were 'approved' boarding-schools, run by boards of managers and accountable directly to the Home Office. The vast majority of these were independent bodies or were run by voluntary organizations but a few were provided by local authorities. For the 'hardened' older juvenile offender, the Prison Department ran Borstals.

The Curtis Committee accepted that questions of criminal justice and the treatment of delinquent children were beyond its terms of reference, but at some points of overlap it felt it appropriate to make recommendations. For example, it was open to magistrates to commit *non*-offenders to approved schools as well as offenders and a small minority of boys and a much larger proportion of girls were dealt with in this way. These were children who had been found in need of 'care or protection', through neglect, cruelty, truancy or moral danger and in their case an approved school order had been made in preference to the more usual committal to the local authority. Curtis questioned whether, in future, many such children would need approved school training, for the education authorities' new powers to provide special education for maladjusted children under the 1944 Act should 'take them in hand before they become a problem for the juvenile courts' and it also hoped that fit person orders would be used more frequently. Nevertheless it saw a continuing role for approved school training 'for the really difficult or unruly child and the child who has been exposed to very depraved influences between whom and the delinquent child the difference is often merely one of accident'.[1] The other side of the coin was the courts' powers to commit *offenders* to the care of the local authority. Again, only a minority of children were dealt with in this way, but it was accepted that the power to provide for some young offenders who were more sinned against than sinning should continue. Curtis clearly recognized that the boundaries between the deprived and the delinquent were blurred, but did not doubt that distinctions nonetheless existed.

Remand homes were also considered by Curtis since they were provided by local authorities, but served the juvenile courts as places of observation and assessment for children on remand, of detention for offenders in need of a very brief term of punishment, and temporary accommodation for children awaiting approved school vacancies, which were in short supply. It was recommended that, in future, they should be used for only the first of these purposes and that, in any case, younger children might well be remanded to reception homes, once children's departments had established them. Neither recommendation was incorporated in the 1948 Act but the children's departments did take over the running of remand homes. By no means every department provided one, but clusters of neighbouring authorities reached 'joint-user' agreements and a fair spread of accommodation was achieved by this means. The only other link between the new service and delinquents, forged in the 1948 legislation, was by means of section 6(4), which enabled local authorities to admit to care children released from approved schools, if they had no suitable home to return to. In practice, this was a power that was used in only a handful of cases each year.

In its earliest years the child care service's peripheral role in relation to delinquency was set against a background of considerable concern about juvenile crime. This rose to a new peak in 1951, when nearly 17 boys out of every 1,000 under 17 were found guilty of indictable offences—a rise of nearly 100 per cent on pre-war figures.[2] Children's departments were involved at the margins. A joint memorandum from the Secretary of State and the Minister of Education in April 1949, urged local authorities to set up conferences to look at local problems of delinquency and to 'secure more effective co-operation among the organisations and services responsible for the welfare of young people'.[3] Just as there were exhortations to co-ordinate in the interests of neglected children, so similar measures were thought desirable to prevent juvenile crime. In 1952, the Children and Young Persons (Amendment) Act embodied the Curtis suggestion of allowing offenders under twelve years to be remanded to reception homes and it also empowered children's departments to undertake the after-care of children released from approved schools. Once again some departments had jumped the gun and, according to the Home Office, 'this has been done informally in the past by some local authorities without express statutory authority'.[4] Nevertheless, the Act had sanctioned two more small breaches in the line which divided the deprived sheep from the delinquent goats.

In general, however, major developments in the field of delinquency in the 1950s took place outside the child care service. In 1949, for example, the police in Liverpool pioneered 'juvenile liaison' schemes and numbers of young offenders were kept out of court by cautioning and advice from selected police officers. Attendance centres also multiplied in this period, again staffed mainly by police officers who supervised the leisure activities of delinquent youngsters. Another new form of treatment was the detention centre, run by the Prison Commissioners and designed to provide 'brisk activity under strict discipline and supervision . . . for the more hardened boy in his teens . . . for the adolescent who thinks that he has come off best in his trials of strength with society and sees no reason why he should not continue to do so'.[5] The first detention centre was opened in Oxfordshire in 1952. Even in the field of approved school after-care, the child care service played a minor part and the probation service gained more ground. In 1954, local authorities were responsible for supervising 18·9 per cent of the boys and 50·5 per cent of the girls released from approved schools, while their probation colleagues supervised 14·5 per cent and 30·3 per cent respectively. By 1959 these positions were reversed; the local authority figures were 11·7 per cent and 28·5 per cent and probation's figures were 22·6 per cent and 53 per cent.[6] The majority of the remainder were supervised by the schools' own after-care agents.

The general picture does, however, obscure some marked local differences and a few children's departments played a much more active role by seizing every opportunity that was presented to work with delinquents. Oxfordshire was outstanding in this respect

H

and it is worth looking in some detail at its attitudes and activities in the fifties and early sixties, for they provide a vivid case-study of policy-making at the local level. The county had, in 1948, a juvenile delinquency rate slightly above the mean for a rural area.[7] The children's department inherited a boys' remand home, but there were no approved schools within the county boundaries. There was, however, a large voluntary 'training school' for adolescent boys, which offered boarding education and a trade training to deprived and disturbed youngsters from all over the country. (The school figures quite prominently in the early records of the Devon department, for instance.) Presentation of 'home surroundings' and school reports to the juvenile courts had traditionally (since 1933) been undertaken by officers of the education department, but in May 1951, the Home Office suggested that the children's department could appropriately take this over and, despite some education department resistance, this was done. Thereafter, child care officers became responsible for preparing and presenting social inquiry reports on most juveniles appearing in the county's courts. For several years they attended regularly in the juvenile courts and became acquainted with the home circumstances of a much wider spectrum of offenders than those who might actually be committed to care. Though, later in the fifties, the probation service staged its own takeover and responsibility for social inquiry reports passed gradually to probation officers, the court setting and young offenders were by then familiar to most child care officers and magistrates were, in turn, well acquainted with the children's department.

From these beginnings, departmental interest in delinquency developed. Service to the courts, remands to the reception home and approved school after-care enabled committee and staff 'to observe at first hand how artificial were the distinctions between the children who were referred for neglect, the ones who were received into care and the ones who appeared before the juvenile court as offenders'.[8] Faced with children with apparently similar needs and coming from similar backgrounds to those of the deprived children with whom it was largely concerned, the department responded by offering its care facilities to offenders. Magistrates learned that, if they wished to remove a delinquent from home, the children's department would be willing to accept him on a fit person order and would, in fact, prefer to try this, before resort was made to an approved school committal. The courts and probation service were co-operative and gradually the balance between approved school orders and fit person orders changed, and the latter became the rule rather than the exception for offenders removed from home. In 1951, thirteen approved school orders were made (ten in respect of offenders), compared with four fit person orders (all for non-offenders). In 1956 there were four approved school orders (three offenders) and eighteen fit person orders (eleven offenders); in 1960 three approved school orders (two offenders) and twenty-five fit person orders (eight offenders).[9] In 1964 only one Oxfordshire child was in an approved school.

As a corollary, the department was also prepared to use its powers under the Children Act to admit troublesome children to care on a voluntary basis, with parental agreement. Persistent truants—'non-offenders' before the law, but seriously at risk of becoming delinquent—were sometimes treated in this way and admitted for relatively short periods of care, to re-establish a pattern of school attendance. Police were also encouraged to refer children who had come to their attention and appeared to be at risk, and child care officers began to offer voluntary supervision and help to such children in their own homes. These policies were reflected in higher than average rates of admission for 'other reasons'—a Home Office umbrella term that covered admissions that were unusual and hard to classify in traditional Children Act terms.[10]

Such policies had important effects upon the department's use of residential facilities. Small, mixed children's homes could not easily absorb more than one or two difficult teenagers and foster homes were not easy to find for this group, so the department sought other means of caring for the older offenders. Its links with the voluntary training school have already been described and, as a complement to its liaison work with the residential staff and with boys from other areas, it placed a number of its own difficult adolescents in the school. The boys had access to the trade training and remedial education that they might have received in some approved schools, with the added advantage of continued contact with their families and their own social workers. Other forms of further education and training, like farm institutes and colleges of further education, were also utilized. Boarding education was sometimes used for school-age children, with holidays spent either at home or, where this was impossible, in foster homes or children's homes. Interestingly, this was a pattern of care that had been advocated by Curtis, when discussing alternatives to approved schools. As the policy of caring for delinquents snowballed, however, pressure mounted for special facilities within the department itself and in 1961 a hostel for twelve working girls was opened, followed by one for fifteen boys in 1964. Also in 1961, a new boys' remand home was opened, designed on 'family group' lines, with house units run by married couples and each accommodating ten boys. A similar pattern was used in a new girls' remand home that was opened in 1964, so the adaptations to institutional living that had been advocated for deprived children were adopted for delinquents. Even these developments did not fully meet the increased demands on a service committed to dealing with offenders, however, and committee minutes and Home Office correspondence of 1966 and 1967 make frequent reference to shortages of residential accommodation and the need to build and extend still further.

Much clearly depended upon the goodwill, commitment and understanding, not only of field and residential staff within the department, but of many other people outside the service. Magistrates needed confidence in the department if they were to commit to care children who would elsewhere be sent to approved schools. The department, without any statutory obligations to do so, offered to supply the magistrates with six-monthly reports on the progress of committed children and there was thus some feedback on the outcome of their decisions. By 1960, visits to the various children's homes by parties of magistrates were being arranged, so that they came to know where some of the children they committed were accommodated and met the staff who cared for them. The field staff also built upon their good relationships with the training school and with other voluntary homes and schools which housed Oxfordshire children. It was a matter of policy that no matter *where* a child was placed, his own social worker would keep in touch by correspondence and by visiting. Continuity and a living link with home was considered of vital importance to the child and to the establishment and took priority over considerations of economy and time. Involvement with numbers of difficult teenagers also spurred the department into experiments with a wider range of treatment methods. Some very disturbed youngsters were admitted for spells of treatment to one or two psychiatric units which specialized in work with adolescents. One of them was a very long distance away, but such facilities were sparsely scattered and in 1960 the county joined forces with Oxford City to press the Regional Hospital Board to expand facilities locally. At a different level, from 1960 onwards several mountain camps were arranged and teenagers in care were taught the rudiments of camping and climbing, under the leadership of a male child care officer and in the company of other members of staff. Even the Children's Officer visited the camps and was remembered 'in a bell tent, with more holes in it than a colander, trying to make sandwiches and keep them dry in a mountain thunderstorm'. The Curtis maxim of the 'personal' element in child care as personified in the role of the Children's Officer was apparently alive and well, even in the 1960s. The idea of an 'intermediate' form of treatment for delinquents, midway between custodial care and supervision at home, can also be seen taking root.

These were all local initiatives but central government watched with interest and gave moral support. In 1957, following a Home Office inspection, the superintending inspector wrote commending several aspects of the department's work, including the visiting of the training school and 'the work of after-care among boys and girls on licence or under supervision from Approved Schools'. In 1960 the department was again inspected and the committee were informed that particular interest had been shown in 'the pioneer work carried out by the staff, both fieldworkers and residential staff, with delinquent children and with difficult adolescents on Fit Person Orders ... the inspectors also commented on the low number of foster breakdowns and the extremely low number of Approved School committals which they considered quite outstanding'. The boarding-out sub-committee, enthused by the commendation, resolved 'to recommend that the Children's Officer be asked to write to the Home Office, commenting on the high numbers of children being committed to approved schools and urging that children's departments should use their powers of dealing with the problem of delinquency to the full rather than have children dealt with by more drastic measures'. The committee had no wish to keep its pioneer work to itself!

Interest spread beyond the Home Office inspectorate. In 1962, the Minister of State, Lord Jellicoe, visited the department and saw two children's homes and the newly opened girls' hostel. The new boys' remand home was officially opened by the Home Secretary, Henry Brooke, in 1963. In 1965, the Minister of State, Alice Bacon, visited the remand home and hostel, met residential and field staff and concluded her visit with a press conference in which she praised the department's 'foresight and success in working with boys and girls who had been before the juvenile courts'. Local experiment had become national policy.

The story would be incomplete, however, without some consideration of the difficulties it created for the county department. Dealing with delinquents mean admitting greater numbers of children to care and keeping some of them in care for a considerable time. Partly as a result the county had a high and rising rate of children in care throughout the fifties and early sixties. It also meant increased use of residential accommodation and for all these reasons it was an expensive policy. As such it was under constant attack from the finance committee and the children's committee had regularly to spring to its defence, arguing its case in terms of its far-sightedness and the long-term benefits of preventing and arresting delinquency. In 1961, for instance, a report to the Finance and General Purposes Committee pressed home the degree to which recommendations by the Ingleby Committee (reporting in 1960) were already being implemented. High costs of committals were balanced by low approved school rates. There were very rarely prosecutions for neglect, because of preventive work, and the last case initiated by the N.S.P.C.C. had been in 1955. Cases where parents brought children to court as 'beyond control' (a procedure that Ingleby deplored and wished to abolish) were avoided because 'both the probation service and child care service have long felt that this is an unhappy procedure for the child'. In January 1964, the committee, in defending the high numbers of children in care, stated 'the main argument is that they believe that their policy with regard to keeping children in care has had a dramatic effect upon the incidence of juvenile crime'. (The county's crime rate had, indeed, been declining at that period, in contrast to national rates, which were climbing rapidly.) However, such arguments were never accepted without question and the department's high expenditure was under close scrutiny from the council throughout its history. There were three separate O and M investigations, a special working party of finance and children's committee members set up in 1965 and a standing 'Finance and Policy Group', created in 1968, 'to investigate at its own discretion any policies, functions or organisation of the Children's department from the financial point of view'. Dealing with delinquents was not all plain sailing.

The logic which led a pioneering authority to pursue such uncomfortable policies sprang from a single basic premise—delinquent children were 'no different' from deprived children who had not been in trouble with the law. They, too, were victims of family and environmental circumstances and suffered from broken, neglectful or unhappy homes. Their offences were seen as a response to these circumstances—cause and effect were assumed—and legal and administrative distinctions between offenders and non-offenders were therefore false and artificial. It was a premise which made sense and was supported by all the evidence, in a county area like Oxfordshire, but it tended to underestimate the importance of socio-economic and cultural determinants of delinquency in urban and inner-city areas, where crime rates are highest. The significance of this over-simplification will emerge later. Nevertheless, there were respectable and well-established precedents for this viewpoint. As long ago as the nineteenth century, reformers had argued in these terms and, in 1927, a Home Office Departmental Committee on the Treatment of Young Offenders had asserted 'there is little or no difference in character and needs between the neglected and the delinquent child. It is often mere accident whether he is brought before the court because he is wandering or beyond control or because he has committed some offence. Neglect leads to delinquency.'[11] Later, the maternal deprivation theorists stressed the links between early separations and family disruption and subsequent delinquency—cause and effect again—while Curtis referred to evidence of the accidental way in which children became classified as 'delinquent', 'neglected' or 'maladjusted'. The day to day experience of child care workers, who saw delinquents in and out of their home environments, reinforced these assumptions.[12]

If the 'character' and 'needs' of delinquents were almost indistinguishable from those of deprived children, it followed that they should also be treated in similar ways. Prevention of neglect through intervention, support and advice in family situations, might also lead to prevention of delinquency. Failing that, young offenders who were removed from home should be offered the same range of care facilities as any other deprived child. As the Oxfordshire Children's Officer claimed, 'there are resources, so far largely untapped, for dealing with delinquents within the ordinary child care service'.[13]

A further, closely related factor was the distrust and dislike of existing facilities for offenders, particularly the approved schools, which was experienced, though rarely publicly articulated, by some child care workers. The very separateness of the approved school system was taken as evidence that they did not share the same assumptions about delinquency. The large-scale boarding-school structure and stress on 'training', 'education' and discipline' that characterized many approved schools contrasted with the child care model of the substitute 'home' where, in theory at least, the emphasis was more on close personal relationships in a small-scale environment. In addition, the uneven distribution of schools throughout the country and the emphasis, in classification, on sending a child to the 'right' school for his special needs, meant that offenders were often placed far from home. This made it harder to sustain and improve a child's relationships with his parents and social workers who were committed to rehabilitation saw this as another stumbling-block. Distrust on these grounds was not new. Carlebach describes the antagonism between probation officers and the approved schools in the 1920s, which sprang from the same dislike of institutional solutions.[14] Social workers who operate in the 'open', in the community, are not easily reconciled to the notion of remote institutions. Confidence in the existing system was also shaken by declining 'success' rates. In 1951, 64 per cent of approved school boys avoided any further court appearance for three years after their release. In 1957 the proportion had dropped to 50 per cent and in 1959 it was only 43 per cent. There were therefore many reasons why some children's departments felt the need for 'a new approach to the problem of the young offender and a willingness to see delinquency as a form of child care problem which might be amenable to more directly child care methods instead of "training"'.[15]

Concern about delinquents was not confined to the child care service. Indeed, the problem of how to deal with young offenders is the theme of a whole series of reports and reappraisals published in the 1960s and it exercised the magistracy, the probation service, police and political parties alike. Cause for concern sprang not only from the apparent decline in the success of the approved schools in rehabilitating young offenders, but also from the rising incidence of juvenile crime. After a reassuring downward trend, following the peaks of the immediate post-war years, delinquency rates (in common with other indicators of social pathology, like the adult crime rate, the illegitimacy rate and figures for attempted suicide) began to climb again in the mid-1950s and continued upwards through the first half of the 1960s. It was the beginning of this rise that so perturbed the Ingleby Committee during its deliberations, and successive reports from the Children's Department of the Home Office published the figures which caused such alarm. By 1959, the proportion of indictable offenders under 17 was 70 per cent greater than in 1938. By 1961 it was 107 per cent, in 1963 125 per cent and in 1965 133 per cent higher than the pre-war figure. Not surprisingly, the Foreword to the Home Office report published in 1964 was entitled 'Against the Evil of Delinquency'.[16]

The Ingleby Report of 1960[17] was the first of several official attempts to analyse and suggest remedies for the growing problem and we have seen already that it was regarded by many critics as too cautious and conservative a document. In contrast, in Scotland, in 1964, the much more radical Kilbrandon Report was published.[18] At much the same time the Labour party, while in opposition, set up its own study group under the chairmanship of Lord Longford, which looked at crime in general and juvenile delinquency in particular. In 1964 it published *Crime—a challenge to us all*[19] and once the party was in power parts of the report were, in turn, translated into the white paper *The Child, the Family and the Young Offender*.[20] This time criticism was in the opposite direction —proposals were too radical to be acceptable to many established interests like the magistracy, police and probation service. A compromise white paper *Children in Trouble* was subsequently produced in 1968.[21] The background debates to all these reports and to the Children and Young Persons Acts of 1963 and 1969 and the 1968 Social Work (Scotland) Act which stemmed from them were fierce and prolonged. Everyone was deeply concerned about the problem of juvenile delinquency but different assumptions were made about the main causes of juvenile crime, about the right procedures to adopt to assess guilt or innocence and about the best methods of dealing with young offenders. Contrary arguments were supported both on idealistic and pragmatic grounds. In effect, two contradictory notions of the juvenile delinquent were in collision: one regarded him as a dependent victim of circumstance whose offence was a cry for help and who therefore needed care and treatment; the other saw him more as a miniature adult with free will and a keen sense of 'right', 'wrong' and natural 'justice', which must be protected by due process of law and if necessary dealt with by control and discipline. The four English reports in particular mirror the to and fro of the debate and the Acts encapsulate the compromises reached and the sometimes futile attempts to reconcile the irreconcilable.

Though no one would accept a uni-causal explanation of juvenile crime, some would lay emphasis upon one factor rather than another. A feature of those who pressed for change in the 1960s was their conviction that family-based explanations of delinquency were of prime importance. In an earlier chapter it was noted that the Ingleby Report laid special emphasis on 'the lack of a satisfactory family life' in the aetiology of delinquency. Longford was more vehement and stated 'it is a truism that a happy and secure family life is the foundation of a healthy society and the best safeguard against delinquency and anti-social behaviour'. It has been seen already that many child care workers were also convinced of the connection between disrupted families and delinquent youngsters.

This basic assumption naturally led the reformers to stress the connection between prevention of neglect and prevention of delinquency (see Chapter 4). Ingleby explored this connection and the preventive powers of the 1963 Act were framed with this in mind. Indeed, in Henry Brooke's Foreword to the 1964 Report on the work of the Children's Department, he welcomed the Act which 'may in the long run prove to be the most valuable instrument of all for reducing delinquency and doing it in the best possible way, by saving family life from wreck'. Longford and the white papers went further and suggested creating a new 'family service', wider in scope than the existing children's service, which would tackle juvenile crime at its roots.

The same assumption also led some reformers to argue for modification or even abolition of the juvenile court system. To Kilbrandon the ' "crime–responsibility–punishment" concept militates against preventive action against *potential* delinquents'. Further, if cause or "blame" was frequently to be found within the family, then the individual responsibility of the child was in question and criminal proceedings seemed inappropriate. An offender who was as much a 'victim' as a neglected or ill-treated child should be spared the stigma of criminality. There were additional arguments for change in the court system, on other grounds. *Children in Trouble* which, like its predecessors, subscribed to the view that family disruption and chronic delinquency were closely linked, also asserted that 'it is probably a minority of children who grow up without ever misbehaving in ways which may be contrary to the law'. If much naughtiness is merely a normal hazard in the long process of growing up, there is little point or justice in using the courts to deal with it. In the words of Longford 'if it is a trivial (offence) such a procedure is indefensible; if a more serious charge is involved this is in itself evidence of the child's need for skilled help and guidance'. There was also the issue of *social* justice. Experience showed that it was predominantly working-class children who appeared before the juvenile court—the wayward children of other classes were dealt with by other means.

Legal and social stigma that were reserved for the most disadvantaged section of the child population were doubly repugnant. Last, but not least, change in the system seemed expedient, since the mounting crime rate suggested that existing procedures were failing either to prevent or arrest delinquency. Something new seemed imperative.

The Ingleby solution was to alter the balance between civil and criminal proceedings in the juvenile courts. By raising the age of criminal responsibility from 8 to 12 (with the possibility of further rises to 13 or 14) the committee wished to make many more young offenders the subject of care proceedings instead of prosecution. 'In its dealings with younger children who commit offences and with children whose primary need is for care, protection or control it should get still further away from the conception of criminal jurisdiction while keeping as far as practicable the sanctions and methods of treatment at present available' (para. 77). There were still to be sheep and goats, but the age at which they could be distinguished would be much higher. In the event, the ensuing legislation was even more conservative than this and the 1963 Act raised the age of criminal responsibility to only ten years.

The Longford Report made more radical proposals. Convinced that 'an appearance on a criminal charge may well aggravate the child's difficulties and be the first step towards a criminal career', it concluded that 'no child in early adolescence should have to face criminal proceedings'. The juvenile courts were therefore to be abandoned altogether. In their place, a new, comprehensive 'family service' would deal with most offenders on an informal basis and a newly constituted 'family court' would hear only a minority of contested, or more serious juvenile cases. *The Child, the Family and the Young Offender* elaborated on this idea, and proposed institutionalizing the informal approach by means of 'family councils' in each local authority area, composed of child care social workers and informed laymen. These councils would discuss the problems both of offenders and non-offenders with the children involved and with their parents and attempt to reach agreement on treatment. Only in cases where guilt was denied, or agreement impossible to reach, would the matter proceed to a family court. There were strong similarities with the juvenile panels, proposed by Kilbrandon, which were subsequently set up by the Social Work (Scotland) Act of 1968.

In England and Wales, however, this challenge to existing methods and institutions was too great and it was poorly argued.

The white paper was a flimsy document, compared with Kilbrandon —insubstantial considering the changes it was proposing. It was resisted on several grounds. First, it was argued that the court was the guardian of civil liberties and the child's freedom and good name were protected by careful procedures for establishing guilt or innocence. The rights of the child—particularly his fundamental right to liberty—were safeguarded by judicial process, and to hand over this function to an executive body was to undermine these rights. If the fate of offenders rested with specialist panels, acting in agreement with parents, the child would be reduced to a position of total dependence on adults. The reformers' reply to this argument was to point out that over 90 per cent of offenders appearing before the juvenile courts pleaded guilty, so the facts of the case were rarely in dispute and the judicial process was therefore superfluous. They also argued that a large number of children already came into public care by agreement between parents and officials, by means of the 1948 Children Act. Abolition of the juvenile courts would merely extend this kind of procedure from deprived to delinquent children.

A second argument against change centred on the *differences* rather than the similarities between offenders and non-offenders. To treat all alike implied that children had no sense of right and wrong and it ignored some real distinctions between the 'deprived' and the 'depraved'. Some form of judicial process and an element of punishment and retribution were necessary for juvenile as well as adult offenders, in order to *define* crime and to express society's disapproval of it. If this lesson were not learned in childhood, it would be all the harder to learn in adult life. In any case, many children already had a strong sense of what was 'fair' and would regard equal treatment for the naughty and good alike as distinctly 'unfair'. When *Children in Trouble* proposed a compromise solution—by retaining the juvenile court whilst attempting to steer all but those whose home life was very unsatisfactory away from it— this argument took on greater force. Critics pointed out that there was real injustice in dealing with the offender from a *good* home out of court and the offender from a *bad* home within it. The 'stigma', if it existed, would then be reserved for the most unfortunate. The reformers again fell back on the argument that this happened already—discrimination existed by means of police cautioning and through the differential treatments imposed by magistrates. It was already most likely to be the child from a bad home who was removed from it and the one with loving parents who was allowed to stay. Nevertheless, the proposed compromise was in danger of achieving the worst of all worlds.

There was also resistance to changes which threatened to throw out the baby with the bath water. Juvenile courts had been in existence for fifty years and magistrates claimed to have accumulated wisdom through experience. Similarly, the probation service had half a century of experience of working with young offenders, yet it was proposed that supervision of delinquents should pass to social workers in the relatively new child care service or even to an as yet unestablished 'family service'. This appeared to many with an established interest in delinquents as a leap in the dark and a wilful waste of existing expertise. The isolated experiments of a few child care pioneers seemed too fragile a basis on which to support such a drastically altered structure. There were also some who asserted that the proposed alternatives to juvenile courts would never work. The necessary resources of manpower, particularly social workers, did not exist and 'the type of parent commonly seen in the juvenile court (is) muddled, inadequate, beaten, pathetic or truculent. Agreement, disagreement and discussion are not very realistic terms to describe the part played by such families which appear before the family councils.'[22] Most social workers had more sympathy with the first part of this particular argument than with the second, and the favourable impression of informality and 'meaningful discussion' gained in due course at the Scottish hearings, seemed to dispose of this objection.[23]

In Scotland, in fact, the reformers carried the day. The old system of juvenile justice was replaced by children's panels, to whom offenders and non-offenders were referred after a preliminary screening by a new local authority official called the Reporter, who was generally legally trained. The probation service was absorbed into the new Social Work Departments—Scotland's version of a 'Family Service'—and delinquents who needed supervision, or care away from home, became the responsibility of these departments. The Scots' acceptance of this radical solution has been explained in terms of the relative weakness of the vested interests involved. Both its juvenile court system and probation service were much less developed than those in England and were consequently more readily overthrown. Clearly this divergence in social policy deserves extensive study in its own right. Here, for reasons of clarity and space, we shall concentrate only on the situation in England and Wales.

The Children and Young Persons Act of 1969 was framed against the background of the debates which have been described and it was closely modelled on *Children in Trouble*. It therefore represented a compromise. The juvenile court system was retained and kept its old twin functions of dealing with both criminal and civil (care) cases. Set against this basic conservatism, the broad intentions of the Act were twofold. As many children as possible should be prevented from actually appearing in the juvenile courts; and offenders and non-offenders should generally be dealt with in the same way, both in terms of the procedures to be followed in court and in the range of care and treatment facilities available to them.

Preventing the appearance of children before the juvenile court was to be achieved in three main ways. First, prevention interpreted in its most fundamental sense meant reaching to the roots of delinquency and, by timely intervention, forestalling the offence altogether or preventing a first offender from becoming an habitual delinquent. The legal foundations for this approach had been laid in Section I of the 1963 Act, which gave children's departments the power to engage in preventive work that would keep children out of care *and* out of the juvenile courts. That this was regarded as good, but insufficient, is clear in the Longford Report and in both white papers. Emphasis upon the family origins of delinquency had highlighted the inadequacies of the personal social services, divided by their specialisms and hence often unable to help the family as a whole. Thus, all the reports on juvenile delinquency in the 1960s assumed that a new 'family service' was a prerequisite of reform. A separate committee (Seebohm) was appointed to make proposals in this sphere (of which there will be more discussion in a later chapter) and its report was timed to coincide with the publication of *Children in Trouble*. The creation of the new family service which it recommended did not fall within the scope of the 1969 Act but was, in fact, the subject of a separate piece of legislation (the Local Authority Social Services Act, 1970). Nor were the new social services departments that were set up designed only for the purposes of preventing juvenile delinquency. Nevertheless, the 1969 Act depended upon this basic restructuring of the personal social services in much the same way as Beveridge's insurance schemes had rested upon full employment policies and a National Health Service. Responsibility for 'primary' prevention would rest with the new family orientated service.

Enshrined in the 1969 Act itself are two more ways in which the number of children appearing before the juvenile courts can be kept down. The first concerns the procedures for dealing with offenders between ten (and thus of the age of 'criminal responsibility') and fourteen. It was the reformers' intention to substitute care proceedings for criminal prosecution for this group of delinquents and the grounds for a finding of being in need of care or control were therefore reframed, to include the commission of an offence. The offence *alone* is not grounds enough, however—it has also to be shown 'that he is in need of care or control which he is unlikely to receive unless the court makes an order under this section'. (Section 1(2).) In other words, the offender's home situation has to be so unsatisfactory as to warrant a court's intervention; if it can be worked with and improved on a voluntary basis there are no grounds for care proceedings and the offender need not, therefore, appear before the juvenile court. The Act thus intended to kill its two birds with one stone. A large number of delinquents from 'normal' homes, or from homes amenable to voluntary help and guidance, would escape court altogether and be dealt with by other means, again frequently involving social workers from the new social services departments; and offenders in the lower age-range who *did* come to court would be dealt with by the same procedures, carrying the same range of court orders, as non-offenders.

The second means concerns offenders in the 14 to 17 year age group. Here, prosecution was to be retained but restricted in ways which would cut down its use and spare numbers of offenders a court appearance. For instance, a prosecution could not be brought if the case could be dealt with adequately 'by a parent, teacher or other person or by means of a caution from a constable or through an exercise of the powers of a local authority or other body not involving court proceedings or by means of proceedings under section 1. of the Act', (Section 5)—that is, the care or control procedure. Local authorities (the new social services departments again) should also be informed and asked for their opinion before prosecution was contemplated, and the Secretary of State might make regulations specifying what kind of cases should be open to prosecution. Thus, by use of a series of bunkers, involving central and local government, the number of adolescent offenders actually reaching court would be considerably diminished and some even of these, might be subject to care proceedings rather that prosecution.

The Act's overall intentions are clear. The juvenile court should

be a place of last resort. Offenders whose delinquency can be
arrested by other means—by cautions from the police, by advice or
voluntary intervention by social workers or teachers, by admission
to care under the Children Act—should be kept out of court
altogether. The delinquent from a 'normal' home, whose parents
can undertake or share the responsibility of guiding him away from
juvenile crime, should not need to come before the magistrates. The
legal process would be reserved for the chronic delinquent with
whom these other measures have been tried and failed and the one
whose home surroundings seem positively malign or beyond the
help of any voluntary initiative. Magistrates would therefore
concentrate upon the most worrying group of juvenile offenders—
those whose delinquency has become habitual and for whom a life
of adult crime is depressingly predictable.

Other measures concern the treatment of offenders and here the
trend is all in the direction of using the same range of facilities for
both offenders and non-offenders, as well as abandoning some of
the more punitive sanctions of the past and experimenting with new
methods of a less extreme kind. The approved schools and probation hostels, for so long separate systems, outside local government,
which catered largely for delinquents, are incorporated in a system
of 'community homes' and take their place alongside children's
homes, hostels and remand homes as part of the total spread of
residential facilities for children in care. Knowing that such
establishments are unevenly scattered throughout the country, the
Act allows for regional plans to be drawn up by Children's Regional
Planning Committees representing several local authority areas. In
this way it is hoped that each region will develop sufficient quantity
and variety of residential facilities to meet its own particular
needs.

The absorption of approved schools by local authorities also
means that magistrates no longer have a choice between making an
approved school order, or a fit person order to the local authority. Instead, if they wish to remove a child (offender or non-offender)
to residential care they must make a 'care order' and the social
services department then decides where the child will be accommodated—whether in an erstwhile approved school or elsewhere.
Thus, the old labelling of sheep and goats is removed—but so, too,
is a great deal of the magistrates' power. Their ability to order
specific 'sentences' is diminished and the details of treatment pass
to the executive—a point to be more fully explored later.

The Act also intended to phase out several of the more punitive forms of treatment. By means of section 7, children of 15 and 16 could no longer be sent for Borstal training—the minimum age would become 17 years. Both attendance and detention centres would gradually be closed down and, on the Secretary of State's notification of this, juvenile courts would cease to have power to make orders in relation to these two kinds of treatment. In their place, new forms of 'intermediate treatment' would be developed, offering something between the potentially long-term removal from home of a 'care order' and straightforward supervision *in* the home. Conditions could be attached to a supervision order, including short spells of residence away from home, daily attendance at some kind of centre, or participation in various kinds of activities. Suggestions made in the debates leading to the Act included adventure training on the 'outward bound' model, community service, group and club activities and so on, but it was up to the local authorities to develop and establish these facilities and the Act did not specify their exact form. Finally, the old 'probation order' for young offenders was replaced by the new 'supervision order', which would apply to offenders and non-offenders alike, and it was the Act's intention that all children under 14 and all those between 14 and 17 not already *known* to the probation service, would be supervised by local authority social workers. The change was not so much in the quality of the order as in the withdrawal of young offenders from their previous association with a branch of the adult penal system.

Taken in its entirety the intentions of the Act are clear. Delinquents and deprived children are all children 'in trouble' and, as far as possible, should be treated alike. The early experiments of incorporating delinquents into the child care system are carried to their logical conclusion. The Act was not, however, implemented in its entirety, for the Labour government, which framed the legislation, fell before it was brought into force and its Conservative successors immediately suspended several significant clauses. With special irony the details of these changes were announced by the Under Secretary of State at the final conference of the Association of Children's Officers. In his words 'the new provisions about care proceedings will come into force; care orders will replace approved school orders and fit person orders; and the new provisions on supervision and intermediate treatment will come into force'. This would enable approved schools to be absorbed in the community homes system, and intermediate treatment to be developed. Set against this,

I

The age for prosecution will not be changed; children from ten upwards will remain liable to criminal proceedings. The courts will retain their present powers to order borstal training, to commit to junior detention centres and to order attendance at junior attendance centres. Probation orders will be replaced by supervision orders for those under 17; but courts will retain complete discretion to select probation officers as supervisors for children of 10 upwards in both care proceedings and criminal proceedings.

The government's long-term intentions were also spelled out. They had no intention at any stage of raising the minimum age for prosecution beyond 12, nor of implementing section 5, which imposed restrictions on the prosecution of offenders in the 14 to 17 year age group. Nor would they dismantle any of the existing forms of treatment until 'satisfied that adequate alternative methods of dealing with these youngsters are available and in full operation'.[24]

It was not an auspicious beginning and, in the words of one Clerk to the Justices, 'conceived by a Labour government and delivered by a Conservative administration, the Children and Young Persons Act, 1969, could hardly be said to have been blessed from birth. . . .'[25] Not surprisingly, it has had a stormy first few years, a bad press and has proved a headline writer's dream. ('Children Act in Trouble', 'Caught in the Act', 'Apprentices in Crime' and so on.) Discontent has been voiced most strongly by magistrates and lawyers, but approved school and remand home staff, police and social workers have all had difficulty with various aspects of its administration. Disillusion has been strong enough to lead some critics to suggest repeal or amendment, only a year or two after its implementation.[26]

One reason is certainly the result of the Conservatives' tampering with the Act as a whole. As a compromise piece of legislation it was already complicated, trying as it did to hold old and new measures in some kind of equilibrium. With the suspension of so many key clauses the balance is badly upset and 'the lesson is clear: tamper with a complex structure and all sorts of strains and defects are created'.[27] The fact that offenders in the younger age bracket can still be prosecuted means that there is little motivation to use the alternative care proceedings instead, since they are more complicated and require the double test of an offence *and* being in need of care or control. The failure to implement restrictions on the prosecution of older delinquents has also put a severe brake on the intention to keep as many children as possible out of court. Some of the reformers' aims have therefore been frustrated, yet despite this the number of children brought to court *has* declined. A 16·1 per cent drop in boys and a 30·4 per cent fall in girls under 14, found guilty of indictable offences was recorded in the first year after the Act, and small decreases in the 14 to 17 year age group (2·4 per cent and 4·7 per cent) were also noted.[28] In Devon, juvenile court appearances, which were running at between four and five hundred a year in the three years before the Act, had dropped to just over three hundred in 1971 and 1972.[29]

An interesting facet of this trend, both locally and nationally, is that it has been achieved, in part, by the largely unanticipated means of police cautioning, which has shown a marked increase. In Devon, for instance, over 70 per cent of juvenile offenders are now cautioned each year.[30] Reflecting this trend, research into the working of the Act, undertaken in the Bristol area, has developed very largely into a study of police cautioning.[31] The use of police cautions as a means of preventing offenders from appearing before the courts was certainly mentioned in the Act, in the unimplemented section 5, but it was not given much prominence either there or in the debates and it was the social worker who was envisaged as the prime agent for dealing with offenders out of court. In practice the balance has shifted and where liaison schemes between police and social workers have developed, a substantial number of referred cases are passed *back* to the police after preliminary investigation, with a recommendation for cautioning, and the social worker plays no further part.[32] That this was not intended seems clear from the Social Work Services Memorandum on its first survey of the administration of the Act, which states 'Following up a police caution ... is one of the most hopeful points at which social work to keep children out of trouble can be initiated and anything that local authorities can do in this way, even if only in selected cases, will not only be valuable in itself but will strengthen general relationships with the police as well.'[33] The implication is clear—the police may be able to keep children out of court but social work is required to keep them out of further trouble. That this is not offered more often means that the idea of prevention has been only partially developed. Police action of a brief but formal and sometimes awesome kind has replaced the notion of social work intervention in many cases and offenders out of court are being dealt with summarily, by another arm of the law. That this distortion has occurred may be because of the pressures on social workers that have made it difficult for them to take on much of the extra work involved or because, in the process of administering the Act, there has been a redefinition of what are 'appropriate' measures for many young delinquents—a point to be expanded later.

More serious distortions of the Act's intentions are also due, in some measure, to its early emasculation. The goal of more liberal, less punitive treatment of offenders suffered with the retention of many of the old orders. While magistrates still have power to send offenders to attendance and detention centres and to recommend Borstal training they will continue to do so—the more so, it seems, since their power to make approved school orders has been taken away and replaced by the unpopular 'care order', giving social workers discretion to choose where the offender shall be accommodated. Faced with a choice between this and the old measures, courts have increasingly used the latter. In 1971, 1,004 15 and 16 year olds were sent to Borstal; in 1972 the figure was 1,117. In 1972, places in junior detention centres were increased by 30 per cent, in response to mounting demand. Worse, the juvenile population in prisons and remand centres has risen from about 1,600 a year before the Act, to 2,000 a year since.[34] This has been partly because of the increase in young people awaiting Crown Court hearings (following a Borstal recommendation) and partly because magistrates have used prisons for 'unruly characters' whom they thought too tough to be coped with adequately on a 'care order'.

The 'care order' is, in fact, at the centre of the struggle between the old and new philosophies of treatment, embodied in the Act— a bone of contention, not least because through it significant sentencing powers have shifted and the 'impartial judiciary have been devalued in favour of the executive'.[35] The direction of change is not peculiar to the sphere of juvenile delinquency. The Mental Health Act of 1959 gave doctors and social workers powers of committal that had previously belonged to J.P.s and there is recurrent debate about confining the business of the adult courts to trials of guilt or innocence, while sentencing powers pass to panels of experts. Indeed, fear of this slippery slope explains why there is such fierce resistance in the juvenile sphere. The magistrates' sense of loss has also been exacerbated by the apparently cavalier way in which social workers have sometimes flouted their intentions by returning a child on a 'care order' to his own home and by their sense of impotence if such a child commits other offences. Punitive measures are sometimes sought or used, not because they succeed in arresting delinquency—the 'success rates' of approved schools and borstals have been as low as 20 per cent—but because they protect society for a short space of time and purport to show offenders that they cannot lightly flout the law. The law, in turn, feels that it has not been made an ass.

The opposing philosophies may never be fully reconcilable but it seems clear that the clash between them is aggravated by ignorance and poor communications between courts, social workers and community homes. Cases where children on care orders have been returned home almost immediately or where committed children have repeatedly offended again (the Magistrates Association have prepared a dossier of examples) may well be the exception rather than the rule, as the D.H.S.S. survey suggests, but they destroy the courts' confidence in the social work service unless the reasons and circumstances are fully understood. Regular meetings of social workers and magistrates to review the progress of supervised and committed children have developed in some areas, much as they did in authorities like Oxfordshire long before the Act, and these provide one way of modifying stereotypes and creating confidence. Similarly, the goodwill of the newly absorbed approved schools was sometimes lost through instances (however rare) of social workers removing children from them without consultation. For their part, social workers were similarly disillusioned in the interim period after the Act when care orders were in operation but when approved schools were not yet part of the community homes system, and when some schools used the breathing space to refuse admissions, leaving social workers 'holding the baby'. Careful procedures for co-operation between the different professional groups are obviously of special importance where areas of disagreement are so wide and where established territorial boundaries have been so recently redrawn and are still disputed. Here, sensitive *administration* of the law is at least as important as its original drafting, since the child becomes the victim of any conflicts that arise. Assessment of the *results* of social work intervention and comparison with older methods is also essential and presumably forthcoming, since the Act is a popular subject of current research. In a modest survey, for example, Devon was able to show that supervision of juveniles by local authority social workers was at least as successful, in terms of checking further offences, as supervision by probation officers.[36] Some magisterial fears may have been allayed in consequence.

Serious shortages of residential accommodation have also hampered the implementation of the Act. These shortages are not new. Earlier in the chapter an instance was cited of some children's departments combining to exert pressure on the Regional Hospital Board to provide skilled and secure care for disturbed adolescents because local facilities were quite inadequate. The Seebohm Report also drew attention to the lack of facilities for very disturbed young people. The Act merely exaggerated the problem because its goal of eschewing traditional forms of custodial care was not matched by any large increase in alternatives. The inevitable delays in incorporating the approved schools and in drawing up and putting into effect regional plans, compounded the basic shortfall. Remand homes and classifying centres became congested with children awaiting placement and some children on care orders were sent home for lack of any appropriate place to accommodate them. The most acute problem was—and is—the minority of persistent and 'unruly' offenders who appear to need secure accommodation if they are to be 'treated' at all. Special units are gradually being added to some community homes and the D.H.S.S. have planned three new 'Youth Treatment Centres', of which only one is so far in operation. Until new-style security is provided more lavishly, the temptation or compulsion to use old-style institutions, like Borstals, will remain.

Shortages of social workers have also produced difficulties. Ironically, the creation of a 'family service', which was to be the basis of the new approach to dealing with delinquents has, in itself, been responsible for much of the difficulty. The foundation stone has proved a stumbling bock, mainly because the idea of an enlarged child care service, which was envisaged in the early blueprints, was overtaken by the much broader Seebohm concept, in which 'families' meant 'everybody'. In the event, many child care officers with training and experience with children were sucked up into the complicated hierachies of the new departments, away from direct work with young people. Those left on the ground have generally had to grapple with 'generic' case loads, containing a far wider range of clients than just children and their colleagues from health and welfare have, in turn, had to cope with child care problems for the first time.

Perhaps as important as this dispersal and dilution of expertise has been the effect of these changes on the social workers themselves. The upheaval of Seebohm, with all its consequent anxieties, has been compounded, in the space of three years, by local government reorganization. Nor is the 1969 Act the only piece of legislation to present a fresh challenge. Coming hard on its heels, the Chronically Sick and Disabled Persons Act also requires extensive new initiatives of a service that, even now, seems heavily preoccupied with its own internal stresses. The effect on social workers has been an unquantifiable but palpable lowering of morale.

The history of the child care service suggests that it is possible to pioneer new methods, even with grossly inadequate resources, if optimism and a crusading zeal prevail. It may be that small and brand new organizations, starting from scratch, can more readily foster such attitudes than a large and complex structure, born of a massive merger. It may even help to be able to concentrate on one thing at a time. Where social services departments have been slow to develop preventive work with delinquents, or where criticism of their handling of young offenders has been justified, it could be because the legislation is not so much misconceived as mistimed. Even Sir Keith Joseph is reported as saying 'we should not have done it all at once'.[37]

A proper evaluation of the Act is impossible while the effects of its difficult birth are still apparent and while research data are awaited. So far it has succeeded in keeping a proportion of offenders out of court, though as much by police cautioning as by social work intervention. Its aim of using care proceedings for most offenders before the court has not, however, been achieved and far from steering delinquents away from some of the old forms of treatment with their 'penal' taint, more young people are currently being accommodated there than before. It has not yet succeeded in making an impact on delinquency rates. Indeed, after a pause in the late 1960s, rates are climbing again and, depressingly, the more serious crimes of violence and breaking and entering are rising particularly fast among the young, despite—or some would say, because of, the Act.[38]

At this stage there are more questions than answers. One concerns the central assumption upon which the Act was based—that repeated delinquency is closely associated with family difficulties and that the intervention of social workers in family situations presents the most hopeful method of preventing and arresting chronic lawbreaking. Research only partially upholds this assumption, for whilst children from broken homes and, more especially, from homes that are intact but severely troubled *are* at great risk of offending and of doing so repeatedly, they still account for only a minority of all delinquents. More than half of all persistent offenders, in some urban areas at least, come from apparently 'normal' families and the origins of their delinquency must be sought in the schools or in the community.[39] It may be, therefore, that the model of treatment that was most highly developed in advance of legislation, in a county area like Oxfordshire, is not easily transferable to the city environment, where most delinquency occurs. The social worker's traditional strategies of intervention, based very largely on an understanding of family dynamics, can tackle only part of the problem in such areas and may be inappropriate in many cases. But alternative methods of approach, involving schools and community groups are, as yet, only just beginning and many opportunities may be being missed. Indeed, the tendency for social workers to pass the 'straightforward' cases, exhibiting no family problems, back to the police for action, suggests that this is the case. Similarly, the very slow development of Intermediate Treatment in some areas results as much from lack of enthusiasm and imagination on the part of social workers (not helped by too many demands and too few resources) as from caution on the part of magistrates. The 1969 Act challenges social workers to develop a very wide range of approaches to delinquency and past practice and current problems mean that, so far, the challenge has been only fitfully taken up.

Research also casts some doubt upon the assumption that *juvenile courts*, as well as social workers, should concentrate mainly upon the delinquent whose home situation is difficult. One of Michael Power's studies in a London borough shows that boys from difficult family circumstances are less likely to offend again if they are cautioned, than if they are brought to court. He points out that 'this is the opposite assumption to that made by the police and by the architects of the 1969 Children's Act . . . In turning this upside down it may be that the children's and society's best interests are served by not further traumatizing those already in a state of shock.'[40] If this proves to be more generally the case it would suggest either a reversal of current 'sorting out' procedures or abolition of the juvenile courts altogether.

Absorption of delinquents into the mainstream of child care finally brought children's departments to an end. In order to create a 'family service' that would underpin the new procedures in the juvenile courts and provide new treatments for offenders, the child care service was itself absorbed into the Seebohm-model social services departments. But, before looking in more detail at how this came about, and with what results, we will turn back to the original aims and methods of the child care service. In the chapter which follows we can see how they were affected by experience, by research findings and by the ever-increasing range of activities that were undertaken.

NOTES

1. Curtis Report op. cit., para. 498.
2. Figures taken from the *Seventh Report on the Work of the Children's Department*, Home Office, November 1955.
3. Quoted in the *Seventh Report*, op. cit.
4. Ibid.
5. Ibid.
6. From Seventh and Eighth Reports on the Work of the Children's Department.
7. Max Grunhut, *Juvenile Offenders before the Courts*, Clarendon, 1956.
8. Oxfordshire's Children's Officer, in a document 'Oxfordshire child care policy, past and present', produced in 1968.
9. 'Approved School or Fit Person Order?' B.J.K. *Child Care*, April 1961.
10. *Child Care: Needs and Numbers*, op. cit., Chap. 13.
11. *Report of the Departmental Committee on the Treatment of Young Offenders*, Cmd. 2831, H.M.S.O., 1927.
12. See also, Harriet C. Wilson, *Delinquency and Child Neglect*, Allen and Unwin, 1962.
13. Approved School or Fit Person Order? op. cit.
14. Julius Carlebach, *Caring for Children in Trouble*, Routledge and Kegan Paul, 1970.
15. Approved School or Fit Person Order? op. cit.
16. Figures from Reports on the work of the Children's Department, 1961, 1964 and 1967.
17. *Report of the Committee on Children and Young Persons*, Cmnd. 1191, 1960.
18. *Report on Children and Young Persons*, (Scotland) Cmnd. 2306, 1964.
19. *Crime – a Challenge to us all*, Labour Party, June 1964.
20. *The Child, the Family and the Young Offender*, Cmnd. 2742, August 1965.
21. *Children in Trouble*, Cmnd. 3601, April 1968.
22. Professor Winifred Cavenagh, quoted in, Marcel Berlins and Geoffrey Wansell, *Caught in the Act*, Penguin, 1974, p. 28.
23. See, for instance, Finlayson, *Social Work Today*, Vol. 2, No. 12, 1971.
24. Mark Carlisle, *The Community, the Family and Children in Trouble*, 21st. Annual Conference, A.C.O., 1970.
25. Brian Harris, 'Children's Act in Trouble', in *The Criminal Law Review*, November 1972.
26. See, for instance, *Apprentices in Crime*, Society of Conservative Lawyers and *Caught in the Act*, op. cit., and Lord Hailsham, in debates on the Children Bill.
27. J. D. McClean, 'Another View', *The Criminal Law Review*, November 1972.
29. Jane Fothergill, *Delinquency in Devon*, Research and Training Section, Devon C.C. Social Services Department, September 1973.

30. Ibid.
31. Philip Priestley, Department of Social Administration, Bristol University, work as yet unpublished.
32. Michael Power and Jean Packman, Data from Devon Family Assessment Study, work as yet unpublished.
33. Memorandum on a survey by the Social Work Service, appended to Home Office Circular No. 130/1972.
34. Figures quoted in *Caught in the Act*, op. cit.
35. Mr. Anthony Marsh, *The Times*, 26 June 1972.
36. *Delinquency in Devon*, op. cit.
37. Quoted in *Caught in the Act*, op. cit.
38. Criminal Statistics, England and Wales, 1973. Cmnd. 5672.
39. M. J. Power, P. M. Ash, E. Shoenberg and E. C. Sirey, Delinquency and the Family', *The British Journal of Social Work*, Spring, 1974.
40. Michael Power, 'Cautions, Hearings and Courts', *Juvenile Justice in Great Britain*, in Press.

CHAPTER SEVEN

New Wine in Old Bottles

The central task of the child care service, at its inception, was the provision of good substitute care for deprived children and, discounting adoption, for which only a minority of children in care were eligible, the preferred method of care was fostering. It was given priority in the 1948 Children Act, emphasized by the title 'boarding-out officer', used for the first social workers in the service, and was encouraged by researches in child development as well as by considerations of economy. We have already seen how children's departments approached the task in the first decade of their existence and how the proportion of children in care who were fostered rose steadily in consequence. From 35 per cent in 1949, the proportion had risen to 44 per cent by 1954, to 48 per cent by 1960 and to 52 per cent by 1963. But this was its high water mark and thereafter, though the actual number of children who were fostered continued to rise slightly for a time, the proportion that they represented of all children in care declined. By 1970 both the absolute and proportionate figures had dropped—the latter to 42 per cent. Such figures are only crude indicators, but they do point to important changes in emphasis which occurred, partly because increased knowledge brought greater uncertainty and caution and partly because the service developed new and sometimes incompatible priorities. Research and experience made departments question their original commitment to fostering and the pursuit of new goals in child care modified and even distorted the original aims and methods of the service.

Experience of fostering—and children's departments accumulated a great deal of experience in their early years—made it plain that it was not always successful. This had been tragically apparent when Denis O'Neill had died at the hands of his foster parents in 1945, but the administrative changes that had been instituted in 1948, and the new training for social workers in child care were designed to avoid such disasters occurring in the future. The fostering failures of the new service were less dramatic but nonetheless disturbing. Children placed in foster homes did not always settle happily. Some had to be removed because their behaviour became intolerable to the foster parents or because social workers were convinced that their needs were not being met satisfactorily. Transplanting a child proved to be as delicate an operation as transplanting any human organ. There was always the risk of rejection.

The extent of failures of this kind was not measured in any systematic way, nor was it widely publicized. The Home Office did not require children's departments to keep any numerical account of fostering breakdowns and no figures were therefore circulated. The *Seventh Report of the Work of the Children's Department* (published in 1955), for instance, devoted only one sentence to the problem. 'Boarding out still has its failures, often with some damage to the child, but increasing attention is being given by local authorities to making sure, as far as possible, that these do not occur.'[1] To their credit, not all local authorities were so complacent. Reference was made earlier, in Chapter 2, to the first report of the county borough of Dudley's Children's Officer, in 1949, in which she drew attention to twenty-six children (out of seventy-one who were boarded-out) who had been in more than one foster home. '(A)n unsuccessful fostering and particularly more than one, can do a child more harm, by destroying his self-confidence and increasing his sense of loss, than institutional care.'[2] It was believed that many of these early difficulties had been overcome, as departments employed more field staff, who could devote more time to selecting and supervising foster homes and as reception facilities developed for the proper assessment of children before placement. But these were only impressions and no figures were collected to support them. The importance of research into the successes and failures of foster care was therefore twofold. It shed light upon the *reasons* for breakdown but it also produced the first estimates of its incidence.

These estimates were far from encouraging. Gordon Trasler studied foster home breakdowns in Devon over a period of three years in the early 1950s.[3] As a background to his study he gathered information from other children's committees in different parts of the country, which suggested an average failure rate of between one-third and two-fifths over all long-term placements. With more precision. Roy Parker looked at all long-term fosterings arranged in Kent in 1952 and 1953, five years after the placement began.[4] In that particular sample, the failure rate was 48 per cent and 'failure' in Parker's terms was rigorous and meant that the child had had to be removed from his foster home during the five-year period. Clearly the proportion of 'unsatisfactory' homes where breakdown might still occur, or where social workers were not entirely happy about the care given, would have been higher still. In Rachel Jenkins's study of placements made between 1958 and 1961 in three northern authorities, for instance, a third were reckoned by social workers, foster parents and/or the researcher as 'unsatisfactory' though the children were still in placement at the time.[5] Nor did research provide evidence of improved techniques leading to fewer breakdowns, once children's departments got into their stride. Victor George looked at placements made in three Midland authorities between 1961 and 1963 and, using Parker's criterion of longevity for measuring 'success', he calculated that the failure rate was 59·8 per cent.[6] Unless there are wide regional variations in fostering failure rates (which is always possible, since most other indices of child care work vary a great deal) things appear to have got worse, rather than better.

The research studies were not all agreed on the reasons for failure, though some common factors emerged over and over again. The chances of successful fostering diminish, the older the child is at placement. In Parker's study, for example, 77 per cent of children placed in foster homes at eleven years and over, failed to settle and had to be removed. Persistent behaviour problems in a child are also likely to cause breakdown—a factor that was explored in some depth in Trasler's study. Both these factors are worth bearing in mind, when we come to look at the way in which children's departments' admission policies were changing over time. There was also some evidence that foster children were less easily assimilated into homes where there were other very young children, or where there were natural children of the family who were close in age to the foster child. More optimistically, older foster mothers (the over 40s) were generally more successful, though as Parker pointed out, the children who were least likely to succeed tended to be placed with them, so that a 'levelling down' of success rates was bound to occur.

The impact of these and other research studies upon the child care service is difficult to estimate, but it was probably of a general rather than a specific kind. Parker constructed a 'prediction table' that could have been used to help child care workers in their decision-making, when planning foster placements, but there is little evidence that it was used much by practitioners (though Oxfordshire's adoption panel, which also dealt with long-term fostering, used it) and it received most attention from other researchers, testing the validity of his original predictions. Victor George was highly critical of the gap between theory and practice, for although careful investigation of foster parents' motivation and interaction with each other and with their own children are stressed in much of the literature on selection, he found little evidence that this was conscientiously undertaken, nor that children and foster parents were properly prepared and introduced before placement. He accounts for these failures in practice in part through 'the lack of adequate knowledge of the factors involved in successful fostering' which suggests that previous studies had had a very limited effect. In contrast, Trasler, writing much earlier, was impressed by Devon's records which were 'detailed, skilfully and accurately written and often illuminated by a keen insight into the relationships and problems of a foster family'. It is impossible to know whether these different evaluations reflect differences in standards over time (the 1950s compared with the 1960s) or of place (Devon, compared with the Midlands) or both.

What *does* seem certain is that research and experience together helped to dampen the early enthusiasm for fostering, with which the service had set out. Gradually, the tone of the Home Office reports changes. The first Report, after the Children Act, draws attention to section 13, with its injunction to board out all children received into care, except 'where it is not practicable or desirable for the time being' to do so. By 1961, the same primary duty is spelled out, but the caveat is emphasized—'a provision which recognises that boarding-out is not automatically and invariably the best course for all children'. By 1964, 'Boarding-out is not necessarily the best thing for every child . . . (and) . . . it is therefore not to be expected that the proportion of children boarded-out should continue to rise indefinitely.' As we have seen, the proportion of children who were fostered not only ceased to rise, but took a marked downward turn and a complementary amendment in the legislation set the seal on the change. Section 49 of the Children and Young Persons Act, 1969, replaces section 13 of its 1948 predecessor, and local authorities are no longer bound to consider fostering as the preferred method of care, but may discharge their duty to provide accommodation and maintenance 'as they think fit'.

A declining emphasis upon foster care and a growing awareness of its limitations were obviously closely related, but other factors lay behind this trend. Of considerable significance were the new

policies of prevention and rehabilitation and the gradual incorporation of disturbed and delinquent children into the child care service.
These changes served to divert attention and effort from the recruitment, selection and supervision of foster homes, with sometimes
detrimental effect. Paradoxically, they also meant that much greater
demands were made upon foster homes. In the circumstances, it is
not perhaps surprising that expansion was halted nor that breakdowns occurred.

We have seen, already, that preventive work, sanctioned by the
1963 Children and Young Persons Act, drastically altered the
balance of work within the child care service. Within a short time
children 'in care' were vastly outnumbered by children receiving
attention in their own homes. Departments grew rapidly and unevenly to encompass the new range of work and a child care officer's
duties spread far beyond the original task of 'boarding-out'. The
time consuming work of recruiting and selecting foster homes
(advertising for foster parents might involve dozens of separate
investigations, many of which would prove abortive) ceased to have
priority. Yet without a surplus of available homes (such as Trasler
described in Devon in the 1950s) some would inevitably be over-
used and perhaps eventually lost, and selection of the 'right' home
for a particular child would be Hobson's choice.

Some of these difficulties are described in the Home Office
inquiry into the Dorset Child Care Service in 1966, which followed
on a case of serious injury to a foster child, of which the supervising department had been unaware.[7] The child care staff had
almost doubled since the 1963 Act 'to meet these new and widening responsibilities', yet only one new clerical officer had been
appointed in the same period—the kind of lopsided development
that produces strain in any organization. So many new social work
staff had been taken on that nearly 75 per cent had been in the
department for three years or less—a proportion that compared
unfavourably with previous experience, but which might not seem
unusual today. Caseloads were nevertheless judged to be so heavy
that 'if they are to find new foster parents and not overburden the
ones in use, additional child care officers will be needed'. Further,
early policies of closing down institutions had now come home to
roost. 'Between 1948 and 1954 the authority closed down several
children's homes and reduced the number of places from 250 to 58.
Since then the demands on the service have changed and the present
number of places is insufficient.' Foster homes were taking much of
the strain.

Some of the same problems were faced in Oxfordshire. Also in 1966, the Children's Officer reported on 'the effects of insufficient residential accommodation on children in care' and cited twenty examples of children who had been moved from foster homes where they were not ideally placed, but where they had been accommodated for want of any institutional alternative. 'This is a very distressing record for a department which fully appreciates the damage that can be done to young children in these circumstances.' As Roy Parker observed when discussing his research findings at a conference of Children's Officers in 1964, research and good training were unlikely to have much effect upon decision-making in foster care, while there was shortage of resources. 'Neither can be fully exploited unless there is a range of possible courses of action and the choice between them is not largely determined beforehand by shortage or emergency.'[8]

The Oxfordshire report also drew attention to some other effects of the new policies. 'As adoption work increases most of the healthy, unproblematic babies will be placed permanently, early and will not feature in the department's boarding-out programme.' In addition, the committal and reception of greater numbers of adolescents—many of them delinquent—produced a demand, not for foster homes, but for more residential accommodation. The high failure rate of older children and children with persistent behaviour difficulties who were placed in foster homes, suggested that this was rarely an appropriate method of care and, indeed, Rachel Jenkins questioned the wisdom of even attempting such placements, when the odds were so heavily weighted against success.[9] With similar effect, the emphasis on keeping children in their own homes whenever possible, meant that those who *were* admitted were 'likely to be the most difficult problem of all, since they cannot remain in the community in their own homes'. Again, fostering might not be the most appropriate method of care and if, despite this, it were used, the risks of failure were likely to be great.

The increasing emphasis on prevention and rehabilitation had more fundamental effects than this, however, for the very nature and purpose of fostering was altered by it. The role of foster parents became more ambiguous as the demands made upon them increased and as their rewards and satisfactions became less obvious. Originally, fostering had frequently been seen as an *alternative* to parental care, when the latter had proved inadequate. Before children's departments existed many children who were fostered lost all contact with their natural families and the fostering became a '*de facto*' adoption. Working with deprived children in Oxfordshire in the 1940s, Claire Winnicott was at first given no idea of the where-abouts of the *parents* of children in care, because this was thought to be irrelevant.[10] The children may well have suffered from the loss, but at least the foster parents' role in these cases was clear. In replacing the natural parents they took on their role. There was some security in this and conflicts of loyalty were partially avoided. The Children Act, moving away from this position, stipulated that children must be rehabilitated with their own families, when this was consistent with their welfare, and we have seen how the concept was increasingly applied. Though fostering was the favoured method of care, promising as it did a 'natural' upbringing and the warmth and intimate relationships that children need, it was now more often a short-term or impermanent arrangement, incorporating a far greater degree of sharing. If children were to be rehabilitated, they must be kept in close touch with their natural parents. In practical terms, this involved visits by parents to foster homes and by foster children to their own families, both of which could be unsettling and disruptive. What was expected of foster parents became at once more subtle and more difficult. They must confer on the child all the benefits of loving family care, but should not seek to replace the parents in his affections. Their compassion and acceptance must be extended from the child himself, to his parents as well—even where the latter seemed 'to blame' for some of his past deprivations. They should act toward him as a good parent, yet give him up when the department judged the time to be ripe.

> For excellent reasons we are increasingly working for the child's return to his own family; we discourage the labels 'Mum' and 'Dad' and prefer 'Auntie' and 'Uncle' for foster parents; we like mothers and fathers to visit their children in their foster homes and so on. It seems possible that in emphasising these desirable objectives we may nevertheless be making it more difficult for many foster parents to reduce or resolve the conflicts which arise.[11]

Some of these conflicts are well documented by Victor George, who questioned long-term foster parents and social workers about the nature of the fostering role.[12] Sharp differences of perception and expectations were revealed. To social workers, the foster parent was generally seen as a 'colleague' and it was expected that all matters of significance concerning the child would be discussed between them. So far as the foster parents' relationship with the

K

foster child was concerned, the majority of social workers characterized this as being like a 'relative' (aunt and uncle?). In contrast,
foster parents usually regarded social workers in a more informal
way, as 'friends' with whom they would not necessarily share
significant events in the child's life (like parents, they would cope
with difficulties themselves) and their relationship with their foster
children, in their eyes, most closely resembled that of a parent or
adoptive parent. Understandably, in view of this, social workers and
foster parents disagreed on some issues of parental visiting—the
former favouring more regular and frequent visits and being 'more
understanding and tolerant of the natural parents' problems'.

In embracing the goals of prevention and rehabilitation the child
care service's expectations of fostering have therefore had to develop in the direction of a 'professional' service, with foster
parents perceived as a species of residential child care worker,
operating from their own homes. Indeed, George would favour the
title 'foster care worker' as one way of avoiding ambiguities. But
the majority of foster parents still conform to an earlier model of
fostering and they are not helped by the ambivalence that still
exists, even in the 'official' view of their role. The form of undertaking which the foster parents sign begins 'We will care for (child)
and bring him/her up as we would a child of our own', yet it goes
on to stipulate that they must be visited, must inform the council
of any change of address, any serious occurrences affecting the
child, and must allow the child to be removed.

> These latter undertakings reflect the authority's ultimate responsi-
> bility for the care of the child and could be described as laying
> down a pattern of roles where the authority is the senior partner
> and the foster parent the junior partner in looking after the child.
> This view is in direct conflict with the parental role which is
> implied in the first clause in the undertaking.[13]

Furthermore, the notion of a professional partnership is not
carried to its logical conclusion. Foster parents are still only rarely
paid a 'wage'.[14] Despite recurrent arguments in favour of paying
foster parents more than a maintenance allowance for the children
in their care (which have been made by researchers and social
workers throughout the history of the child care service) the nineteenth-century principle of 'no profit', for fear of baby-farming, has
only been partially eroded. Interestingly enough, the majority of
Victor George's sample of foster parents were at odds with the
social workers on this issue and thought maintenance and costs

were all that were required—a view consistent with their perceptions of fostering and a most convenient attitude for local authority treasurers. Nor do foster parents always share very significantly in the decision-making about children in their charge, or about foster children in general. A recent B.A.S.W. survey[15] showed that in only 9 out of 81 authorities did foster parents themselves participate in discussions about rates and policy and, as one of George's foster mothers remarked

> A foster parent tries to make a child a part of their family and usually the casework is left to the child care officers. It is, I think, their decisions not the foster parents' that are acted on. The foster parents often being told what to do or what has already been done.

There is a clear link here with the recent mushroom growth of Foster Parent Associations and with one of the stated aims of the National Foster Care Association (founded in 1974), 'to work for foster parents to have an effective share in policy making in child care'.

Fostering has thus developed, and is still developing, along lines that were not envisaged when the Curtis Committee expressed its almost unqualified approval. On the credit side there have been encouraging experiments in fostering handicapped and disturbed children and in placing families of children together in one home (an achievement which prompted a Home Office letter of congratulations to Oxfordshire's department). These have usually been made possible through the payment of special allowances and local authorities have broken out of their nineteenth-century straitjackets in this respect. There has also been an enormous increase in the temporary fostering of children who are in care for a matter of weeks or months in time of family crisis—an intelligent and humane use of community resources. (Because these are short-term cases they make little impact upon the total percentage of boarded-out children and their significance is therefore likely to be underestimated.) Further, there have been attempts to draw foster parents into closer involvement with their local authorities, so that their vital contribution can be acknowledged and their 'professionalism' enhanced. Foster parent group meetings are one way and 45 per cent of children's departments were arranging such meetings in 1966, and 70 per cent by 1970.[16] As we have seen, participation in decisions and in policy discussions has been the exception rather than the rule, but it *has* occurred in small ways. Oxfordshire, for instance, for years used a Christmas newsletter to keep foster parents in touch with departmental policy and gossip and, in 1969, broke new ground by asking for their views on how the boarding-out allowances could be most effectively raised. A year later, a foster parent recruitment campaign was discussed and a working party which would include foster parents was proposed.

On the debit side, social workers have been accused of failing to find foster homes for all the children who could conceivably benefit. *Children Who Wait* suggested that in 1971 there were as many as 7,000 children in the care of statutory and voluntary agencies throughout the British Isles who, on their social workers' own admission, needed a substitute family, but were still in residential care.[17] Many possible reasons for this have already been discussed and the difficulties of social service reorganization have probably compounded the problem. The re-emergence of specialist 'foster care' posts within social services departments are clearly one way of tackling the problems afresh and there are signs of a new drive to extend fostering again in many authorities throughout the country.

The clash of perspective between foster parents and social workers has also produced its victims. New wine has been poured into old bottles with sometimes explosive effect, as the much publicized 'tug of love' cases show. Between the traditional 'permanent' foster home and the explicitly 'temporary' placement, an inter-mediate group of placements has grown up where these conflicts are most apparent. The social work aim has been eventual rehabili-tation with the child's family, but years may pass before this becomes possible. Maria Colwell was just such a case. Unless foster parents and—no less importantly—the child can believe in and hold on to the aim throughout the years, 'rehabilitation' may be achieved at the expense of the child's welfare. Goals that are compatible in the short term—loving care in a substitute family and restoration to the natural family—may become incompatible in the course of time. A child's (particularly a young child's) 'natural' bonds may weaken as his allegiance to his foster family grows and ultimately rehabilita-tion becomes unrealistic. Ironically, it is the special benefits of foster care—its capacity to keep alive and to stimulate a child's ability to feel and to 'relate'—which may ensure that the goal of 'restoration' is never achieved.

It is for this reason that the Houghton Report proposes that foster parents who have looked after a child for five years should be allowed to apply to adopt. For the same reason, commentators like Parker stress the need for more positive and long-sighted planning for deprived children, which will get away from 'an essentially passive and reactive attitude . . . the temptation to decide as you go —and little by little . . .',[18] which is often responsible for the impermanent fostering of indeterminate duration. Several clauses in the new legislation deal with these points so, in future, some of the tensions might be resolved and fewer children suffer in consequence.

The same developments in policy which have had such a profound effect upon fostering have produced changes of equal significance in the residential child care sphere. In terms of the scale and scope of residential provision, the needs and problems of the children admitted and the aims and functions of all types of child care institution the service has come a long way from the original Curtis conception. Most obviously, residential care has not dwindled to the residual, last-resort service that the Children Act seemed to envisage. As we have seen already, drastic reductions in the number of residential places were made in the earliest years of the child care service to match the initial fostering drive, but subsequent increases in the proportion of boarded-out children were achieved, not at the expense of the total in residential care, but as a result of steadily rising overall numbers. Indeed, the number of children accommodated in all types of local authority children's homes has remained remarkably constant since the mid-1950s (21,941 in November, 1955, and 20,548 in March, 1972.)[19]

Latterly the pressure has been to expand, rather than contract, though financial constraints have made this extremely difficult for local authorities to achieve. Dorset's problems have already been mentioned and Oxfordshire's struggle to increase its numbers of residential places in the 1960s was constantly thwarted by freezes on the one hand, and soaring building costs and land prices on the other. In 1966 and 1967, for example, the council were deadlocked on how they might reconcile the White Paper on Prices and Incomes Standstill with the Children's Committee's desire to expand residential provision. A senior Home Office administrator and the Chief Inspector of the Children's Department came down to express their views on current inadequacies and the urgency of need—the county's proportion of residential accommodation in relation to numbers 'in care' was well below average—but their role was purely advisory and central government's relationship with the local authority was spelled out with great delicacy. 'They made it clear that the financial decisions and the allocation of priorities between committees was entirely a matter for the Council alone to decide, but they wished to be sure that before taking final decisions the Council was fully apprised of the Home Office views.' In October, 1967, we even find the finance committee urging the children's department to look again at its old, long-discarded cottage homes in a desperate attempt to suggest cheaper ways of increasing accommodation, but the Home Office declared them unsuitable. Many other local authorities must have found themselves caught in this unenviable dilemma—attempting to reconcile the incompatible policies of different arms of central government and no doubt regretting, in some measure, the earlier policies that had led them to dispose of such valuable capital assets.

One way of solving this dilemma was to make greater use of voluntary homes. It had always been possible under section 13 of the Children Act for departments to place children in their care in voluntary establishments and a minority of children were accommodated in this way. Voluntary homes sometimes offered specialist care of a type that a local authority did not provide ('training homes' for difficult adolescent girls, for example) or they might be chosen because they were situated in an area that was specially convenient for maintaining contacts with a child's family. A substantial number were preferred because of their religious bias, which enabled local authorities to fulfil their obligation to see that children were brought up according to their parents' own persuasion. Numbers of Roman Catholic children, for whom foster homes were often hard to find (generally because Catholic families tend to be large) were accommodated in this way. Thus, Dorset made greater use of voluntary homes than any neighbouring county and over half of the placements were of Roman Catholic children, 'usually members of large families. All the voluntary homes are outside the county and the Roman Catholic homes are particularly distant. There can be little doubt that the extensive use of the voluntary homes is influenced by the authority's inadequate amount of residential accommodation.'[20] Clearly the use of the voluntary sector was regarded as a mixed blessing by the Home Office and by many departments, since it sometimes meant that the child's needs were not ideally met and it also reduced the sense of urgency in some authorities about providing adequate accommodation of their own. Nevertheless it was one way out of the problem of building and adapting new local authority premises in a period of economic crisis and the total number of children housed in this way crept steadily upwards throughout the 1960s (3,677 in 1962; 4,877 in 1967; 5,411 in 1970).[21]

The failure of residential care to keep pace with increasing demands was felt throughout the whole child care system. Full and overcrowded homes meant that the area of choice in vital decision-making about placements was seriously constricted or even non-existent. Simple or sophisticated assessment procedures which determined what *kind* of residential home was suitable for a child were worthless if there were no places available, or if the first bed to fall vacant had to be seized, in whatever establishment, to make room in the reception home for the next admission. We have seen this kind of congestion occurring in relation to the 1969 Act, but the problem existed before the new legislation. Shortage also diminished the quality of care that the service was anxious to give. A study group, reporting on the *Residential Task in Child Care* in 1968 (the *Castle Priority Report*) asserted 'residential establishments caring for children should have a wide enough margin of empty beds to allow for newcomers to be accommodated without requiring constant changes of beds, rooms and other arrangements in order to receive them'; and again 'every child needs his own particular territory and the movement of children from bed to bed or room to room which at present so frequently happens, due to lack of accommodation, is to be deplored'.[22] An inadequate supply of residential establishments clearly put in jeopardy the whole aim of sensitive and 'personal' care for which the service had striven since Curtis.

Preventive policies, the extension of foster care and the incorporation of delinquent children have also meant that the residential sector of the child care service has had to deal increasingly with heavier concentrations of disturbed and handicapped children and with a higher proportion of adolescents. The widespread use of foster homes for very young children, for instance, has meant that the residential nurseries which remain have been used for children needing extra skilled attention—sickly babies, victims of 'battering', toddlers who have already suffered breakdowns in foster care and so on. Similarly, as many of the more 'straightforward' deprived children have been restored to their families or have been successfully fostered, those that remain in children's homes are often handicapped mentally or physically or have behaviour difficulties that are not easily tolerated in an ordinary family home; or, again, they are families of siblings whose best chance of remaining together is in a children's home setting. John Stroud describes the twenty-three inhabitants of a children's home in 1971.[23] Thirteen were teenagers and there were five pairs of siblings, a family of three and a family of four. Three were described as subnormal and one had a physical disability. Eleven had difficulties displayed variously through delinquency, out of control behaviour and incipient mental illness. Their admission to care had often followed on long periods of disturbance after parental desertion or mental instability.

The increasing stress upon maintaining family links and attempting rehabilitation has also had its effects upon residential care. It is one reason why the demand for places has not dwindled, for fostering has sometimes proved impossible for children whose loyalties to home have been very strong or whose parents have been too difficult or demanding to be acceptable as regular visitors in a private household. It has also involved residential staff in the same subtle shift of role that has been required of many foster parents— from substitute 'Mum' and 'Dad', to affectionate, caring but undemanding adults, who can help sustain a child's original affective links and can let him go when the family is ready. It has sometimes been responsible, also, for exacerbating the tensions between field and residential staff, when the former have seemed to ride roughshod over the knowledge, perceptions and feelings of the latter, in their anxiety to get children out of residential care.

One obvious result of the changing demands on residential care has been the development of a far wider variety of children's homes than were at first envisaged. We saw that Oxfordshire and some other authorities responded to the needs of some of the difficult adolescents in their care, by opening hostels for working girls and boys. Many departments found, too, that the original Curtis model of a home for no more than eight to twelve children was too restricted to meet many of their needs. The Castle Priory Study Group's Report, which has already been mentioned,

> regretted the large scale development of homes of the size and type known as 'family group homes'. Too many authorities had put all their eggs in this one basket. Family group homes tend to ape family life instead of recognising the value of small groups within the general structure of somewhat larger establishments. They over-emphasise the traditional family concept without in fact providing the security which a real family gives. Staff are often isolated and unsupported within them and too many roles have to be played by them.[24]

The rejection of the simple assumptions of the 1940s is quite explicit. In practice this has meant that some children's homes are of medium size, housing twenty, thirty or forty children divided into smaller living groups (and are thus incidentally close to Bevan's 'ideal' for old people's homes than to the Curtis model for children). It is thought that this enables a staff of sufficient size to be employed to offer a useful range of personality and skills to the children and a basis for support and professional development amongst themselves.

Under the 1969 Act the incorporation of approved schools into the 'community homes' system has further extended the range of establishments for which local authorities are responsible. They vary enormously in size and type but the fact that they are boarding-schools with a single-sexed pattern of living contrasts with most children's homes and adds another dimension to residential child care. Following the assumptions and aspirations of their founders, their boards of managers, or of their headmasters and head-mistresses, they have developed in a variety of ways. A few, for younger 'junior' children, stress homeliness and a substitute family style of living that is close to the children's home model. Others favour a highly structured programme of learning and activity that fills most waking hours. Others again are closely modelled on a pattern of service life, while there are some which are run on the lines of a 'therapeutic community', with shared decision-making, extensive group work and a degree of free expression that is closer to the style of care developed in some schools and hostels for maladjusted children.[25]

How the schools ('community homes' in current terminology) themselves will develop as they settle down in the new structure is still an open question. It is no secret that they have often been unpopular with social workers in the child care service who have regarded many of them as punitive, old fashioned and unimagina-tive. They, in turn, have viewed their incorporation with mixed feelings—defensive about any suggestion that they are to be taught to suck eggs by a service whose experience with delinquent children is much less extensive than their own and suspicious of the power that social workers now have in relation to the children in their charge. The recent development of three new community homes has provided an experiment in joint planning which has involved the local authorities concerned and the Development Group of what was the Children's Department of the Home Office (now part of the D.H.S.S.). The underlying philosophy and architectural guidelines have been published and although it is repeatedly stated that the pro-ject 'does not attempt to lay down a blueprint for all community homes' the hope is also expressed 'that they would have wide relevance and application'.[26] Their conclusions are therefore of considerable interest. The pattern envisaged combines boarding education for both sexes, a living style that emphasizes individual needs (privacy, personal possessions, flexible routines and so on) and 'treatment' through explicit therapy and by means of the 'planned environment' itself. Considerable attention is paid to staff structure and deployment and to buildings—their use, scale and balance. The influence of many different styles of care, deriving from mental hospitals, special schools, the child care service and the approved schools themselves is evident and the resulting model is a far more complex one than the homely, domestic solution for deprived children with which the child care service started out. To what extent it will become a practical reality depends, of course, upon many factors—not least the adaptability of staff who are already in post in community schools.

Developments in child care policy over a generation have thus significantly altered the nature and importance of residential care. It was seen first as a regrettable necessity, second best to foster care and quite distinct from it, yet copying so far as possible the small-scale style of living that was believed to be fostering's great strength. The concept was of an enlarged, imitation substitute home, where the emphasis was upon *nurture*. Now, residential care for children is regarded as both an important and integral part of the service and it covers a wide range of establishments of different size and specialism. The 'family group home' at one end of the continuum merges almost imperceptibly into the kind of 'professional' foster home that has developed as needs have changed or been better appreciated. (Indeed, American child care literature treats family group homes as part of foster care.)[27] The barriers between residential and day care are also being gradually eroded; assessment centres are encouraged to admit children on a daily basis and some residential nurseries run playgroups for their own and neighbourhood children, for example. At the other end of the continuum are special homes and schools for children who are severely disturbed and/or anti-social, some of them equipped with secure units and most of them, as yet, old approved schools under a new name. Throughout the whole spectrum of care, as the difficulties of deprived children have been increasingly appreciated, the notion of 'treatment' has been added to the basic task of nurture—at least in theory and intention. '(B)ecause both nurturing and remedial care are likely to be needed by all children in residential homes help must be provided on two levels, i.e. the level of the normal warmth and affection which a child needs in any case and the additional help and treatment which a child in difficulties needs particularly.'[28] It follows that residential staff are no longer required to be merely home-makers, but must possess therapeutic skills of a high order. Inevitably, this development in expectations has brought with it some alteration, together with demands for much greater changes in the whole status of residential work and the staff who undertake it.

The changes that have been sought and partially achieved have been concerned with training, living and working conditions, salaries and greater participation in policies affecting individual children and the service in general. We have seen, in an earlier chapter, how training for residential child care was modest in conception and how it failed to keep pace with needs and with wastage through high staff turnover. Though one or two advanced courses developed and the basic courses became more ambitious and demanding, at no point in time have more than a small proportion of residential child care staff been qualified. The Williams Committee's[29] suggested solution was to develop common courses for all forms of residential work—a sort of residential equivalent to the 'generic' social work courses that were proliferating in the 1960s. An alternative line of development came from the child care service itself. Workers were, on the whole, lukewarm about the idea of a generic residential training and believed they had much more in common with their fieldwork colleagues in child care. The Castle Priory Report asserted that 'residential work needed as high a calibre of staff as field work', and suggested a joint two-year training for both branches of the child care service in which all teaching would be shared and field and residential workers would be differentiated only by the balance of their practical placements.[30] Parity of esteem would be based on parity of training. The Central Training Council in Child Care promoted a similar scheme shortly afterwards and a few experimental courses were established. With the Seebohm reorganization a new pattern is emerging, however, which merges the Williams's plan and the child care experiments in one. A CCETSW working party, alarmed at the vast training needs of residential care in general (only 4 per cent of the staff caring for 395,000 people in residential institutions have an appropriate training) has proposed joint training for all field and residential workers. The title of its Paper—'Residential Work is part of Social Work' —expresses a hope and determination that the gap between field and residential workers, that has persisted for so long, will be closed. It also underlines that the problem has not been peculiar to the child care field, but has been common to all branches of social work.[31]

Gradually, over the same period, residential workers have seen some improvements in their conditions of work. In many homes their own living space has been restricted or lacking in any privacy so that work has invaded their home life to a tremendous degree. This is, of course, consistent with the 'family' model of residential care but emphasizes how little the strains imposed were properly appreciated. (To many laymen, looking after deprived children was like being a 'parent'.) As authorities adapted premises or built afresh attempts were made to improve staff accommodation by providing self-contained flats, with separate entrances, equipping single rooms with simple cooking facilities, allowing space for staff to entertain and accommodate visitors and so on. As the emphasis on faithfully reproducing a family atmosphere has waned, so too has the insistence on an all-resident staff. Many homes now employ a mixture of resident and non-resident staff though few, if any, have gone so far as to engage everyone on a non-resident 'shift system' basis, on lines not uncommon in the United States. Perhaps this is seen as too close to a medical model of care to be readily acceptable here though, as Williams[32] pointed out, chronic staff shortage may force experiments of this kind, whatever the 'ideal' might be.

Hours of work have also set residential workers apart from their field colleagues. Although both kinds of work spread beyond normal 'office hours', producing an untidy working day, this is obviously particularly so for residential staff and their average working week has been consistently longer. The Williams Committee[33] revealed that most children's home staff were working between 60 and 80 hours a week at a time when the 'official' working week of a child care officer was $38\frac{1}{2}$ hours. (In practice, with overtime, this was usually between 40 and 50 hours, on average.) In 1968 a circular from the National Joint Council recommended that employing bodies should attempt 'gradually' to reduce the hours worked by residential staff to 45 per week but for many authorities this was seen as a fairly distant goal. In 1969, for instance, Oxfordshire's Heads of Homes reminded their committee of the circular and, in reply, the committee recorded 'their appreciation of the friendly, helpful and constructive attitudes of the Heads of Homes' and set a target of a 50-hour week by 1970. By 1974, the national target was 42 hours, with a further reduction to 40 hours in 1975, though it is unclear how far this is attainable in practice.

Salaries for residential work have also been strongly criticized;

for being too low (often a 'woman's wage' that fails to attract men into the service); for encouraging turnover because of small and slowly-won increments; for rigidities and anomalies in standard charges for board and lodging made for varied and often inadequate accommodation. There have been improvements, particularly where departments have been able to argue that establishments are 'special' in some way, and have paid higher salaries in recognition of special difficulties in the work, but the ideal proposed in the Castle Priory Report of 'parity between field and residential staff' is not yet achieved.

Gains in the status of residential workers are best illustrated, however, by the changes that have taken place in their relationships with lay members and with field social workers—changes which have often been formalized through new committee structures and administrative procedures. Oxfordshire's experiences illustrate this well, though its particular pattern of development is not necessarily 'typical'. In the early years of the child care service each children's home had its own house committee of elected and co-opted lay members which met regularly and concerned itself with the detailed running of the home. Top officials of the department—the Children's Officer, Deputy and the Administrative Officer responsible for residential establishments, for instance, attended all such committees and therefore had a total view of residential care in the county, but the homes staff themselves attended only their own committees, had no direct 'links' with a central committee and no regular formal relationship with the staff of any other home. Their own 'overview' of the county's residential situation was therefore gained informally or received at second hand. Residential business was referred on from house committees to the finance and general purposes subcommittee of the main committee (which was clearly concerned with other matters besides residential care) and Homes staff did not attend. In contrast, fieldworkers put in detailed reports and were often in attendance at the boarding-out subcommittee—the other main subcommittee of the children's committee. In some ways residential staff were thus under much closer lay scrutiny than their field colleagues (members regularly visited the homes and actually saw residential staff at work, whereas child care officers visits were 'confidential' and sacrosanct) but their links were all at a *local* level, with no means of achieving a corporate identity or voice, which might turn this close contact to their own advantage. The pattern sprang, in part, from the separation and isolation of residential units in a county area and it reinforced that isolation and underlined the primacy of foster care in the department's scale of priorities.

Several important developments altered this pattern. 'Heads of Homes' meetings were established which were at first spasmodic, largely social gatherings to enable residential staff to get to know each other and their establishments. (They took it in turns to act as 'host'.) As these gained momentum they became a regular feature and even split into two—the 'Lady Heads' (Matrons) meeting separately to discuss domestic issues. They also enabled the residential staff in charge to share experiences and views and to develop the corporate voice that had been lacking. Initiative for changes and improvements relating to residential care shifted from field or 'office' inspired plans to proposals which came direct from the homes themselves. We find, for instance, a document on a new maintenance scheme for working adolescents in residential care, drawn up by the Heads of Homes and presented to fieldworkers for comment and observations.

The committee structure was also changed in 1967. House committees were abolished and two new subcommittees of the main children's committee were formed to replace the old divisions—a 'fieldwork' subcommittee and a 'residential work' subcommittee. This not only reflected an *equal* concern with the residential and field aspects of the service but also acknowledged the vast range of field social work that had quite outgrown the original 'boarding-out' title. The residential subcommittee maintained contact with the establishments by meeting in each home in turn and the residential staff for their part were also able to keep in touch more regularly. We have already seen the Heads of Homes jogging their committee about working hours—no longer reliant upon other departmental officials to put their case for them.

Changes are also apparent in the development of formal links between homes and 'the office'. The Children's Officer maintained a special interest in and responsibility for residential care from the earliest days of the service but other official positions were created in due course to augment this. The administrative officer with special responsibility for homes was joined in the early 1960s by a social worker with Assistant Children's Officer status, whose concern was with the 'professional' aspects of residential care. The task involved being a convenor and chairman of case conferences on children in residence, channel and arbiter of requests for vacancies, arranger of relief in times of staffing crisis and, in particular, interpreter and buffer between field and residential staff. Typically the first appointment was of a field social worker with only limited residential experience. Later the role was filled by a worker with extensive residential experience and training and later still, in the last stages of the children's department's existence, a Head of a residential establishment moved into the position of Deputy Children's Officer. The rights of residential workers to consult and to be 'managed' by professionals they could respect was thus explicitly recognized.

Residential staff also took a growing part in redefining and articulating their own roles and functions. From the beginning of 1969 working parties on residential care began to meet regularly. The first arose directly from a crisis and the temporary closure of one of the homes and residential staff from other establishments joined top administrators in lengthy discussions about future plans and the best procedures for reopening and re-establishing the unit. Thereafter monthly meetings were held in the various county establishments and the staff of each home were involved in detailed consideration of a wide variety of issues; the how and why of daily routines, for instance, and how 'institutional' tendencies might be eliminated; a splitting of 'domestic bursar' roles from 'child care' ones to enable trained residential workers to deal more directly with children; relationships between field and residential staff and how the former might be persuaded to consult the latter more frequently and sensitively. (Great bitterness was expressed by some residential workers that field staff would happily remove a child who had been in residence for several years with very little consultation with residential staff—yet there would be outcry if a child was wrenched away from a foster home after the same period of time.) They also considered relationships with the wider community—the unwanted pressures of worthy organizations who wished to 'adopt the Home, take children on outings and to parties and shower them all with anonymous gifts' and thus pushed the homes into a 'humble but grateful' posture. At the remand and reception homes the likely repercussions of the 1969 Act were considered, the future of the nursery was discussed exhaustively and at the hostels the problem of helping adolescents who were 'still struggling, dirty, disorganised and dependent' at 18 and seemed likely to become depressed and inadequate parents in their turn, was confronted. A means had been found for residential staff to look very carefully at what they were doing and to participate in determining the direction of future changes in which they would be involved. The working parties were also a clear prototype of residential exercises which are now promoted by the Development Group of the D.H.S.S. where all the staff of selected establishments, together with members of the group, spend several days dissecting and redefining their tasks and methods.

Thus, by the time children's departments came to an end, considerable change had taken place in the nature and expectations of both foster care and residential care and in the balance between them. In broadening their initial, narrow, sharply defined focus on providing good substitute care, departments found that preventive work, more vigorous rehabilitative efforts and the inclusion of delinquent as well as deprived children, put their accepted methods under fresh strain. They were forced to rethink priorities, to diversify and to redefine roles and tasks. In the process relationships between field, residential and administrative staff, between staff and lay members and between staff and foster parents were all affected. It is perhaps a sign of the changing balance of relationships between field and residential workers, for instance, that field staff who had been willing to spend large amounts of time helping out in the homes in the pioneer days of the service ('rescuing' the staff as well as the children?) were no longer so willing in the late 1960s. 'Why is it always us? Why don't residential workers ever help *us* out in times of staff shortage?' It seemed to them that equality of status ought to cut both ways.

None of these changes has been smooth or clearcut and the service still wrestles with the problem of trying to preserve families, while providing good substitutes for them, and with the inbuilt tensions between those who look after deprived children and those who work mainly with their families. These problems have been carried over into the new social services departments and may even have been amplified by them. It is to these large new departments and their role in relation to child care policy and practice that the following chapter will turn.

NOTES

1. *Seventh Report on the Work of the Children's Department*, Home Office, H.M.S.O., 1955.
2. County Borough of Dudley Children's Committee. First Annual Report of Children's Officer. August 1948–February 1950.
3. Gordon Trasler, *In Place of Parents*, Routledge and Kegan Paul, 1960.

4. Roy Parker, *Decision in Child Care*, Allen and Unwin, 1966.
5. Rachel Jenkins, 'The Needs of Foster Parents', *Case Conference*, January 1965.
6. Victor George, *Foster Care*, Routledge and Kegan Paul, 1970.
7. 'Dorset County Council Child Care Service', Report to the Secretary of State for the Home Department by the Chief Inspector, Children's Department, Home Office. H.M.S.O., 1966.
8. R. A. Parker, 'Foster Home Care', in the *Proceedings of the Fifteenth Annual Conference of the Association of Children's Officers*, 1964.
9. 'The Needs of Foster Parents', op. cit.
10. Personal communication from Claire Winnicott.
11. Foster Home Care, op. cit.
12. *'Foster Care'*, op. cit. Chap. II.
13. 'The dilemma of the foster parent role and the potential of foster parent groups for its resolution.' Dissertation for the Diploma in Social Work, Exeter University, Cynthia Canniford, 1974. (Unpublished.)
14. According to a B.A.S.W. survey, described in 'Cut Price Fostering' (Joan Fratter, *New Society*, 1 September 1974) a few local authorities in the North-East pay a basic allowance to foster parents, on top of the allowance for the foster child. Some authorities also recognize a few 'professional' foster parents and pay a 'wage'—the most generous was £15 per week.
15. Ibid.
16. G. Adamson, *Social Work Today*, 2 December 1971.
17. Jane Rowe and Lydia Lambert, *Children Who Wait*, Association of British Adoption Agencies, 1973.
18. R. A. Parker, 'Planning for deprived children', National Children's Home Convocation Lecture, 1971.
19. Local Authorities' Returns of Children in Care, Home Office and D.H.S.S. N.B. The earlier figure is for England and Wales but the 1972 figure is for England only as the form in which the statistics are presented has now changed; if the Welsh figures were to be included the two totals would be even closer.
20. 'Dorset County Council Child Care Service', op. cit.
21. Local authorities Returns of Children in Care, op. cit.
22. *Residential Task in Child Care*. Report of a Study Group. R.C.C.A., 1969.
23. 'Residential Care', in *Services for Children and their Families*, ed. John Stroud, Pergamon Press, 1973.
24. Op. cit.
25. See Spencer Millham, Roger Bullock and Paul Cherrett 'After Grace—Teeth', Human Context Books, 1975.
26. *Care and Treatment in a Planned Environment*, Home Office Advisory Council on Child Care, H.M.S.O., 1970.
27. See, for instance, Alfred Kadushin, *Child Welfare Services*, Collier Macmillan, 1974.
28. *Residential Task in Child Care*, op. cit.
29. *Caring for People*, op. cit.

L

30. *Residential Task in Child Care*, op. cit.
31. The same document also proposes a 'two tier' system of training, however, and a minority report suggests that the 'lower' tier will almost certainly be used much more widely for residential workers, so that differences in status will persist.
32. *Caring for People*, op. cit.
33. Ibid.

CHAPTER EIGHT

Seebohm—Snake or Ladder?

Developments in prevention and work with delinquency not only strained, modified and redefined the original aims and methods of the child care service; they also contributed directly to its eventual demise. The pursuit of both policies increased the children's departments' involvement with and dependence on other agencies and threw into relief their relationship with one another and the illogical and wasteful effects of the fragmented pattern of personal social services. As the two policies drew closer together, with prevention of neglect being seen more and more as a key means of forestalling delinquency, the pressure to change that pattern and to provide an integrated 'family service' in its place mounted. The child care service was thus, in a very real sense, a prime initiator of 'reorganization' whereby it (alongside other departments and sub-departments of local government) ceased to have a separate existence. In the event, the form of reorganization was much more radical than the early child-centred blueprints envisaged, so that the service lost its identity in a way which was not anticipated. That it was nevertheless responsible for much of the impetus for change, is very evident.

Commitment to preventive work meant an increasing amount of work with families in their own homes and a greater degree of involvement with other, interested agencies. In the process child care workers were made more aware of the common ground between them and workers from other departments, both in terms of problems tackled and methods used.[1] More pertinently, they were also reminded of their dependence on facilities and resources which were not within the power of their own departments to provide. Examples are day care for young children (nurseries and child minders) and the home help service—which offered great

155

potential for support in family situations, but which came under the health department umbrella. Temporary accommodation for homeless families was another resource for which child care officers often expressed a need, but which was the responsibility of welfare departments. Indeed, some residential establishments, a network of foster homes and a team of field social workers, which made up the major resources of most children's departments, were well suited to the 1948 aims of providing good substitute care for deprived children, but were of more restricted value once policies of prevention and the promotion of good child care in the community were adopted. We have already seen that the 1963 Children and Young Persons Act gave the service more scope, particularly where material and financial help was concerned. Nevertheless, departments felt frustrated by the many related means of supporting families which were outside their control. Co-ordination between departments was one way of mustering these resources and the joint circulars of the fifties and the 1963 Act itself all advocated this approach. Where it failed, demands for a restructuring of personal social services and a regrouping of responsibilities became more vociferous.

Concern about delinquency gave those demands a much more cutting edge. Arguments for preventing family breakdown and child neglect had considerable force and much heart-appeal, but by taking a further step and linking such efforts with the prevention of juvenile crime, the cause appealed to the head as well. The upward trend in juvenile delinquency rates, which began in the mid-1950s and only levelled out in the mid-1960s gave cause for concern in at least two ways. That a growing number of children and young people committed crimes was troubling and troublesome enough in itself: but it was also known that some adult criminals had once been juvenile offenders. Forestalling delinquency might therefore have long-term benefits, both in terms of the crime rate as a whole and in terms of the numbers of people, expensively housed in Borstals, prisons and the like. There were therefore good law and order *and* economic grounds for making any changes that would facilitate more effective preventive work.

The emergence of the idea of a 'family service' has already been touched on in earlier chapters. Some of the witnesses who gave evidence to the Ingleby Committee[2] (the Fabians, Donnison and Stewart, for example) hoped for a restructuring of the personal social services which would redraw departmental boundaries and give children's departments new responsibilities in relation to unmarried mothers, homeless families, day-care facilities and so on. Ingleby failed to do this, though it acknowledged that 'it may be that the long-term solution will be in a reorganisation of the various services concerned with the family and their combination into a unified family service'. Because it foresaw 'obvious and formidable difficulties' and because it believed such radical changes to be 'well outside our terms of reference' it merely urged 'the importance of their further study by the Government and by the local interests concerned'. The idea was not buried, but shelved for the time being.

Four years later in *Crime—a Challenge to us All*[3] it appears again as a key proposal in the Labour Party Study Group's plan to combat crime. In its chapter on 'Forestalling Delinquency' it declares that 'the administrative structure of the social services is ripe for review. . . . The first step needed is the establishment of a new Family Service'. Again, what is envisaged is clearly an enlarged children's department—'this will incorporate and develop some of the functions of existing central and local government departments relating to children and families, including the present children's departments and parts of the health, welfare and education departments'. There are strong echoes of the original Curtis proposals as well. 'Each local authority will be required to set up a Family Service Committee and to appoint a chief officer. The head of the Family Service should be a skilled and experienced social administrator, with the same status as other chief officers of the authority, such as the Medical Officer of Health and the Director of Education.' Work with handicapped children, with unmarried mothers and their children and the setting up of family advice centres are all mentioned as coming within the bounds of the proposed new service.

A year later, in a white paper *The Child, the Family and the Young Offender*[4] the government announced its intention to pursue the proposal further.

(E)very advance in dealing with the young offender helps also in the attack on adult crime. . . . The proposals made in this paper for the reform of the law and practice relating to young offenders emphasise the need to improve the structure of the various services connected with support of the family and the prevention of delinquency. The Government believe that these services should be organised as a family service, but the form and scope of such a service will need detailed consideration. The Government therefore propose to appoint a small, independent Committee to review the organisation and responsibilities of the local authority personal social services, and consider what changes are desirable to ensure an effective family service.

Four months later, in December 1965, the Seebohm Committee was set up with precisely those terms of reference.

The focus at the time Seebohm began its investigations was thus clearly on the child—particularly the delinquent child—in his family context. This is not to say that pressures for change had not come from beyond child care circles as well. Since the mid-1950s, for instance, training for social workers had been moving steadily against the specialist implications of the separate welfare services. Following an L.S.E. experiment, 'generic' courses, providing a common training for social workers in probation, child care and hospital services gradually evolved and fresh impetus was given by the 1959 Younghusband Report,[5] which recommended a new, common basic training for all social workers in Health and Welfare services. Later, as we have seen, the Williams Committee[6] wanted a similarly 'generic' training for all residential social workers. The view of the trainers was that there was a common core of knowledge and skill that all social workers needed to acquire, whatever their administrative setting, and this, in itself, suggested that departmental boundaries artificially divided an emerging profession and might therefore be changed. Proposals to reform the whole of local government also had repercussions. The first Maud Report on Management in Local Government,[7] for instance (published in 1967), deplored the proliferation of committees and small departments, which made efficient management so difficult. One of its proposals was a drastic reduction in such departments, to a mere five or six—and a merger of 'health and welfare services' was one rationalization that was suggested. Education services were also highly critical of the current muddle of personal social services and both Newsom[8] and Plowden[9] urged simplification, so that schools and other referring agents would know better where to turn for help with social problems.

There was therefore a general interest in reorganization as well as a particular concern with children and their families and the views of the child care service and its professional associations were only some amongst many that were considered by the Seebohm Committee. Nevertheless, in the light of subsequent changes, it is interesting to see what these views were. The Associations of Children's Officers and of Child Care Officers and the Residential Child Care Association were all in favour of gradual change, phased over some years, and they clung to the original notion of a child-centred service as a necessary first step. The ultimate goal, in their view, should be a family service, which in the words of the Children's Officers, 'should embody eventually those parts of the social services (other than medical and educational services) which can be defined as *personal* rather than general and in which the *family unit* is the essential element in the background of the individual' (my italics). This presupposed, in the Children's Officers' view, 'a casework service closely tied in administratively with residential accommodation to which immediate and easy access is constantly available' and, in the opinion of the child care officers, 'to be effective, social work must be the basic activity of the service and not a subsidiary activity'.[10]

Aware that there were strong arguments for a radical reorganization, including all forms of social work—mental welfare, for example, and care of the elderly, handicapped, sick and deviant—they were nevertheless opposed to immediate and wholesale change, which they felt would create more problems than it solved. The Children's Officers, for example, pointed out that one special element of child care was that 'the service is required to provide extremely long-term care . . . it necessitates the sort of responsibility similar in implications to that of a parent'. For this reason, the service must be highly personal with a strong element of continuity, and rapid absorption into 'too large and complex an organisation' would put this in jeopardy. They also argued that other services which might eventually be integrated—Probation, for instance—needed a period of consolidation, to cope with new duties imposed by recent legislation, before they faced the upheavals of reorganization themselves. The fears of residential workers were that precipitate administrative change, unsupported by increased resources, would merely perpetuate, or even exacerbate the service's failure to meet needs. 'It has been characteristic of the social services in recent years that they have lived from day to day and from hand to mouth and have had to undertake what was expedient rather than what was necessary for the well-being of each individual client.' R.C.C.A. reiterated again and again its fear that, without extra resources of money and manpower, any reorganization would be useless. Both A.C.O. and A.C.C.O. proposed a three-stage change, which differed only in the order of its last two phases. The first phase involved integration of all personal services concerned with children—the child care service itself, work with unmarried mothers and homeless families, juvenile court work, the approved schools and so on. At two later dates, services for the elderly, the mentally ill and handicapped, and for offenders would be absorbed in their turn. The child care officers, following the logic of human development, put the elderly last; the Children's Officers—perhaps more shrewdly aware of likely resistance—proposed that absorption of the Probation Service should be the final step.

Though stoutly in favour of the benefits to be derived from a new family service (the child care associations dwelt more on the positive gains from a family approach and less on the deficiencies of existing fragmented services than most other bodies which gave evidence) they were also aware of the dangers of reorganization. Insufficient attention to the need for increased resources, breaks in continuity and loss of the vital 'personal' element have already been mentioned. Too large a structure, embracing too many functions was feared by A.C.O. because 'to attempt to combine general social services, personal social services and income supportive services in one very large organisation, whether at local or central level would, we believe, merely reproduce the present fragmentation of services under an inevitably impersonal leadership'. At the local level, similar fears were more strongly expressed. Oxfordshire's Children's Committee, in preparing its own evidence to Seebohm, said 'it would in our opinion, for instance, be damaging to the highly personal type of work done by the child care service to place it in such a large and general group of functions that the old pattern of the former Public Assistance Service might recur, with the disadvantages that would entail'. The spectre of the Poor Law still haunted the local councillors. The service was also nervous of any reorganization that might place social workers under the leadership of professional administrators or of members of a profession, other than social work. The child care officers were quite explicit about their horror of being managed by the Medical Officers of Health (and the Medical Officers made no secret of their dislike of child care officers, in *their* evidence!) and all the child care associations recommended that the head of the new service must be a qualified social worker or social administrator. In this, they were at one with other social work groups, valuing their independence and fearing the effects of subordination to any other profession.

In the light of subsequent developments, many of the reservations about reorganization, expressed by child care workers in their evidence to Seebohm, assure considerable significance—a point to be explored later. In the event, however, the child care lobby failed to sway the committee on several important issues and other evidence from different quarters had considerable influence. The suggestion that change should be phased and gradual was rejected in favour of radical reorganization at one fell swoop. The committee obviously thought that the suggested model smacked too much of self-interest—a takeover bid which would place child care firmly in charge. The emphasis on the 'family'—and hence on casework as the primary method of help—was also modified by the committee's eloquent commitment to the notion of 'community'. It had been argued (by the psychiatric social workers, for instance) that many isolated people living outside families were also in need of help. The committee agreed, and wished to include 'everybody'. In addition, a group of Islington social workers—influenced, no doubt, by the patent *dis*integration of the urban community in which they worked—stressed that many problems 'could be dealt with to a much greater extent by the community. . . . People should be encouraged to become their own social workers', and the new service should be 'wider than a rescue service and even prevention'. It should 'assist change in the community'. The same group expressed 'frustration with the limited potential of individual relationships' and wanted to incorporate more extensive groupwork and community organization methods within the new service. They also favoured the 'general social caseworker', backed by specialist consultants. In tune with this view was the powerful voice of Professor Titmuss, who declared that much preventive thinking had been 'too family and child-centred'; the new department should emphasize provision of *services*, rather than support for the family or any other pattern of relationships.[11] Seebohm reflected all these views very clearly, and the concept of a 'family service' was thus swallowed up in something much larger and more ambitious, before it was even born.

The Seebohm Report, recommending a new local authority Social Services Department, 'community based and family oriented', was published in July 1968.[12] The new structure was to comprise children's departments, welfare services for the old, handicapped and homeless, mental health social work services, education welfare and child guidance, home-helps, day nurseries and other social welfare work carried out by health and housing departments. But its responsibilities were to go beyond those of existing departments. Integration was to be accompanied by a reaching out 'far beyond the discovery and rescue of social casualties; it will enable the greatest possible number of individuals to act reciprocally giving and receiving service for the well-being of the whole community'.[13] It was a 'universal' concept in several senses of the word. It was to be available to all classes of person, whatever their means, and thus preserved the tradition, established in 1948, of a complete break from any kind of Poor Law. It was also envisaged as meeting a wide variety of human needs, along the whole age spectrum and in a multiplicity of ways—through material assistance, domiciliary, day and residential care and social work support of every kind— casework, groupwork and community organization. Community involvement would break down barriers between the 'givers' and 'recipients' of service and deterrence and stigma, hopefully, would be minimized, and communities revitalized in the process. In one way or another it would therefore involve the whole population— much as the Education and Health Services do, and would no longer be directed solely at minority groups with particular personal problems. The chief officers of the new service at local level would ideally be social workers with administrative experience and/or training and only one department would be responsible at central government level.

The response of social workers to the Seebohm plan was generally very favourable and child care workers joined colleagues from other specialisms in pressing for implementation when action was delayed. Doubts and reservations were still apparent, especially but not exclusively among groups of social workers like the probation officers and medical social workers, who were not included but looked as if they might be. But the excitement and potential of Seebohm (significantly it was dubbed the 'social workers charter' by some—status and career prospects were clearly going to be much brighter) carried along most of those concerned. In addition, premature reorganization of welfare services in some boroughs, in advance of legislation, which put Medical Officers of Health in charge, created alarm and increased pressures to reorganize the Seebohm way.

The Local Authority Social Services Act was eventually passed and came into effect on 1 April 1971. In integrating previously separate local authority departments it followed the bare bones of the report fairly faithfully, but it lacked most of its flesh. Recommendations about methods of work, forms of organization, about research and intelligence requirements, about community involvement and—most importantly—about the need for more resources, were untouched by the legislation. Such matters were left entirely to the initiative of the local authorities themselves. Indeed, the

R.C.C.A.'s gloomy prognostications about reorganization without resources seemed all too realistic in the light of the preamble to the bill, which declared that 'the increase, if any, in expenditure of local authorities will prove to be so slight as not to be quantifiable' and also that 'the Bill is not expected to have any appreciable over-all effect on public service manpower requirements'. The scale of social services department budgets now and their continuing thirst for more money and manpower should bring a blush to the cheeks of the government advisers concerned.

It remains to consider child care policies and practice since re-organization took place and since the child care service, as such, ceased to exist. There is no doubt that they have been the subject of widespread public concern and criticism for the past two or three years, on a scale and with an intensity that has not been experienced since the ferment of the 1940s. The attacks on the 1969 Children and Young Persons Act, expressing disquiet about its principles and its implementation, have already been discussed in an earlier chapter. Alongside this, a growing unease has been expressed about the consequences of the 1963 legislation, with its powers to give material aid. Has preventive work with families now become an alternative and inferior income maintenance service and has personal social work suffered in consequence? More dramatically, a series of scandals in which children have been injured or killed by parents or caretakers have led many to question both the organization of services designed to protect children and the assumptions on which they operate. Where the death of a child has involved a 'tug of love' situation as well—as in the Maria Colwell case—criticism has been passionate and severe. Public services are being accused of neglect, ineptitude and insensitivity towards the needs and rights of the child and new legislation is being enacted in the hopes of rectifying the situation. In some ways we are therefore back where we began a generation ago, and it is necessary to explore the reasons why. Disentangling cause and effect—especially how far the current situation stems from policies and practices developed in the early days of the children's depart-ments and how far it is a direct result of reorganization (either because of temporary upheavals, or because the new structures do not support good child care) is a difficult and hazardous enterprise. The evidence is confused and witnesses disagree.

To take, first, the criticisms of the way 'preventive' work has de-veloped; an earlier chapter has traced the struggles of children's departments to prevent family breakdown both before the 1963 Act gave them specific powers to do so, and after its implementation. The emphasis in Section I of that Act was on the 'advice, guidance and assistance' (in other words family casework) that social workers should give to avoid the reception of children into care and the appearance of children before the juvenile court. Material and financial assistance was subordinate to the social workers' personal skills and influence and, in the case of cash, was to be offered only 'in exceptional circumstances'. Child care workers had pressed for this power because they experienced the inflexibility of the N.A.B. in meeting the exceptional and crisis needs of their clients and because problems of management and budgeting were evident among many of the multi-problem families that they were attempting to preserve. It seems clear that neither they, nor the legislators, envisaged the new power as involving large sums of money, nor regular supplements to the poor, for as the accompanying Home Office circular stressed 'it is not intended that the power to give material assistance under Section I of the Act should be used to provide an alternative to National Assistance or a child care supplement to national assistance payments'.[14] Awareness that this was nevertheless what was gradually beginning to occur and uneasiness about its effects was being expressed by the late 1960s, well before administrative reorganization took place.

At the 1967 Conference of Children's Officers, for instance, Sylvia Watson, their President, said that social workers should be used to provide a personal service for individuals and families with *special* problems. They should not be used to solve *general* problems, created by an inadequate social structure. To promote the children's welfare and prevent family breakdown children's departments might be asked to supplement the man's wages. Was this the right way for this social problem to be tackled? Fears of becoming inappropriate dispensers of poor relief were quite explicit. A year later Joel Handler, an American commentator, coined the phrase 'the coercive Children's Officer' to describe the way in which clients' behaviour was being controlled by the giving or withholding of Section I monies and material assistance.[15] Similar points of concern emerge from Heywood and Allen's research into financial help under the 1963 Act, which was undertaken during the same period.[16] They noted that expenditure was rising fast (by 200 per cent between 1966 and 1969) and that social workers were often confused and distressed at being faced with clients 'in desperate need'—all of whom they would have wished to help. But, given restricted local authority budgets and the enormity of need being presented, this was impossible and child care officers were forced strictly to ration assistance—and they often used social work notions of 'helpability' to do so. These seemed peculiarly inappropriate when many clients were being referred (or referring themselves) whose major or perhaps *only* problem was lack of money. Should and could a social work agency therefore be dealing with them?

These trends have become much more marked since reorganization and seem to reflect a deliberate shift in responsibility for certain income maintenance functions from the supplementary benefits commission to social services departments. Bill Jordan, one of the severest critics of this policy, points out that the latter are, in many instances, providing an alternative and *inferior* income maintenance service.[17] Persuaded into making emergency payments or into meeting exceptional needs (for both of which the S.B.C. itself has responsibilities, with discretion) they are, in effect, doing the poor and themselves a grave disservice. Unlike the S.B.C., social services departments have no uniform policy to guide them (Heywood and Allen show how social workers themselves often groped towards the formulation of such policies in their own areas) and no appeals procedure which disgruntled clients can invoke. Many of their payments for food and fuel and household goods are very small and some operate extensive loan systems in preference to grants. Social workers may imagine that they offer a more flexible and sympathetic service but this is not necessarily how clients experience it; especially if it involves probing into their personal relationships in an attempt to discover whether there are underlying emotional reasons for poverty—or whether the poor are merely poor.

> The systematic referral of people who are in a state of financial crisis which frequently bears no relation to emotional stress of the kind helpfully dealt with by social work has reduced claimants' rights to exceptional needs grants from the Supplementary Benefits Commission, whilst at the same time, undermining the confidence of social workers in the usefulness of their skills.[18]

American experience supports these contentions for, as Jordan points out, a number of commentators (Keith Lucas and Piven and Cloward among them) have deplored the effects of the combination of public assistance and social work functions in their own country, which leads to 'the arbitrary, insulting and insidious effects of employing casework as a method of rationing and controlling the dispensing of public assistance'.[19] Social workers in this country are also expressing growing disquiet. A 'poverty special interest group' of the British Association of Social Workers has, for example, recently investigated Section I payments in a number of London boroughs and has found that almost half of all the money given went to help people already receiving Supplementary Benefit, or other State benefits.[20] In some boroughs as much as one-fifth of the sum was for such basics as food. A system which was never designed to 'top up' supplementary benefit (national assistance, as it then was) seems nevertheless to be developing fast in that direction.

In the same way, children's departments and now social services departments have come to support an enormous financial burden on behalf of the homeless. In areas of housing shortage by far the largest proportion of Section I money is spent on paying off rent arrears or on paying for bed and breakfast (often for weeks or even months) for families who would otherwise be homeless.[21] As with poverty, many families are homeless because of gross housing shortage and not because of their own relationship problems or mismanagement.[22] Certainly they are in danger of breaking up because of their lack of a roof, and hence their children are at risk of coming into care, so that application of 1963 Act powers is understandable. But the fault lies in the sphere of Housing and not in themselves. Again, therefore, social workers are in contact with many people whose need is not for family casework (or, indeed, groupwork or community work) but for accommodation (which they cannot provide), and social services budgets are drained for want of proper expenditure by other departments of local and central government. The recent circular[23] which recommends the gradual transfer of responsibility for homelessness from social services departments to housing departments is a modest move in the direction of a more logical division of responsibilities.

Preventive policies in child care have therefore led social workers a long way from the original concept of intensive personal assistance to families whose children might otherwise be admitted to local authority care. The power to give material and financial aid, which seemed so necessary in order to be able to respond helpfully to family crises and to make rehabilitation a reality, has brought social workers in contact with 'the poor' as a class, rather than with troubled families, some (but not all) of whom happened also to be poor. Understandably they have felt outraged at the material deprivation they have witnessed and have used their powers to meet material need whenever possible. The expansion of such policies has also been encouraged by their conviction that they have a more sensitive and sympathetic approach to people than either housing or supplementary benefits officials and that the dignity of applicants is thereby respected.[24] If their purse were bottomless this might, indeed, be so, but as it is severely limited their inevitably strict rationing has often been experienced as offensive and arbitrary. One must also question what would have happened if they had *not* paid the rent arrears or cleared the debts or bought furniture, clothes or food for all the families in question. Would these children then have come into care or been brought before the court? In some cases they undoubtedly would but commentators like Jordan suggest that in many more situations the appropriate services would have *had* to help and responsibility would have been pushed back where it belonged. Certainly, the relatively unchanging numbers of children admitted to care, despite all this activity, suggests that there is some truth in this contention.[25]

As it is, social workers in the new social services departments have given the impression of being swamped with referrals for material help (intensified by the Chronically Sick and Disabled Persons Act, with its provision for radios, telephones, household aids and so on) and many have felt they have much less time to give to 'real' social work. They have thus felt themselves to be effective neither in the sphere of income maintenance, nor as social workers. On the credit side, however, their awareness of the extent of poverty, poor housing and homelessness has probably been sharpened. It has certainly led social workers to be more conscious and knowledgeable about their clients' 'welfare rights' and to be more critical and vociferous in their protests about social injustice. This, in turn, may have given impetus to more radical approaches to social problems—to the kind of community work, for instance, which seeks to help people to combine to protest against their environment. In this way, Seebohm's ideal of a service which involves and revives whole communities could be realized.

Sadly, it also seems that such developments may have been at the expense of the personal care and continuity that was thought so important in a good child care service. Attention may too often be focused on the financial circumstances of parents and less on the needs of the child. Recently, for instance, there were moves on the part of a number of influential workers to form a pressure group to publicize falling standards in child care practice. Paradoxically, too, Seebohm's other important aim of creating a truly 'universal' service may be receding out of reach, as social services departments are seen more and more as agencies for the poor. If the direction taken by preventive policies is merely a temporary phenomenon, the disturbance and reappraisal that it has caused may produce considerable long-term benefits. If it becomes a permanent feature, child care pioneers may have to face the possibility that they have helped to create, in Jordan's phrase, 'a public welfare agency'—an agency not unlike the old public assistance departments, which children's departments replaced and whose memory they sought to erase.

In a much more dramatic and emotive way, a series of child care tragedies which have received enormous press coverage in the 1970s, have also been disturbingly reminiscent of the 1940s, when scandal was a spur to legislative and administrative change. The most notable of all—Maria Colwell's death at the hands of her stepfather—does, in fact, bear an uncanny resemblance in a number of ways to the death of Denis O'Neill in 1945, and there are several points of similarity in the analysis of what went wrong and of what should be done to avoid future tragedies, in the reports of the inquiries into both cases. Both children came into local authority care from neglectful home situations and were the subject of court orders. Both were under child care supervision at the time of their death (Denis, because he was in a foster home; Maria, because she was at home again with her parents under a supervision order). In both cases there had been a crucial six months' gap in supervision prior to their death, through misunderstanding between agencies about who was or was not visiting. In both cases the children's school attendance began to fall off badly and eventually ceased altogether for several weeks before they died and both were undernourished as well as brutally treated. They even died at the same time of year—early in January. There is evidence in both reports that the children had become subdued, withdrawn and ill-looking in their last months and that visiting officials had failed to talk to them on their own, to explore the reasons for this, and had left the initiative for taking them to a doctor with the parents and foster parents. Both reports blame disastrous failures of communication between departments and between the many different persons involved and both show how the urgency of situations of risk was insufficiently appreciated and how concern became dissipated as messages were passed from person to person.

The differences in the two cases are no less significant than their similarities. Denis O'Neill was neglected in his foster home and killed by his foster father, having lost all contact with his own family. Failure was in the substitute care offered. Maria Colwell was neglected by her own mother and killed by her stepfather. Failure was within the 'natural' family with which she had been in contact and to which she had returned after six years in a foster home. Contrasting policies had a similarly tragic outcome. Further, when Sir Walter Monckton was investigating the O'Neill tragedy there was no child care service and no qualified social workers were involved in the child's placement or supervision. He blamed the visitors' ignorance and lack of experience for the initial lack of investigation of the foster parents and for the subsequent failure to appreciate the seriousness of Denis's predicament just before his death. The complicated division of responsibility between different local authority departments had also contributed to confusion and failure in vital communications, but more importantly 'the administrative machinery should be improved and informed by a more anxious and responsible spirit'.[26] In contrast, qualified social workers were involved in the supervision of Maria Colwell and 'there was no question at any time in our view of anyone deliberately shirking a task; there was no shortage of devotion to duty'.[27] Yet qualified social workers, devotion to duty and the accumulated experience of a quarter of a century of specialized child care did not prevent the tragedy occurring, and for many of the old, familiar reasons. It is therefore important to try to analyse why; whether some tragedies are inevitable, whatever our administrative structures, our policies and our expertise; whether reorganization and the extinction of the child care service has exacerbated old difficulties or created new ones, which hamper good child care practice; and whether policies in relation to deprived children have developed which are misconceived and damaging and therefore need revision.

In Maria Colwell's case a cumulative series of errors suggest that her death might well have been prevented, but this cannot hide the fact that tragedies will occur and that some children will be neglected and ill-treated, whatever our preventive efforts. To expect otherwise would be as unrealistic as to imagine the police will some day prevent all crime or that doctors will eliminate all disease. Only a twenty-four-hour-a-day surveillance could ensure that no

M

child comes to any harm and we know that, even in the relatively exposed conditions of institutional care, children can still be hurt. It is all the harder, therefore, to ensure that no damage is done to them in the privacy of an ordinary home. The task of the social worker in supervising situations of risk, where neglect or cruelty seem likely to occur, is also extremely delicate and taxing. Supervision that is ill-judged, obtrusive or unsympathetic may even precipitate the violent behaviour that it is seeking to prevent. A study of seventy-eight battered children by Skinner and Castle, for instance, showed a much higher rebattering rate among families known to a protective agency than among those who received *no* supervision and 'the findings suggest that multiplicity of workers and over-frequent observation of battering families can increase family stress, and a type of supervision of a family which is limited to an anxious watchfulness without specific treatment goals is not in the child's interest'.[28] One wonders how far the numerous unco-ordinated visits paid to Maria Colwell's home by a variety of officials in the last weeks of her life may have exacerbated her situation in the same way. Danger signals may also be open to a variety of interpretations and may be recognized as such only after the event. As Roy Parker points out in his commentary on the Report, 'different judgements may be formed, despite the closest mutual attention to the available evidence'—the division of opinion among the three members of the inquiry in their interpretation of events being a clear example of this.[29] Evidence itself may be obscured or distorted, since parents who ill-treat their children are often evasive and adept at offering plausible explanations for the child's injuries. There is also the common problem of exaggerated or malicious complaints against families, which must be distinguished from those demanding a proper concern. Sometimes, if a family has become a neighbourhood scapegoat, complaints of their behaviour become so frequent and various that an element of 'cry wolf' creeps in and a genuine expression of alarm may be overlooked. For all these reasons, therefore, no system of investigation or supervision is likely to be foolproof and some disasters are unavoidable.

Nevertheless, there are many indications that child care practice is failing badly in circumstances where child abuse or child distress is, in fact, preventable and the Maria Colwell Report provides us with a number of examples. One is the worrying breakdown in communication and in swift co-ordination of effort on behalf of children at risk. A major argument for Seebohm reorganization was that small, fragmented services were dangerously rivalrous, they led to gaps and overlaps in provision and attempts to co-ordinate their efforts were time consuming, wasteful and often ineffective. Integration was to be a vital remedy. Yet the report observes 'it is salutary to note how little the recommendations of the Seebohm Committee and subsequent legislation altered the situation in Maria's case'.[30] In fact, it may have made matters worse. Communications within social services departments must now negotiate a much more complex organizational structure that is still relatively new and unfamiliar to those within it. Messages pass through more hands and many social service personnel are unacquainted with child care matters. The dangers of misdirection, distortion and loss of a sense of urgency become that much greater. In addition, the new departmental boundaries are no less artificial than the old. There are still numerous other agencies which have vital contact with children such as Maria—schools (and particularly the education welfare service, in her case), the N.S.P.C.C., police, doctors and neighbours. Effective communication between them depends upon a clear appreciation of each other's roles and responsibilities and mutual *respect*. No administrative reorganization will automatically create either of these. Indeed, since the new departmental boundaries embrace territories previously belonging to others, old rivalries may be intensified for a time.[31] The complaints of magistrates against social workers, after the 1969 Act, illustrates this— and doctors and educationists have been no less critical since Seebohm. Co-operation may therefore have been made more difficult.

But reorganization cannot be blamed entirely, since many breakdowns occurred within small agencies, unaffected by it—the local branch of the N.S.P.C.C., for instance, schools and a doctor's practice, and we have seen how a similar chain of mistakes occurred thirty years earlier, among a very different cluster of organizations. The size and boundaries of administrative structures therefore may be only one factor determining their responses to communications received. Are complaints of child neglect so painful and unacceptable that they produce a particular defensive reaction in any system to which they are directed—analagous, perhaps, to closing the eyes and stopping the ears? The lamentable failures in all shapes and sizes of organizations concerned suggest this may be so. Remedies then lie, not only in restructuring organizations, but infusing them with Monckton's 'anxious and responsible spirit'. *All* staff within social agencies need to be sensitised to situations of risk —'anxious' in the degree of priority, urgency and proper suspicion with which complaints are viewed and 'responsible' in the decisiveness with which action is taken. The scale and wide variety of functions that social services departments now perform may, of course, make this a far harder task than it is for a small, specialized agency. On the other hand, there is evidence that social workers do not pay enough heed to 'the commonsense reactions of deeply concerned ordinary people'[32]—one of the bad effects of professionalism. Here, Seebohm may be positively beneficial, if its ideals of greater community involvement are put into effect so that departments have an 'ear to the ground' and a greater respect for what the ordinary citizen can offer.

The report also suggests that shortage of resources is adversely affecting child care practice. This was felt to be the case long before reorganization (indeed, reorganization was recommended because it would attract *more* resources) but if the experience of Maria Colwell's social worker is typical then caseloads of today's social workers are as high as they were for child care officers in the 1950s, and higher than the workloads carried by many in the mid-1960s.[33] This fallback in standards may well be a result of social worker losses (not least through promotion) and higher referral rates since reorganization. Shortage of aids is not new either. 'Investment in secretarial resources and mechanical aids to communication would pay heavy dividends in efficiency and could release professional staff for their proper task.'[34] Similar observations were made eight years earlier, when a Dorset child suffered injury in his foster home.[35] Arguments in favour of more resources are naturally popular with the social work profession, though they tend to obscure important factors that are more readily within their grasp. The opinion column in *Social Worker*, for example, in commenting on the report, put as its major remedy 'the time when social work is given money for development on something approaching the scale accepted as normal for other services, like health and education'.[36] A good deal of bitterness has been expressed about a society which demands that social workers perform difficult child protection duties on its behalf, which severely censures them when they fail, but which is reluctant to pay the requisite rates and taxes to support them adequately in their work. Such defensiveness when under attack is understandable, and there is some justice in these sentiments but, as Roy Parker points out, 'we should not necessarily assume that more resources for the social services will reduce the dangers of another Maria Colwell catastrophe'.[37] As with administrative reorganization, increased resources are of little value unless they are properly applied and unless we have 'a better basis for ordering the priorities in day to day social work'.[38] This depends less on having more social workers, than on the development and support of social work skills, and leads to another cause for concern—the loss of specialisms within the new departments.

The report points out that 'since the reorganisation of the local authority social services the average field level social worker, with a wider range of cases, has inevitably less experience than her predecessor in Children's Departments and it may be that less attention is paid in training to this particular aspect of the work than heretofore'.[39] Fears that genericism in training and practice might lead to a lowering of standards seem to have some foundation. There is a sense in which *repetition* of a task increases expertise, by adding to the bank of experience on which a worker can draw. In the words of one consultant paediatrician, 'I rue the day when the old Children's Department disappeared, because there is a skill needed in essential work which only comes with experience.'[40] Not all social services departments have insisted that their staff carry fully mixed caseloads. In some the old specialisms are maintained under the enlarged administrative umbrella and, for children at risk, there may be some strong arguments for this.

One of the social worker's needs, in working with vulnerable children, for instance, is an ability to communicate with them and to understand the significance of their own verbal and non-verbal communications. Many of Maria Colwell's signals of distress seem to have been overlooked or misinterpreted and in this, not only lack of specialist skills, but a blunting of perceptions, may be to blame. Social workers' tolerance of trauma in others may become too great and their suspicions too slight, because of over-exposure to distressing situations. Specialization may do little to guard against this coarsening of perception and, as well as more sympathetic consideration of 'man in the street' reactions (which has already been mentioned) support and supervision by experienced social workers may be of key importance. The 'old fashioned value of close professional supervision', as *Social Worker* terms it, is also vital in reinforcing the *courage* social workers need in these cases. Investigating complaints of neglect is unpleasant, difficult and occasionally dangerous. Those who do it need moral, and sometimes even physical support from professional colleagues.

Skills and structures are, in fact, inextricably linked. Social workers are dealing daily with situations of human distress where the level of uncertainty is high, and predictable outcomes are few.

In sociological language, they are best served by a 'normative' organization,[41] in which they can share and develop their skills and values, and can reaffirm their commitment within a close-knit group of colleagues, in which morale is maintained by a sense of togetherness and common purpose. This is less easy to achieve in large, multi-purpose organizations than in small, specialized ones. Indeed, anticipating this, sociologists like Claudine Spencer urged departments to allow for this in their structure.[42] The degree to which they have so far succeeded seems very variable. Specialist consultants are often seen as performing this supportive function, but are sometimes placed in a position so remote from the workers at field level that their influence is diluted. A more hopeful development may be in the cohesion of area teams. The frequent expressions of discontent among social workers, often in terms of a sense of alienation and lack of worth, suggest however that many social services departments still have a long way to go in creating an atmosphere conducive to good social work, and thus to good child care.

The conclusion of the Maria Colwell Report emphasized that it was a failure of the *system* which lay at the root of this, and presumably many similar tragedies. 'What has clearly emerged, at least to us, is a failure of a system compounded of several factors of which the greatest and most obvious must be that of the lack or ineffectiveness of communication and liaison. A system should so far as possible be able to absorb individual errors and yet function adequately.[43] Many of the inefficiencies have already been discussed. But it can be argued that child care *policies* are equally to blame. Commentators, like John Howells,[44] have accused social workers of clinging too slavishly and simplistically to theories about the ill effects of maternal deprivation; of transforming these into an undue reverence for 'the blood tie' and therefore of pursuing policies of rehabilitation to impossible lengths, thus disregarding the welfare of the children concerned. The reaction of Olive Stevenson, social work spokesman on the committee of inquiry, to this kind of allegation is twofold. Social workers are less simpleminded than Howells suggests and she gives a cogent explanation of their position.

The issue is seen more in terms of the development in a child of a good self image and sound sense of identity. There are two elements in this; first that a child shall know who his parents were; secondly that his perception of them, coloured as it is by the adults who care for him, shall not be such as to make him feel he comes of 'bad stock'.[45]

Clearly such a position does not lead inexorably to rehabilitation—merely to a careful and sensitive maintenance of a child's sense of his own origins. In Maria Colwell's case this was impossible because of the bitter feud between her mother and the relatives who fostered her. She was, however, returned to her family after six years in her foster home, and despite exhibiting signs of extreme distress at the prospect. Social workers, Olive Stevenson argues, are the victims, not the perpetrators of the policies which allow this to happen—the 'legal and social system' assumes that parents will resume care of a child if their circumstances improve, however long they have been away, and social workers act within those terms of reference.

This seems to imply that social workers have had no hand in shaping the current legal and social system and that they are powerless to influence its operation—both dubious propositions against which this book provides a lot of evidence. Indeed, it seems a trifle disingenuous to place responsibility upon a prevailing climate of opinion, concerned with the importance of restoring children to their parents, when social workers have contributed so much to its development. Certainly it did not exist, so far as neglected children were concerned, before children's departments came into being. On the contrary, neglected children like the O'Neills were deliberately fostered out of their own home area, to sever the connection with their natural family and make a 'fresh start'. Nor has it been impossible for social workers to influence the courts. It has always been the duty of the latter to decide on cases where parents apply for revocation of committal orders, but the law does not make it clear how they are to decide whether previously 'unfit' parents are now fit to have care of their child, they are also bound to 'have regard to the welfare of the child' and it is social workers who provide the reports which inform them. Opportunities to modify a harsh and over-simplified application of the rehabilitation principle have therefore been available and the failure of the local authority to grasp such an opportunity in the case of Maria Colwell may have been its most significant error. Indeed, all the evidence about developments in child care policy over the past thirty years suggests that at least some social workers have been far from passive and that there has been room for manoeuvre within the letter of the law. Differences between departments, not only over the use of court orders, but over admissions and discharges, fostering and adoption, prevention and delinquency all testify that the area for *choice* has been considerable—if not for individual social workers, then for their departments as a whole.

The most important general issue which the Maria Colwell Report highlights, therefore, is how far child care policies have, through their growing commitment to the 'family', ultimately failed the child. Critics believe that the focus upon the child, which was so sharp in 1948, has been blurred rather than enhanced by the increasing attention to his family context and the strenuous efforts made to preserve family ties. Defenders would argue that the reverse is true, but none would deny that there have been tragic instances when practice has actually harmed children, despite good intentions. It is this issue which lies at the heart of the new legislation, with its emphasis upon children's 'rights', and it is these arguments which have been in evidence in the debates which have accompanied it. Once again we are back in a situation akin to the forties, when important legislative changes are occurring in the wake of intense public disquiet and child care scandal. It is to these developments and their relationship with what has gone before, that the final chapter will turn.

NOTES

1. In *Portrait of Social Work* (O.U.P., 1960), Barbara Rodgers and Julia Dixon show how little social workers in one Northern town understood of each other's work.
2. *Report of the Committee on Children and Young Persons*, Cmnd. 1191, 1960.
3. *Crime – a challenge to us all*, Report of the Labour Party's Study Group, 1964.
4. *The Child, the Family and the Young Offender*, Cmnd. 2742, 1965.
5. *Report of the Working Party on Social Workers in the Local Authority Health and Welfare Services*, H.M.S.O., 1959.
6. *Caring for People*, Allen and Unwin, 1967.
7. *Management of Local Government*, Ministry of Housing and Local Government, H.M.S.O., 1967.
8. *Half our future*, Report of the Central Advisory Council for Education (England), H.M.S.O., 1963.
9. *Children and their Primary Schools*, A report of the Central Advisory Council for Education (England) H.M.S.O., 1967.
10. All quotations are from the written evidence of the various child care associations to the Seebohm Committee.

11. 'Social Work and Social Service: A Challenge for Local Government', Lecture delivered by R. M. Titmuss to the Social Workers Conference at the Health Congress, Eastbourne, April 1965. First published in the *Royal Society of Health Journal*, Vol. 86, No. 1., 1966.
12. *Report of the Committee on Local Authority and Allied Personal Social Services*, Cmnd. 3703, July 1968.
13. Ibid., para. 2.
14. Home Office Circular No. 204/1963.
15. Joel Handler, 'The Co-ercive Children's Officer', *New Society*, 3.10.68.
16. Jean S. Heywood and Barbara K. Allen, *Financial help in Social Work*, Manchester University Press, 1971.
17. Bill Jordan, *Poor Parents*, Routledge and Kegan Paul, 1974.
18. Ibid., p. 91.
19. Ibid., p. 95.
20. Draft Report of 'Survey in the London Boroughs of Section I Children and Young Persons Act 1963 Payments', Tony Emmett and Maurice Hawker, October 1974.
21. According to the B.A.S.W. Report, two London boroughs were spending between 80 per cent and 90 per cent of their Section I money on Bed and Breakfast charges. In one, the total budget ran into thousands of pounds—in the other, into hundreds of thousands.
22. See, for instance, John Greve, 'London's Homeless', *Occasional Papers in Social Administration*, No. 10, 1964.
23. Circular 18/74 (Department of the Environment) Circular 4/74 (Department of Health and Social Security) Circular 34/74 (Welsh Office), 7 February 1974.
24. These issues are fully discussed in Olive Stevenson, *Claimant or Client?*, Allen and Unwin, 1973.
25. According to the Home Office Returns of Children in Care, the number admitted in 1968, 1969 and 1970 (before the 1969 Act altered the basis of admissions) in England and Wales was 50,938; 51,262 and 51,542.
26. *Reported by Sir Walter Monckton K.C.M.G., K.C.V.O., M.C., K.C., on the circumstances which led to the boarding out of Dennis and Terence O'Neill at Bank Farm, Minsterley, and the steps taken to supervise their welfare*, Cmd. 6636, May 1945, para. 54.
27. *Report of the Committee of Inquiry into the Care and Supervision Provided in Relation to Maria Colwell*. Department of Health and Social Security, H.M.S.O., 1974., para. 240.
28. Angela Skinner and Raymond Castle, *78 Battered Children: A Retrospective Study*, N.S.P.C.C., 1969. Quoted in Jean Renvoize, *Children in Danger*, Routledge and Kegan Paul, 1974.
29. Roy Parker, 'Maria Colwell: the lessons', *New Society*, 12 September 1974.
30. Maria Colwell Report, op. cit., para. 150.
31. Roy Parker discusses problems of co-operation between social welfare organizations, including the problem of 'domain' in 'Caring for Children', ed. M. L. Kellmer Pringle, Longmans, 1969.
32. 'Maria Colwell: the lessons', op. cit.

33. In *Workloads in Children's Departments* (a Home Office Research Unit Report) field officers in nine sample authorities were carrying, on average, between forty and fifty cases each. Miss Diana Lees, Maria Colwell's supervising officer, was stated to have had a caseload of between sixty and seventy.

34. Maria Colwell Report, op. cit., para. 154.

35. 'Dorset County Council Child Care Service'. Report to the Secretary of State for the Home Department by the Chief Inspector, Children's Department, Home Office., H.M.S.O., 1966., para. 51.

36. *Social Worker*, Vol. 3, No. 119, 12 September 1974.

37. 'Maria Colwell: the lessons', op. cit.

38. Ibid.

39. Maria Colwell Report, op. cit., para. 209.

40. Dr. Eric Jones, at a Joint Conference of the Health Visitors and Scottish Health Visitors Associations, reported in the *Guardian* on 12 October 1974.

41. See Amitai Etzioni, *A Comparative Analysis of Complex Organisations*, Glencoe, III. The Free Press, 1961.

42. Claudine Spencer, 'Seebohm: Problems and Policies', *Social and Economic Administration*, Vol. 4, Nos. 3 and 4, 1970.

43. Maria Colwell Report, op. cit., para. 240.

44. John G. Howells, *Remember Maria*, Butterworths, 1974.

45. Maria Colwell Report, op. cit., para. 315.

46. See Jean Packman, *Child Care: Needs and Numbers*, Allen and Unwin, 1968.

CHAPTER NINE

Whose Children?

The tragedy of Maria Colwell, together with other recent instances of child abuse and death, added considerable impetus to the demand for new legislation, which was presaged by the Houghton Committee. Such scandals and well-publicized 'tug of love' cases in fostering, adoption and divorce and custody proceedings, have done much to engage the interest and concern of the public at large. Amongst the 'experts' research findings have also been marshalled as evidence of the need for change. Longitudinal studies by the influential National Children's Bureau, for example, have highlighted the vulnerability of disadvantaged children who, through illegitimacy, family breakdown, poverty, poor housing and so on are 'born to fail',[1] and their deprivation has been compared with the much happier lot of many adopted children who have been 'rescued' from similar circumstances.[2] That adoption is too little used and that many more deprived children in local authority and voluntary society care could benefit from a permanent substitute home is the contention of *Children Who Wait*,[3] with its figure of 7,000 children living in temporary foster homes or residential care, who really need a permanent substitute family.

Concern that children are suffering because bonds with parents are too tenaciously preserved and either cannot be or are not broken often enough or soon enough led to the formation of pressure groups (the Adoption and Guardianship Reform Organization—AGRO—formed in November 1973, for instance). In lieu of any signs that the Conservative government intended to act, Dr. Owen's private members bill was introduced during the same winter but Parliament was dissolved in February 1974, before it received its second reading. Two elections later, legislation was framed and debated in the 1974/75 Parliamentary Session. Articles and letters to the press abounded and their focus was firmly on the rights and needs of the child which, it was argued, should be recognized as paramount in our legislation—if necessary at the expense of the rights and needs of natural parents. A major piece of child care legislation is now being enacted, as important in its implications as any since the 1948 Children Act.

Parallels with the situation in the 1940s are easy to draw and are salutary to contemplate but there are at least two differences between then and now which are important. One is that, for all the grave deficiencies in care that have recently been revealed, child care practice in general is much more careful and sensitive than it was thirty years ago, when amateurism and the Poor Law principle of 'less eligibility' combined to produce minimal and sometimes disgraceful levels of service for many children in public care. For that reason, current failures seem all the more distressing and contradictory. In addition, there is now in existence a powerful body of trained professional social workers, who are responsible for the services which are currently being criticized and who have strong and sometimes conflicting opinions on the proposed reforms. Their resistance on some issues led to modifications in the draft legislation at an early stage but these have, in turn, been criticised for their conservatism. No such organized professional body existed in the 1940s and, indeed, the child care profession was created to bring about the improvements that were desired at that time. Thus, in the space of a generation, the 'crusaders' on behalf of deprived children have, to some extent, become the 'establishment'—uneasy and resistant to some of the changes now proposed. This has led to accusations of reactionary self-interest and a failure to appreciate the needs of the child. The painful irony of this situation, with all its complications, deserves investigation.

Many of the Houghton Report's recommendations (which have already been outlined in an earlier chapter) met with general support and approval. The need to integrate adoption services within the mainstream of child care provision is widely recognized. Thus, local authorities will be obliged to provide an adoption service as part of their general child care and family casework provision and will also have a duty to ensure, in co-operation with voluntary societies, that a comprehensive service is available throughout their area. In future adoption will be seen as one of a whole range of possible means of helping deprived children and their parents and, by outlawing private arrangements, it is hoped to avoid some of the risks and the worst examples of poor service. The transfer of responsibility for welfare supervision to the placing agency and the *optional* appointment of a *Guardian ad Litem* will save duplication and waste of scarce social worker resources and may mean better support for adopters as well. More stringent requirements for the registration of voluntary agencies will help ensure a more consistent level of service. The proposed changes are a logical extension of the Curtis Committee's original purpose in creating a comprehensive, professional service for deprived children. Indeed, in view of the irrevocability of adoption and the care with which it should be arranged and supported it is something of an anomaly that it has remained for so long on the periphery of the public service.

Thus far social workers are united in support of the new policies, but they would also prefer stronger central government control over both voluntary agency and local authority practice than is apparently contemplated. It was proposed, for example, that voluntary agencies should be registered with central government (in the same way as voluntary children's homes are) but that such registration should be granted on the basis of reports made by the local authorities. This was strongly resisted by the British Association of Social Workers (B.A.S.W.) which believed that 'registration and inspection must go together . . . the power should fairly lie and be seen to lie with the Secretary of State'.[4] The social workers also suggested that 'the standards of practice of local authorities in the adoption field need to be reviewed in the same way as the standards of voluntary agencies'.[5] There was no evidence of smug self-satisfaction here and they also questioned the assumption that had been made since the old Home Office Child Care Inspectorate was incorporated in the Department of Health and Social Security—that 'the Social Work Service in most fields does not function as an inspectorate', but is of an 'advisory and promotional nature'. 'Perhaps the Social Work Service *should* function more as an inspectorate!' was B.A.S.W.'s response.[6] This is an interesting example of the value that many professionals place upon the role of central government. Their suspicion that too much local autonomy can lead to unacceptable variations in service and that inspection can be an ally of good professional standards is again in the Curtis tradition and was re-echoed by Seebohm. Both the well-documented existence of variations in local authority provision and the achievements of the child care service in comparison with other local authority welfare services, after 1948, lend strong support to this view.

However, most controversy has arisen over a cluster of proposals, aimed at protecting the welfare of children in care, providing them with greater security and making it possible to formulate long-term plans for them, despite parental opposition, prevarication or indifference. Advance notice of a parent's intention to remove a child from care will be required, to avoid precipitate and unsettling changes for the child or even, in less favourable circumstances, to give the caring authority a chance to forestall removal by the assumption of parental rights. Linked with this is the amendment which makes it possible for a local authority to assume parental rights over any child who has been in its care (or the care of a voluntary organization) for a period of three years or more, regardless of the parents' fitness or capacity. Local authorities will also be able to apply to a court to free a child for adoption, with or without parental consent, which may be dispensed with in some cases. A child may also be protected against removal from his foster parents, by anyone (including a local authority or voluntary organization)—after he has spent three years in their care, if they apply for custodianship, and after five years, if they apply for an adoption order. In such cases, the court will hear all parties and the views of foster parents of longstanding will, for the first time, receive equal judicial consideration with those of the natural parents and the caring authority.

What is proposed makes a clear break with the old law's assumption that voluntary admissions to care should leave the parents free to withdraw their children as and when they please, and that parental rights should be removed only in cases where parental unfitness, incapacity, abandonment or persistent failure to discharge their obligations can be established. It introduces, instead, the notion of a series of 'stages at which, with safeguards, the rights of natural parents should weigh progressively less heavy'.[7] It recognizes that children—especially very young children—operate on a different time-scale from adults and that emotional bonds formed in a substitute home may come in time to supplant the ties with natural parents. When this happens it may be more important for the child's welfare to preserve the substitute home than to restore him to his natural home. Hence the needs and rights of the child may come into conflict with those of his own parents and, in such cases, the former must be regarded as paramount.

Reaction against the tendency, over recent years, to regard a child's interests as inextricably bound up with those of his natural family is clear and the impact of 'tug of love' cases is also evident. Indeed, in one of the consultative papers on the new legislation it is suggested that 'in the two years since the Committee formulated their cautious recommendation there has been some shift of opinion against the rights of natural parents in favour of substitute parents with whom the children have formed bonds'.[8] The proposals are also a response to criticisms of the lack of *planning* for children in care. Social workers themselves, as well as some academic commentators, are conscious that they often adopt a short-term and essentially reactive approach to the problems of deprived children (frequently for want of adequate resources and a real choice between alternatives), and that in this they collude with the uncertainties and unreliability of many parental plans. Time limits, though arbitrary, may be one way of stimulating decisiveness.

The protection of the *child*'s interests, where these may conflict with those of his natural parents, is also the aim of a proposal to ensure separate representation for the child in care or custody proceedings. For example, in cases where a parent applies for revocation of a care order (as in the case of Maria Colwell) the child should be separately represented, to avoid the danger of the court hearing only the parents' or the local authority's view of the situation. An independent social worker and/or lawyer will be appointed *Guardian ad Litem* in such cases. The implication is clear. If local authority social workers are parties to the case—as initiators of care proceedings or as representatives of the caring agency which has the child in its charge—they are no longer regarded as being objective enough adequately to represent the child's interests. (Dr. Kellmer Pringle goes further, arguing that proper representation of a child's interests requires *Guardians* to be appointed from outside social work altogether.) An independent voice will therefore be sought, on the child's behalf (as was always the case in Adoption hearings and will continue to be so in all contested cases). In the process, there are signs of an attempt to shift back towards greater judicial involvement with child care cases, despite the recent trends in the opposite direction which place more and more responsibility on the executive. (One suggestion—squashed by social work opposition—was that no committed child should be returned home without court approval.) Thus it seems that, by widening the focus of their work from the child to his whole family, social workers have unwittingly forfeited public confidence in their ability to judge what is in the child's best interests and, for this reason alone, they need to reassess their policies and practice at the present time.

Opposition to these changes comes from various quarters. At one end of the spectrum there are those who object both to existing law and to some of the changes now proposed because 'nothing in the Acts indicates that independence and self-regulation among children is an idea to be pursued'.[9] They stress the right of children to be consulted directly and condemn 'the salvationist attitude of protecting children from "bad" families or associates', instead of giving 'support to the idea that a child has a right to keep contact with his family and friends even though it is in care'.[10] In fact, the burden of the 'Children's Rights' movement is that we are over-protective and paternalistic (maternalistic?) in our concern for children and leave them too little room for self-determination— an attitude that is shared by some writers on delinquency.[11]

Some members of the legal profession are also likely to view the changes as undesirable, partly because of their belief in the importance of the blood tie (in Lord Justice Sachs's words 'the bond between mother and child is perhaps the strongest that nature forges')[12] and partly because they perceive the difficulties of arriving at a true assessment of what is in the interests of 'the welfare of the child'. Such an assessment implies predicting the child's likely long-term future, as well as weighing all aspects of his present circumstances and, as such, is far more problematic than merely establishing parental fitness or failure. Again, Lord Justice Sachs warned of 'the dangers of a whole class of adoption cases being in effect decided by the psychiatric specialist profession. Moreover, to decide these cases on such a basis can only too easily result in the courts' descending the slippery slope of a custody type welfare contest between mother and foster parents'[13]—a slope that his Lordship clearly regarded as one to be avoided.

B.A.S.W's objections are on rather different grounds. For instance, it resists the conflict or 'adversary' model between parental rights and children's rights that is implicit in a number of the proposals and which it believes over-simplifies the situation. Whilst acknowledging the importance of bonds formed with substitute parents, it also lays emphasis on 'a child's sense of identity, cultural and personal and his feelings about his parents and his situation'.[14] It fears that changes in the law will ignore the subtleties of the child's attachments—though it might be argued in return that social workers have sometimes been so concerned with the subtleties, that the obvious has escaped them. Fear is also expressed that the greater powers to be given to local authorities will merely discourage parents from placing their children in care and will certainly make them nervous and suspicious of the benefits of fostering. The child care service may therefore be turned from a predominantly supportive and 'helping' service, offering 'shared parenting', to a coercive and threatening one, severing the links between parents and children. According to B.A.S.W. it is *practice*, not the law, which needs to be improved and changed. It is argued, for instance, that existing powers to assume parental rights are adequate but that local authorities vary enormously in their use of such powers. Firm guidance and inspection could ensure a more acceptable uniformity.

The arguments will doubtless continue, even after the new legislation is implemented. The measures to protect children more adequately and to offer them a greater degree of security may discourage and alarm some parents, but equally they could be used to help parents to understand the needs of children better, and they may stimulate social workers to make much greater efforts to preserve and rehabilitate families. Research evidence shows that, despite social workers' attitudes towards the maintenance of a child's family links, the amount of work done in this sphere is often minimal.[15] Guilt about this may underlie the vehemence with which social workers currently argue in its favour, and is certainly reflected in their contention that it is practice which must change. Legal reminders of the consequences of allowing children in care to 'drift' may spur them to greater efforts in this direction. The device of 'custodianship' may also enable some conflicting views to be reconciled. Because it gives the child and his substitute parents security without extinguishing parental rights, it is clearly much more acceptable to many than adoption, for it offers children in long-term care and children who are the victims of divorce a similar chance of stability, without denying them all contact with their original family network.

Less easily reconcilable may be the fundamental unease with which many regard, not the details of the new legislation, but its general direction and its apparent relationship with wider social policy issues. In the past two years the phrase 'the cycle of deprivation' has been much used to describe the transmission of social problems from one generation to the next. Since the concept was popularized by Sir Keith Joseph it has become the subject of a massive programme of special research and is seen as a proper target for future statutory intervention. There is, of course, nothing new in the notion that how a child is brought up will affect how he himself performs as a parent and that deprived infants may grow into depriving parents who will, in turn, produce another generation of deprived infants. It has, in fact, been a basic assumption

N

upon which most of the work of the child care service has rested. Supported by the maternal deprivation theorists, child care workers have developed preventive family casework and substitute family care, both with a view to meeting the child's immediate needs for love and security, and with the long-term aim of enabling them to grow into stable and affectionate adults and parents. They have received ample confirmation that problems can (but need not) repeat themselves from generation to generation; that battering parents have often themselves been abused as children; that neglected children sometimes become neglectful parents and that illegitimate children may become unmarried mothers. Many of their arguments in favour of more resources and more preventive powers have, in fact, been in terms of breaking the cycle and thus avoiding such problems in the future.

Current disquiet arises, not from these familiar 'cycle' theories as such, but from the strategies of intervention which are now proposed. In an understandable swing away from policies which may have kept too many children in home conditions that were positively damaging, the trend of the current legislation is in the opposite direction—in securing a child's future *away* from his natural family. The relative success of adopted children has been used to show how beneficial 'rescue' operations can be, and social workers are faced with the uncomfortable probability that their skills in providing substitute care may be better developed than their abilities to sustain and improve relationships within some deprived and depriving homes. The direction in which this imbalance of helping skills may push child care practice clearly smacks of 1984 to some social workers. 'It is also dangerous to imply that parental rights should rest upon a balance of probabilities about a child's future welfare; the logical extension of this could be arbitrarily to decide which families within the community are the most suitable for bringing up children and to transfer children from other families to them.'[16]

These fears are sharpened by the way in which the 'cycle of deprivation' theory has come to be particularly associated with 'the poor' as a social class. As Bill Jordan has pointed out, neither harmful child-rearing practices nor various indices of social deviance are the exclusive preserve of the poor—poverty and maladjustment are not synonymous.[17] Yet Sir Keith Joseph's speeches—in particular the one about the decline in the nation's morals, with its reference to the 'threat to our human stock', to the high proportion of births in social classes 4 and 5 and to the need to 'remoralise whole groups and classes of people'[18] create a powerful impression that this is, in fact, the case. Again, as Bill Jordan and others have reminded us, there is nothing new in this view either. Nineteenth-century thinkers were deeply concerned about the birth rate of the poor, and made strong links between a high birth rate and moral degeneracy.

The analogy is not a pleasant one and many social workers are naturally suspicious of policies which not only tend to favour more drastic interventions in family life, on behalf of children, but which seem to be directed at only one section of the population—the poorest. Their fears are set against the background of the social services departments' increasing involvement in meeting people's financial and material needs, as described in the previous chapter. Indeed, the Finer Committee on One Parent Families would take this process several steps further, for it urges a wider interpretation and more generous use of the power to give financial help under Section I of the 1963 Children and Young Persons Act, and also states 'the case can be argued for straightening out the situation (of overlap between social services departments and the supplementary benefits commission) by arranging for all exceptional needs payments for families with children to be made by social services departments, leaving only weekly subsistence allowances to be paid by the S.B.C.'.[19]

Thus, inexorably, social services departments appear to be dealing more and more *directly* with problems of poverty and homelessness as well as with child neglect and cruelty. The dilemma posed is whether they can do both kinds of work successfully and sensitively or whether both will suffer by being harnessed together. For instance, will rate-bound budgets and lack of appeals machinery mean that families in financial distress are assisted *less* adequately than they would be by the notionally bottomless purse of the S.B.C.? Will the close association between social work help and financial aid deter *non*-poor families with problems from seeking assistance? And—the other side of the same coin—how far will the families which *are* helped suffer from the stigma of a service which, though it began with Seebohm ideals of 'universality', appears, inadvertently, to be moving towards a selectivity based on economic status? This last dilemma is further complicated by a long tradition of thinking in social policy which emphasizes the 'demoralization' caused by too much 'giving' on the part of state or charity, and too much 'dependency' on the part of those who are specially helped. Sir Keith Joseph again—'Parents are being divested of their duty to provide for their family economically, of their responsibility for education, health, upbringing, morality, advice and guidance . . . when you take responsibility away from people you make them irresponsible. Hand in hand with this you break down traditional morals.'[20]

The challenge is therefore to find ways of helping children, without undermining their parents and without *reinforcing*, instead of *breaking* the 'cycle of deprivation' and some of the current unease springs from a suspicion that we may be moving in the opposite direction. A child care expert, Mia Kellmer Pringle, states 'Bringing up children is too important a task to be left entirely to those parents who are patently in need of support, guidance and, where necessary, sanctions on the part of the community'.[21] To be able to agree we have to be sure that we are accurately identifying those who are 'patently in need' and that we really are offering 'support and guidance' as well as exercising sanctions. If we are using the crude indicator of 'poverty' as our guide to the former and if we now swing too violently and uncritically in a 'protective' and 'rescuing' direction this will not be the case. On the contrary our policies could then prove destructive and repugnant—a return, not to 1948, but to 1834.

There are several growing points in current child care practice, however, and not all are as beset with difficulties as those discussed so far. One concerns experiments with direct work with children —a development which, paradoxically, seems to have come from outside the child care tradition. Perhaps partly in reaction to the 'family casework' bias of much of the preventive work of the old child care service, community workers of various kinds have encouraged the setting up of holiday playschemes, adventure playgrounds and on-going group activities for children and adolescents in deprived areas. Such schemes may offer as much benefit to the parents suffering from overcrowding and the stress of poor living conditions, as they do to the children and, in this way, are a valuable complement to family casework. To their credit, social services departments have been concerned both with the organization of such activities and with supporting voluntary and self-help groups and there is clearly scope for further development. From a different direction, the 'playgroup movement'—inspired largely by middle-class parents in response to the dearth of statutory nursery education—is spreading gradually to include some disadvantaged and handicapped children. Again, since Seebohm

transferred responsibility from education to social services departments, the latter have been involved in a supportive role and, again,
the scope for development is enormous.

Intermediate Treatment also focuses directly upon the child,
and social services departments are beginning to implement the
1969 legislation. Challenged to develop imaginative treatment for
juvenile delinquents that involves more than supervision but less
than long-term removal from home, they have responded in
different ways. Some offenders are introduced to existing statutory
and voluntary facilities—clubs, adventure schools, holiday schemes
and so on—in the belief that new creative activities and fresh peer
group experience will bring long-term benefits. Social services
departments are also slowly developing or supporting special new
facilities. Day centres, staffed by teachers and social workers, are
one kind of experiment, where attention can be concentrated on
relatively small numbers of offenders, out of the normal school
environment, but avoiding total removal from home, In other cases
'one off' solutions, tailored to an individual situation, have been
used. The young vandal who was required to repair the bus shelter
he had wrecked is one example, where I.T. has been used to encompass the notion of 'reparation', with overtones of making the
punishment fit the crime.

Developments in I.T. are already raising fundamental as well as
practical problems, however, and these are likely to continue. One
stems directly from the dual purpose of any measure aimed at
delinquency, and involves striking a balance between care and
control. As Olive Stevenson has pointed out, 'one is concerned with
law and order and with the preservation of the social structure,
even of property. The other is concerned with the desire to speak
to the condition of children who suffer.'[22] The two may not always
be compatible and the public is unlikely to be sympathetic to treatment which enriches a delinquent's life experience, without also
demonstrably controlling his anti-social behaviour. Since I.T. is
generally 'in the open', in full view of the community, it may be all
the harder to give proper weight to the 'caring' dimension. This is
also linked with difficulties associated with 'positive discrimination',
which are probably more acute when practised on individuals than
when applied to whole communities. As some I.T. gives (and is
designed to give) the offender new and exciting experiences he has
never before enjoyed, the effect upon non-offending youngsters from
a similar environment has to be considered. Already social workers
report rumblings from some poor areas, where delinquency is now

seen as being 'rewarded' by such experiences, whilst conformity is not.

Once again, the dilemma is not new. Nineteenth-century Reformatories were criticized for providing better education for inmates than the poor child outside received and children's departments were sometimes challenged for providing high material standards for children 'in care'. But the penalty of being 'put away' probably offset the advantages, in the eyes of the community, whereas in I.T. that penalty has disappeared. The problem of using well-motivated but highly selective policies against a general background of deprivation and unequal opportunities is once again made clear. Development of facilities and opportunities for whole neighbourhoods of youngsters may therefore be more important than designing schemes specifically for offenders, if I.T. is not to create more problems than it solves. The scope for extensive community work is obvious.

Still more scope for development is suggested by the Finer Committee on One Parent Families.[23] A large part of the report is concerned with the financial, employment and housing needs of lone parents, but a final section concentrates on the specific needs of their children. 'There are more children than parents in one parent families'[24] (over a million in fact) and the committee considers that they are particularly vulnerable. Finer is anxious that parents in this situation shall not be forced into full-time employment, through lack of an adequate income. This is one reason for its suggestion of a 'Guaranteed Maintenance Allowance', which is designed to be adequate enough to enable a parent not to work, or to work only part-time, but neither so mean nor so generous as to tempt them into full-time employment if this is against the interests of good child care.

As a complement to its financial provisions, the committee recognizes an 'urgent need for considerable expansion of day care services',[25] which will remove some of the stress and social isolation from parents 'caged in the home', whilst offering extra care and stimulation to the child. The committee favours expansion of play-groups and nursery schools, rather than day-nurseries, which it feels are too health-conscious and resistant to parental involvement to be an ideal 'support' facility. It also suggests developing a 'day fostering' service and wants social services departments to educate and assist daily minders and to interpret the regulations 'with more emphasis on the suitability of the child minder herself for the task as opposed to the present emphasis on the suitability of her premises'.[26] Other suggestions are day care for school-age children in the awkward out-of-school hours—perhaps by social services and education departments in co-operation—and more imaginative use of boarding education, on grounds of social need.

The creation of social services departments has prepared the ground for pursuit of all these developments, for day care was not previously a part of the child care service, yet it is clearly a vital resource if a wide range of flexible support services is to be offered to families in difficulties. Its potential for prevention of total family breakdown is tremendous. Finer also adds its voice to the many which are now emphasizing that the needs of the *child* must not be swamped by our increased concern for and sensitivity to the needs of families as a whole. By refusing to look at problems *only* 'through adult eyes', it makes the point that parental and children's needs, though closely interwoven, are sometimes in conflict and where this is the case it argues that the latter should be seen as paramount. Its links with the proposed legislation on other aspects of child care are striking and consistent.

Thus there is a sense in which, in the space of one generation, we have come full circle. In the 1940s failures in public care, scandal and a review of existing provision led to a heightened appreciation of the needs of deprived children. The result was a new, specialist service whose focus was firmly on the child and on the provision of good substitute care. Swiftly and inexorably that focus widened to encompass the child's family—his need for them and theirs for him —and measures to support families became as important as finding substitutes for them. Now, once more, failures in practice, scandal and review have brought the focus sharply back on to the child and his needs as an individual in his own right. In the process, substitute care has again come to the fore and new legislation confirms this emphasis.

Yet to describe child care policy simply in terms of a cycle is to do less than justice to the complexities of what has taken place. The task set in 1948 was clear cut and circumscribed. Children deprived of a normal home life were to be provided with good substitute care by a new professional, personal service. The provision of such a service perhaps made it inevitable that a process of expansion and redefinition was immediately set in train. The task was steadily enlarged, both through the inclusion of fresh categories of needy children (most notably the delinquent) and through the development of a much wider range of helping methods. Experience and training also taught social workers that the needs of

deprived children were subtle, complex and difficult to assess and
that provision to meet these needs must necessarily be flexible and
varied. There were no simple problems nor simple answers. In
addition the specialist service has been replaced by a multi-purpose
agency with a vast range of responsibilities. For all these reasons
what is expected of services for deprived children today and of
the social workers who staff them, is much more ambitious and
difficult than was the case in 1948. Current inadequacies and
failures must be seen against this background and though many
old lessons undoubtedly have to be relearned, there have also
been substantial achievements. Movement along a spiralling course
may better describe what has occurred than the simple analogy of a
circle.

There is no sign, either, that the difficulties will diminish,
despite new legislation. To date, developments have taken place
against a background of shared assumptions about families and
about childhood. Belief that families are the right and proper place
in which to bring up children has been an integral part of all recent
child care policy. Even the Poor Law shared this belief, using its
deterrent policies and its punishing care of the 'undeserving' to
try to encourage the 'deserving' to look after their own. More
positively the policies of the last thirty years have stressed measures
to support and sustain families in difficulty and, where all else
fails, to provide children with substitute care on a model as closely
resembling the 'normal' family as possible. Families which produce
deprived, damaged or delinquent children have been seen as unfortunate failures of an accepted system. The concept of the family
as an essential and generally benevolent institution has gone un-
questioned.

Similarly, child care policy has been based upon a notion of
childhood as a distinct and vulnerable period of life, requiring considerable protection and special care and treatment not accorded
to adults in our society—a concept in stark contrast to the 'miniature adult' status of children before the Industrial Revolution.
We have moved steadily further and further in the direction of
extending childhood and increasing the years of dependency and
diminished responsibility. The age of criminal responsibility has
been raised and may be pushed higher and children can remain 'in
care' until they are eighteen or even older. Some Children's Officers,
conscious of the immaturity of some of their adolescents, would
have liked to keep them until twenty-one. Again, such policies
have accorded with the values of the wider society and have been in

line with other developments, like the raising of the school-leaving age.

Now, both assumptions are being challenged. Laing and Cooper,[27] amongst others, question the benefits of family life and support quite different patterns of relationships; and some writers on delinquency and on 'children's rights' dispute the protective stance of the 'child-savers' and want far more self-determination for the child. There are few signs that these views have influenced child care policy so far (though the new legislation places emphasis on the child's right to a say in his own future) and they may well continue to be held by only a minority. Nevertheless, they suggest that future developments in child care will rest less securely than in the past on a consensus view of what is good and desirable, and the direction of future change will be all the harder to discern, to determine and to defend.

True to Donnison's description of a social service as 'a continually developing response to continually changing needs and problems'[28] services for children are facing fresh difficulties, even as they attempt to solve existing ones. Dilemmas arise in policy, in practice and in the organizational framework—many as a direct result of previous solutions to past problems. Resistance to deprivation by separation may have led the service too far in the direction of supporting insupportable families. Can the balance be redressed without swinging too far in the opposite direction? Enthusiasm for prevention has drawn social workers deep into the fields of income maintenance and housing provision. Are these appropriate activities for social workers or do they do more harm than good? Policies for delinquents have been emasculated by government and are unsupported by fresh resources. Can they be salvaged or are they doomed to failure and a consequent backlash? Can social workers narrow the gap between theory and practice in all branches of child care and how far can training and supervision help? Can social services departments develop a framework that is supportive to social work instead of one that is too often positively damaging and are they *able* to do this within the huge structures of the newly reorganized local authorities? This last may be the most important problem of all, for upon its solution so much of the rest depends. As Claudine Spencer has said

> Commitment is closely related to morale; disillusion with social work as an activity blunts commitment and makes it harder to subscribe to its values and standards. What this all means is that

the problems of organization in a social work department, particularly in relation to the objective of a 'professional service', are not simply concerned with 'getting the job done', but significantly involve the *orientation* employees bring to that job.[29]

There may be real lessons to be learned from the past, for commitment and morale were high in the child care service.

Looking back also reminds us that those who administer a service play as much part in shaping policy as those who draft the legislation. Many of the developments in child care sprang directly from local experience and experiment. Indeed, much social legislation is drafted in the broadest terms to enable such developments to take place. Local administrators and social workers are therefore involved, not only in providing the vital 'personal' element in any child care service, but in determining the direction of change. Though they frequently feel powerless their responsibility is considerable and may be dangerous if exercised unconsciously. For this reason alone, they need to look back in order to understand where they have come from, how they have arrived here and where they are going next.

NOTES

1. Some of the findings of the Bureau's cohort studies are brought together and summarized in P. Wedge and H. Prosser, *Born to Fail*, Arrow Books, 1973.
2. Eileen Crellin, M. K. Kellmer Pringle, Patrick West, *Born Illegitimate*, National Foundation for Educational Research, 1971.
3. Jane Rowe, Lydia Lambert, *Children Who Wait*, Association of British Adoption Agencies, 1973.
4. Comments by B.A.S.W. on the first D.H.S.S. consultative paper on the Report of the Departmental Committee on Adoption.
5. Ibid.
6. Ibid.
7. Consultative Paper on proposals relating to foster children and children in care generally. D.H.S.S.
8. Ibid.
9. Nan Berger, *Children's Rights*, Elek Books, 1971, Chap. 5, p. 164.
10. Ibid.
11. See, for instance, Anthony M. Platt, *The Child Savers*, The University of Chicago Press, 1969.
12. Part of L. J. Sachs's judgement in Re. W (an infant) in All England Law Reports (1970).
13. Ibid.

14. B.A.S.W. Comments on Third Consultative Paper on Adoption and Guardianship Law Reform.
15. See, for instance, Victor George, *Foster Care*, Routledge and Kegan Paul, 1970; and Robert Holman, *Trading in Children*, Routledge and Kegan Paul, 1973.
16. From B.A.S.W. Comments on Third Consultative Paper on Adoption and Guardianship Law Reform.
17. Bill Jordan, *Poor Parents*, Routledge and Kegan Paul, 1974.
18. Speech given in Birmingham on 19 October 1974.
19. *Report of the Committee on One-Parent Families*, July 1974, Cmnd. 5629, para. 8.88.
20. Birmingham speech, op. cit.
21. Mia Kellmer Pringle, *The Needs of Children*, Hutchinson, 1974, p. 160.
22. Olive Stevenson, 'Care or control: A view of Intermediate Treatment', in *Social Work Today*, Vol. 2, No. 4, 10 May 1971.
23. Finer Report, op. cit.
24. Ibid., para. 8.12.
25. Ibid., para. 8.118.
26. Ibid., para. 8.135.
27. See, for instance, R. D. Laing, *The Politics of Experience*, Penguin, 1967; and David Cooper, *The Death of the Family*, Penguin, 1972.
28. D. V. Donnison, Valerie Chapman, *Social Policy and Administration*, Allen and Unwin, 1965, p. 27.
29. Claudine Spencer, 'Seebohm: Organisational Problems and Policy Proposals', in *Social and Economic Administration*, Vol. 4, No. 3, July 1970.

Index